The Mystery of Christian Marriage

The Mystery of Christian Marriage

PETER JEFFERY, CSSp

GRACEWING

Paulist Press
New York/Mahwah, N.J.

First published in 2006

Gracewing
2 Southern Avenue, Leominster
Herefordshire HR6 0QF

Published in the United States of America in 2006

Paulist Press
997 Macarthur Boulevard
Mahwah, New Jersey 07430

www.paulistpress.com

UK ISBN 0 85244 622 5

Library of Congress Cataloging-in-Publication Data

Jeffery, Peter, CSSp.
The mystery of Christian marriage / Peter Jeffery.
p. cm.
Includes bibliographical references.
ISBN 0-8091-4419-0 (alk. paper)
1. Marriage--Religious aspects--Christianity.
2. Family--Religious aspects--Christianity.
I. Title.
BV835.J44 2005
234'.165--dc22
2005030583

Typeset by Action Publishing Technology Ltd,
Gloucester GL1 5SR

Printed in the United Kingdom by Antony Rowe Ltd,
Chippenham, Wiltshire SN14 6LH

Contents

Fr Peter Jeffery CSSp

An Appreciation

Fr Peter Jeffery was a man of many talents which were often concealed behind a shy exterior – he never boasted of those talents, but he left behind him in this world much evidence of them, both here in Europe and in Nigeria, where he spent thirteen years as a missionary of the Holy Ghost Congregation.

It was when he was appointed to be in charge of the candidates for the priesthood of the Holy Ghost Congregation in Britain, that his long and fruitful association with the Missionary Institute London began. He succeeded in first getting a Licentiate in Moral Theology and then a Doctorate; he taught these subjects at the MIL while also holding down important posts of responsibility in its administration.

His unexpected death at the age of sixty-six has left a large gap which has not been easy to fill. The typescript of his latest book on marriage was recovered from his personal papers and virtually completed. As a tribute to the life, work and achievement of Fr Peter Jeffery CSSp we are very happy to offer this deep and penetrating reflection on the mystery of Christian marriage.

On a personal note, I wish to thank most sincerely Professor Peter Millard whose commitment and dedication have made the publication of this book possible. I am sure it will be a valuable addition to our understanding of Christian marriage at a time when it is under so much pressure.

Fr John McFadden CSSp
Provicial Superior,
Holy Ghost Fathers

Foreword

by The Right Reverend Christopher Budd, Bishop of Plymouth

A book on marriage coming from a Catholic author will understandably be scrutinized to see what solutions it offers to the significant number of Catholics who are involved in irregular and difficult marriage situations. A question always in the forefront of a pastor's mind is whether a particular situation may be resolved so that the couple may be re-admitted to the sacraments. Strange things happen in this area! Many a second irregular marriage develops a stability that brings a couple to silver, ruby or even golden jubilees. Despite best efforts, ecclesiastical tribunals have not been able within their terms of reference to bring to a resolution many of the situations and so such jubilees are celebrated outside the sacraments of the Church. There is a widespread feeling that pastorally and theologically something is not right!

Father Jeffery in this book *The Mystery of Christian Marriage* makes no claim to have easy solutions to such situations. However, true to his calling as a theologian, he explores in depth the Catholic tradition which over centuries has shaped our teaching and our living. Our teaching about marriage has been heavily influenced by law and the need for clear and correct processes and disciplines. But can law really cope with the mystery of marriage?

Marriage as contract, so amenable to legal concerns, is

an inadequate way of understanding a relationship of love that, in Christ, has become a mystery of faith. Marriage as a flesh and blood instance of Christ's love for his Church is not conforming to an external reality but is participating in it. The Catholic sacramental tradition speaks to us of realities that are gifted to us by Christ, and so touch the heart that they bring people together as the Church, Christ's Community.

This book explores two principal themes – marriage as covenant and family as domestic church. The work of theologians, the teachings of popes and Council have helped us to 'rediscover' these essential elements of our tradition. They have yet to influence fully our thinking and practice so that we can find more fruitful ways of supporting pastorally our people in their marriages and family relationships. The grip of law leaves many people unsupported and ensures that those who, for whatever reason, find themselves in irregular situations feel even more out in the cold despite exhortations by bishops, popes and others that they do belong and should feel they belong.

The reality of covenant is at the centre of God's relationship with us in Christ. We become immersed in it through baptism; it is renewed every time we celebrate the Eucharist and it is the defining reality of marriage between two baptized Christians. A particularly pleasing aspect of this book is that it teases out some of the effects on marriage of being touched by Christ in his Church through the sacrament of baptism. It becomes an ecclesial reality. Conjugal love, such a deeply human reality, through baptism becomes a part of our on-going story of salvation, which is the Church. Marriage, very naturally, becomes the foundation of family, and family touched by baptism cannot but become the Church in its domestic form. In this way all family relationships become engraced and thus the domestic Church is not a 'holy huddle' of two and 2.5 children but a dynamic, outward-looking unit that is able to give witness to marriage that attempts to be truly ecclesial by breaking out of the narrow confines of what we call 'the nuclear family'.

Among the many seams explored, Fr Jeffery conducts a dialogue with the Eastern Traditions. He explores the important common ground that we have with the Eastern Churches when we allow our sacramental tradition its proper voice. From this source we can challenge some dominant elements in our present society that seem to promote excessively the individualism of our age. Genuine human love, especially in its conjugal form, shapes community through being self-giving rather than self-promoting. Ironically the Christian tradition will always say that genuine self-promotion can only be achieved through self-giving.

This book is an invitation to think 'big, deep and differently'. It provides a solid theological basis for marital and family spirituality. It is particularly good in addressing the wider issues of family and does not hesitate to use the notion of sacrament in the broader sense to embrace a wider set of family relationships while keeping in view that marriage must always be at the heart of the family. Perhaps many of the irregular and unfortunate family situations of which many people have first-hand experience will be more fruitfully addressed as we re-appropriate the best of our theological tradition.

The Church's major concern is 'the salvation of souls'. This book is a welcome contribution to articulating what that could mean for those deeply personal relationships that constitute marriage and family.

† Christopher Budd
Bishop of Plymouth

Introduction

Beware of friends suggesting that you explain how marriage is a covenant. This is what started this book. Although I knew that there were a whole series of questions that are rarely discussed, such as: Why was the definition at Vatican II that marriage was a covenant so important? What consequences did this have? What did remarks mean, like: 'the sacrament continues throughout life and brings about a domestic church'? Most of all why is marriage always presented as an image of the marriage between Christ and His Church? It was only when the theological content of the term covenant was closely examined that the real import of saying marriage is a covenant became clear. As the research for this book took place, it became evident that there were a whole series of doors that were known to theologians, but seldom opened. When I opened these doors, I found I had wandered into an array of riches known to the early Fathers of the Church, rediscovered again at the Second Vatican Council in the 1960s, yet practically unknown today by the ordinary Christian.

To reveal the riches of the theology of marriage necessarily involves some theological archaeology. But there are always two dangers in this. The first danger is that the past will be searched for texts to prove the point without taking into account the context in which the text was written. To correct this the second danger takes over

where the examination degenerates into a historical trea-
tise. Hopefully this has been avoided as far as possible. Yet
when misinterpretation and misrepresentation is abroad,
the past needs exploring and the original texts need re-
examining. The biggest error is translating these texts to
overemphasize your own point of view. This has
frequently occurred; I can only hope I have not made the
same error.

It is commonly said that 'marriages are made in
heaven'. As regards the choice of partners, I have sometimes had my doubts whether this is true. But as regards
the invention of marriage, it is certainly true. The fundamental truth regarding marriage has always been that God
invented marriage not merely as a sexual institution so
that children might be born, but by marriage He wished to
reflect His own family of Father, Son and Spirit. Thus, the
basis of marriage is always family and relationships with
love at its heart. It is clear that humankind has found
conjugal love a difficult task, yet it is this concept of
marriage, having its basis in relationship, which this book
explores, not in a psychological sense, but in a theological
sense. It is not the purpose of the book to investigate
marital ethics or sexual ethics, although these flow from
marital theology. This is because, due to an overemphasis
on sexual morality today, the theology of marriage has
been obscured, with the result that some even see marital
theology flowing from sexual ethics. The reverse is true.
Sexual morality flows from marital theology. In addition
there are many books on sexual ethics already, and the
position of the Roman Catholic Church is well known.
This book is about the theology of Christian marriage,
which is not so well known, where marriage is understood
as a heterosexual union. In brief, it tries to answer the
question: What is God's vision of Christian marriage?

Examining the past to illuminate the present involves
grappling with the previous terms and explanations used
to express the theology of Christian marriage. Sometimes,
seminal phrases are found; sometimes, it is clear the terms

used have so determined future thought that they have become a hindrance to future development. The clearest examples of the latter are the canonical terms of contract, institution and indissolubility. As canonical expressions of theological truths, they are perfectly acceptable. But they become an obstacle when they are applied to the theology of marriage, as was clearly stated at the Second Vatican Council. Instead, theology uses the terms covenant, family and permanence to express the same reality. This in no way denies the truths the canonical words express; rather it illuminates the broader reality, which form their basis. It is this broader theological reality that this book seeks to express.

The necessity for such an exploration is easily visible today. A person who has no understanding of the past and no framework for telling their own story will be at the mercy of whoever decides what the options will be, and from where they must select them. Nowhere has this been more evident than in marriage. The past has been replaced so that marital values depend upon the prevalent ideas of a good marriage. Changes have taken place particularly in the role of the partners so that expectations are considerably altered to the extent that the purpose of marriage has been transformed. Personal fulfilment and enjoyment have largely superseded family ideals. Furthermore, as each generation believes its arrangements are superior to those of their parents, there is a real danger that the past together with its values is sidelined, mere history, irrelevant to the present. Marriage can be reinvented at will. But such a revolution tends to confuse cultural expression with values. The reaction is often painted as ultra conservatism – 'the young don't think like us any more', or rejection of all that went before – 'the world has changed, we must keep up to date'. Yet there are a large number of married Christians relying on family tradition. Mothers often hear their daughters telling their children exactly the same things as they did, and in many cases in exactly the same words. Nearly always this is about dos and don'ts.

There is continuity in moral tradition that is not so easily lost. Family values remain based on a kind of folk-religion where values are cut adrift from their roots. But this is dangerous. Rootless values die. Truly, those with no past and no framework are at the mercy of opinion makers.

This dangerous situation has already alarmed many politicians, who foresee the dissolution of society if family values die. But they are ill equipped to deal with the situation. The churches that are equipped to give guidance are ineffective. In fact, what is remarkable is that the churches' influence in this area has almost disappeared. The cause of this phenomenon is complex, but certain factors that have caused this ignorance are clear. Most prominent of these are: the tendency in the Western Church to understand marriage through the optic of a contract; and the negative Augustinian approach to marriage where having sex could only be justified by the intention to procreate. These two factors so impoverished the theology of marriage that from the time of the 1917 Code of Canon Law until the Second Vatican Council there was scarcely a theology of marriage. The shortness of life and the large number of children who died in infancy made this theology seem a reasonable approach in the past. However, a longer life-span, where child-bearing years formed only one period of life, meant that the relationship between a couple became increasingly important. When this was combined with the advent of the birth-control pill, a whole new area of marriage came to the fore. Marriage could no longer be described in the contractual terms. There was need to clarify the personal basis of marriage.

It was the realization that the old approach was incapable of revealing the sacrament of marriage that caused the major change in the approach to marriage at the Second Vatican Council in the 1960s, clearly evident in the document *Gaudium et Spes*. It rejected a purely contractual vision of marriage. Yet since then, those who say a covenant is the same as a contract have largely hidden this transformation. The result is that for many Christians, the sacrament of marriage is still a one-day wonder, where the emphasis is on the wedding vows. It is a ceremony that takes place in church where more attention is paid to the flowers, the attire of the wedding party and the party that follows than to the sacrament being received. This leaves the struggle to fulfil the personal vision of marriage to psychology that can be seen in the numerous books on 'How to get on as a couple'. While a psychological approach is valuable and necessary, and marriage counselling can help to solve relationship problems, there is still a whole area that is absent in such an approach. Christian marriage as a sacrament has been overlooked.

The main consequence of this secularization of marriage is that marriage is seen as a contract binding a man and a woman based on biology and social custom. Sociology, anthropology, and psychology illuminate marriage so that marriage has no need of a religious dimension. This impoverished view has been made worse by the attitude that canon law adequately describes and regulates marriage. There is a failure to realize that marriage possesses both a legal and a personal dimension, and the sacrament belongs to the personal dimension. While it is true that in marriage the personal dimension becomes a legal reality, the progression from a personal reality to a legal entity does not of itself make marriage, otherwise marriage is a piece of paper. Rather, the nature of the personal relationship makes a marriage, and is the basis of the sacrament.

Obviously, this relationship can be over-romanticized and lead to unreal expectations in living happily ever after as in fairy tales. Yet the perverseness and self-seeking of human nature soon brings any couple face to face with reality. The meaning of the self-gift of each other then becomes only too clear. Conjugal love goes beyond eroticism or human drive, because it is the gift of persons, not of organs. Its explanation is beyond biology and is found deep within the couple. It goes beyond attraction because conjugal love is a very special form of personal friendship where, within reason, everything is shared. It is not based on what is received, but what is given because it is the gift of oneself. Thus, the personal element in marriage is at the heart of marriage.

However, the significance of this self-gift cannot be limited to personal relationships, forgetting its religious dimension. The divine dimension is not an added extra, dependent on the religious conviction of the couple. Instead, this element has its origin in God, who invented marriage and made it in the image and likeness of His family. Marriage has fundamentally a divine dimension, which is clearly seen in the self-sacrifice found in human love. Love goes so far beyond human reason that the care of a husband for his sick wife, or the care of a mother for her disabled child, runs contrary to most human attitudes. Truly, conjugal love is a sign of being made in the image and likeness of God, who is love. It is this conjugal love that is elevated so that marriage becomes a Christian sacrament. This was the ground plan of God, which could be seen in the love of God for his chosen people – a people he had married.

But this was only the beginning. Marriage was to be elevated to a new level. With the coming of Christ, membership of God's family went beyond physical creation as a human person to being His sons and daughters in the New Creation through baptism. When these sons and daughters marry, they participate in God's family in a new way and have a special place in creation. They are the instruments of new life, both biologically and spiritually. Through their family they bring about a new order of relationships where all who meet them participate in the love of Christ. As children of God they take part in God's life, which means participation not only at a physical level, but also at a religious level, because sacraments need involvement. This is the radical difference between Christian marriage and non-Christian marriage; Christian marriage is about being a family participating in Christ's saving mystery by being part of the Church; non-

Christian marriage is just about being a family. Christian marriage is not just about receiving a blessing, but about belonging because Christ is always present in this marriage. This radical difference is not signified in the term contract, which only indicates its human dimension, but in the term covenant that shows the divine dimension of Christian marriage. This is the thesis of this book.

To explore such a vision, it is first necessary to examine the debate that took place at Vatican II over marriage, where it was insisted that marriage is a covenant, and that the essence of marriage is found in conjugal love. Revolutionary though this concept was in defining the limits of the contractual concept of marriage, and overturning Duns Scotus' definition that the contract was about the exclusiveness of sexual relations between the partners, it was only a return to the Scriptures and the teaching of the Fathers of the Church that renewed the concept of Christian marriage. The concept of covenant necessarily brings out the personal dimension of marriage, yet describes the merging of the human with the divine. It was the Second Vatican Council's interpretation of the biblical phrase 'two in one flesh'.

The return to the biblical concept of marriage underlined marriage as a community of life and love, showing the theological basis of marriage. This did not mean that marriage was purely about love. The bishops at the Second Vatican Council in the 1960s had no intention of restricting marriage in this sense. Nor did it mean that childless marriage was promoted. Instead, the intention was to underline the centrality of the gift of self in marriage, the basis of conjugal love. Certain important conclusions flow from this. First, as conjugal love can only be understood from the marital covenant, sexuality cannot be understood simply in a biological sense, but rather in a full human sense of being the source of community. Second, the marital covenant means that self-giving is not any one act, or the blessing of fertility, but a dynamic force for the whole community of life. Just as the original covenant brought about the people of God, the marriage covenant brings about a new concept of being the people of God by partaking in the community. From this flows the third conclusion, that Christian marriage is a domestic church, not in the sense that there children learn about God, but in the sense that the Christian family is church, an incarnation of the Church.

It is into these facts that the concept of marriage as a sacrament must be threaded, for the sacrament is not exterior to marriage, a blessing on family life, but is interior and is part of the marriage. Christian marriage is a participation in the new creation brought about by Christ. As Ephesians teaches, the flesh of Christ brought about the gift of new life so that the Gentiles participate in a new creation and new temple because they are now members of the household of Christ. This new creation achieved through their baptism is the foundation for the new relationship of Christian marriage where the relationship between husband and wife takes on a new dimension as they participate in the mystery of Christ. The spouses participate in the love of Christ because they become part of the love of Christ for His Church through their marriage. In addition, incorporation into Christ takes place through incorporation into the Church. Christian marriage shows forth the Church, is part of the Church and occupies a special place within the Church. Thus, the Christian vision of marriage finds its model in the domestic church, God's family.

In every way, family is the true sign of marriage. Family is where life is handed down, and lineage is created, because family is the base unit of human society – not only because it underlines the fundamental relationships that affect a person, but also because it is the image God revealed of Himself. Christian marriage adds a further dimension to this notion, because there the priestly role of the Christian couple is carried out. In living out the nuptial mystery of Christ, they meet Christ, portray Christ and give Christ to the family and the world. They are a living image and historical representation of the mystery of the Church. Within the home their priestly function is one of service and witness to faith and the values of a Christian life. By bringing their children up in faith and nurturing them in love, they are witnesses to the world of Christ's love. Thus the family with all its relationships is sacramental; it is here that Christian marriage goes beyond creation to salvation. This is the dynamic sign Christian marriages give to the world.

Some years ago the Laity Commission asked that the Church teach marriage, not give rules. This is what this book is about, discovering the mystery of the sacrament of marriage. Thus married Christians can understand the presence of God in their marriage and grasp the central place of marriage in the life of the Church, and the Church in the life of the family. Obviously, a single book cannot fulfil such a purpose, and so it should be immediately evident that this book is incomplete. Rather, it paints a picture where certain areas are illuminated. Much more is still unexplored. Nor does this book claim to be a reference book where the footnotes form an integral part. Instead, the book can be read ignoring the footnotes. The footnotes are only there for those who wish to research the matter further.

It has taken a long time to research the book, and I must thank Mr John Harwood, librarian at the Missionary Institute London for his assistance in finding texts, especially those referring to the Orthodox Church. Thanks must also go to fellow lecturers, and lay people I have consulted, too many to mention. Finally there are the unseen proofreaders, who deserve the greatest thanks and have made the book possible.

Chapter One

Relationships, Theology and Marriage

Everyone knows in his or her heart that mutual under-standing and respect make a marriage. Everyone knows that marriage has to be worked at to overcome as far as possible human failings. We are beings that carry gifts in fragile containers and are afflicted by weakness and sinfulness. Yet the gifts are there, especially the gift of love. This gift, the foundation upon which marriage is built, holds a mystery that needs exploring. Part of the mystery is why such a gift exists at all. Love is a peculiar human attribute that goes beyond our animal nature. This already suggests that its origin is beyond our evolutionary capabilities, as love cannot be reduced to eroticism or a human drive. If this is tried, love soon departs as the real-ities of married life dawn. Love is between persons not organs, and so its explanation is beyond biology. It is also beyond psychology for though psychology can remove the barriers to love, it cannot explain it because love goes beyond attraction. Love is a very special form of personal friendship where, within reason, everything is shared. It is not based on what is received, but what is given because it is the gift of oneself. For the Christian, it is the sign of a being made in the image and likeness of God. God gave us love. It is because of this that the depths of love depend on a spiritual dimension.

2 The Mystery of Christian Marriage

However, for many people the spiritual dimension is a lovely thought: unreal, unworldly, far from the reality of marriage with all its stress and strain, quarrels and fights. The result is that a theology of marriage is quietly disregarded and discarded by priests and laity. The priest finds canon law much simpler and more practical. The laity thinks the interpersonal point of view of marriage only finds its meaning in the interplay between the partners. Theology is irrelevant, a belief compounded by the conviction that priests, having no experience of marriage, should leave the subject to others. Priests are window shoppers, admiring the goods, but never buying them. What is needed is experiential knowledge of conjugal love and psychology. However, to reduce married life to this would be seriously incomplete. There is a need to understand marriage holistically.

Marriages can only be understood if people are seen in their world. Yet this is difficult because the complexity of marriage necessarily involves many disciplines. Thus, it is necessary to examine its biological basis because surely the mental state, the gender-orientation, and the ability to cope with daily living must be taken into account. Likewise, from a psychological point of view, the ability to relate, the motivation and the possibility of putting these motives into action so that expectations become realities are important elements. Again, the wider community of relationships within which a marriage has to work can be illuminated by sociology and anthropology making it possible to understand the backdrop of the marriage. Yet the value system the couple bring to marriage and their understanding of its obligations are crucial to the way a marriage is lived. These do not come from sociology or anthropology but flow from an inbuilt spirituality, whether the couple realizes it or not. This does not mean that sociology or anthropology are irrelevant to understanding marriage. Rather, it means that all of these elements are important, whether applied to medicine, to produce holistic medicine, or applied to marriage in order to understand the complex reality that marriage is. Only a bio-social-anthropo-psycho-spiritual model of marriage can give full insight.

Yet such an approach is rarely seen. Most of the specialist literature concerning marriage ignores this complexity and thus presents incomplete models of marriage. There is a real danger where marriage is concerned that many disciplines examine the question in isolation. For example, when sociologists and anthropologists examine marriage, they consider social attitudes and changes in society. Principal among these are the changed attitude of women, the disposability of relationships, the emphasis on self-realization, and the effects of the contraceptive pill, which brings freedom to conceive or not to conceive. Yet when psychologists examine the same crisis, they concentrate on the depth of the relationship and find the cause of the difficulties in the inability of many men and women to truly relate. Historically the Church has similarly failed, by simply presenting a single model of marriage modelled on Roman custom. Marital problems were examined in the light of this model and a condemnatory tone pervaded many Church documents. Thus, Church documents before Vatican II always included a long list of sins against marriage. Little attention was paid to the reason for these sins except to comment that they constituted a grave danger to the Christian ideal of marriage. Rarely were questions asked concerning the cause of these aberrations, and why people acted in a certain way. Making an analogy with medicine, the Church has been treating symptoms rather than diseases. Thus, the answers were inadequate for the problems people faced.

Since the 1960s, the time of John XXIII, a different attitude can be seen in the Church where answers are given to the signs of the times, and theology establishes why certain actions should be rejected. This new attitude called for the recognition of the spiritual dimension of marriage. Strangely, this spiritual dimension is rarely mentioned even by believing Christians, due to a rejection of the role of theology in life, and the 'privatization' of religion: the belief that religious values must not affect public life. Pluralistic society respects everyone and expects humanistic values to be sufficient for human life even though it is clear both to sociologists and anthropologists that such an approach cannot succeed. They both acknowledge the importance of belief in family life, but can only illuminate the external workings of this belief. In this way sociology's and anthropology's answers are limited. Even if the concepts of biology, sociology, anthropology and psychology are combined together, they are unable to satisfy the demands marriage presents. This is clear because although the present situation does not lack for sociological and psychological research, the situation of so many marriages does not improve. There is a need to accept that these disciplines alone cannot solve the lack of an understanding of marriage. The depth of marriage is found elsewhere, in theology. Theology is an essential criterion. This does not mean that biology, sociology and psychology are redundant; rather their findings need theology to be complete.

This point is even clearer if the extent of these disciplines and what they show is examined. Critical reflection and analysis of society depends on the tools used for such a work.[1] Historical analysis reflects on the social system and its causes, concentrating on external structures and institutions, or on the value systems that underlie these structures. Thus analysis of the social system can be both objective and subjective or even both in its findings. This complexity leads to many misunderstandings. First, the methods used do not provide immediate answers: instead they are diagnostic in that they can identify social trends. A further examination is necessary based on other criteria before an answer is forthcoming and action taken.[2] Second, social surveys can only provide a picture at a particular point in time, and as society is in constant change, this view may later be inaccurate. Third, they are a nuanced view of society, which may not include all the complexities, so generalizations are hazardous.[3] Finally, social research is not a value-free analysis. It is based on preconceived values that are used to criticize policies and practices and these pre-values are often not without bias. Hence social analysis is both a useful tool and a misleading tool and cannot provide answers on its own.

Likewise, psychology has its limits coming from its methodology. A non-directive or client-centred approach can help a person to realize what is their inner self, but the basis of this approach is the acceptance of that person. The depth of the person may be illuminated, but that person alone can change their inner self. Likewise, the basis of a relationship can be clarified, and the reason for various difficulties revealed, but only the couple themselves can correct and heal the relationship. Marriage counsellors are well aware of these limitations. Furthermore, they know marriage is with this person, in this culture, at this time, so that the full human reality contains many levels of meaning that depend on the person's value system. However, it is not easy to gain an insight into this value system even though it is the heart of what makes a person what they are.[4] Partly this is because it is at the centre of the person, and partly because the system depends on the way a person has internalized values. Literally, a person cannot operate without values, whether these are acceptable to others or not. Yet such a concept does not imply that the person openly believes and practises a faith, rather it implies values accepted, often through custom or family tradition.

It is the basis of these values that is all-important for married life. While humanists may claim their origin is in the natural goodness of human beings, human experience finds this an inadequate explanation as the perverseness of humankind causes considerable strain on any loving relationship. Instead, anthropology, sociology and psychology find the basis of values is in religion. This means the depth of marriage is found in theology. Unfortunately, the reaction to this statement often is: 'the

Church should keep out of the bedroom' because the Church is seen as a bringer of rules not a revealer of God's loving plan found in marriage. So, the experience of the ordinary married Christian in finding a supportive theology of marriage in the Church is very poor.

The reason for this negative impression of the Church in its attitude to marriage is not just based on its sexual ethics. The legalistic approach of the clergy also has to answer for this. So often the clerical approach to marriage is based on canon law where marriage is described as a 'contract' and an 'institution'. In both cases, these terms conceal rather than reveal the theology of marriage. The problem is not that marriage is not a contract or an institution, but that marriage is much more than these terms are able to convey. In addition, further obscurity is caused by the double description of marriage in canon law where it is described both as a covenant and a contract.[5]

Considerable confusion is caused by this statement, which is compounded by the fact that many canon lawyers see no difference between a contract and a covenant. For example, Orsy says: 'Contract or covenant, they belong to the same legal model: there must always be an agreement. Agreement can have a sacred dimension, and covenant certainly has that; but the agreement also has a legal content and contract says that well enough even after Vatican II.'[6] Yet covenant is a theological concept based on love; while contract is a legal concept based on consent. Furthermore, such a position obscures and ignores the double nature of marriage. Marriage is both a personal and a social reality. As a personal reality it is expressed in conjugal love, and in this sense of daily living marriage comes about through a covenant. But as a social reality it is a family, a legal entity, and an institution, and in this sense marriage comes about through a contract. Thus, a contractual relationship and a covenantal relationship express different realities. They are not interchangeable terms.

These different realities are well known. Contract is

concerned with what constitutes marriage, while covenant expresses what marriage is. The difference is crucial. Marriage lived as a contract is well known to marriage counsellors. One such story is the man who came for counselling because of difficulties in his marriage. He told the counsellor: 'You would understand why I am here if you saw our house. Nothing ever seems to get done. The washing is always late. Last week I dropped a dirty sock by the bed in full view and left it there. A week later it was still there.' When the counsellor suggested that he pick it up himself and put it in the dirty linen basket, the reply was: 'That's her job not mine.' This marriage had become a contract based on job descriptions, rather than a covenant based on conjugal love.

From the idea of marriage as a contract flows the idea of marriage as an institution because marriage is a state of life entered into through mutual consent freely given. However, marriage is more than an institution, even an institution made holy, because it has personal, practical and spiritual dimensions. The personal dimension is summed up in the phrase conjugal love. The spiritual dimension is found in the concept of a domestic church. The problem is that canon law by its own admission is incapable of expressing conjugal love and so reduces marriage to an agreement, and concentrates on what constitutes a legal marriage. Likewise, the term institution is an insufficient description of marriage, which cannot describe the domestic church. Yet there has been a tendency to reduce marriage to an institution alone and to believe that by exactly defining this in law, canon law expresses the essence of marriage. The falsehood of this position was made very clear at Vatican II which defined marriage as the intimate partnership of life and love.[7]

Thus theologically, marriage cannot be presented through the optic of canon law. Even when canon law applies the insights of sociology and psychology, it only applies these findings to define the necessary consent and consummation for a marriage to take place. Marriage is a lived reality and these legal aspects do not address the day-to-day reality of a living marriage. To inspire married life demands appreciating the centrality of the theology of marriage, and understanding that a marriage's value system gives life to the marriage. This value system depends on the cultural and religious values the couple have. This dimension needs exploring. Yet this exploration cannot begin by taking a view from above. The hidden forces manipulating people today must be uncovered. There is a real necessity to discern the signs of the times using biology, sociology, anthropology and psychology and taking into account their limitations: limitations that mean these disciplines only provide a picture of a particular instance in time and are nuanced in that the tools they use have preconceptions. They do not give a value-free analysis, but a picture of the forces at work moulding modern marriage. As Orsy points out: 'Marriage is a drama in its original classical sense of the word: an action performed on scene where the participants are often moved by hidden forces and energies.'[8]

It is these forces and energies that must be discovered, and at the same time combined with the forgotten truths of marital theology. To discover these forces, an examination of the present understanding of today's catalysts is necessary. Behind modern marriage lies a series of fears and hopes that determine the ideal of marriage. Among these are certainly the disposability of relationships, the multiplicity of relationships and the economics of relationships. An understanding of these elements underlines the importance of relationships.

The Disposability of Relationships

In 1976, Jack Dominian noted that the traditional ends of marriage remain children, permanency and faithfulness. Currently they are greatly enlarged in the direction of the quality of the relationship of the couple and between parents and children. Marriage is seen primarily as a community of love. In addition, this community of love is being influenced by revolutionary changes in the duration of marriage, the man–woman relationship, procreation and the expectations of the couple.[9] It can be seen in the phenomena of couples living together before marriage, the disposability of relationships and consumerism. Thus some hold that the typical family has vanished. *The Toronto Star* in 1995 claimed this is true, quoting *Statistics Canada*.[10] Likewise, a British newspaper had as its headline: 'Marriage – Never more Popular, Never more Risky'. The cause is divorce and common-law marriages to the extent that today one third of all marriages end in divorce and one third of children are born out of wedlock.

This secular evaluation is echoed by religious surveys reporting that 50 per cent of Catholic couples coming for marriage preparation are already living together. The result is that not only has this made the sequence of changes – leaving home, courtship, getting married, having children and being grandparents – more complicated, it also has created a reluctance to make commitments on a long-term basis and altered the concept of what marriage is about. In fact, there is a kind of vicious circle where the reluctance to marry erodes the idea of Christian marriage: so much so that those involved in preparing couples for marriage are often struck, even frightened, by the gap between what Christian marriage really is and the vision many young couples asking to be married have of it. This does not just apply to those who choose to marry in church because it looks nice, or make their marriage into an event that should be blessed or solemnized in a cultural practice that is empty of its real meaning; there is a real ignorance even among practising Christians as to what Christian marriage is about.

The reasons for these phenomena are complex, but certainly among them are the changed expectations of women and their role within a marriage. In Victorian times, marriage found its ideal in the middle classes where children were separate from adults, and looked after by a nanny. Fashion made women look weak and in need of protection, able to play the piano to provide entertainment. The reality was very different. Among the wealthy, women were able to play the piano but at the same time they were the managers of the household and not wilting flowers; among the poor they were an essential part of a family economic unit where to survive everyone worked. An unmarried woman worked in the factory or the shop, and even after marriage continued to work until the birth of her first child. Even then she had to supplement the husband's wage by taking in piecework, boarders, or laundry. The grim reality of survival determined marriage, not the patriarchal ideal. Economics determined the woman's role. The man's role was also dominated by economics, particularly in the sense that the man saw himself as the breadwinner. War challenged this social ideal by changing the economic role of women.

In Britain, the 1914–1918 war brought women out of the family or domestic service into the munitions factories, taking over work previously done by men. When the armistice of 1918 took place, men once again wanted to take their place as breadwinners, and this occurred. Yet economic freedom and the absence of men had altered women's perception of their role in life. In America the phenomenon was even more pronounced, trumpeted as the arrival of the 'new woman'. The Second World War reinforced this new role. In 1939 women were urged to enter non-traditional professions – the Land Army in Britain, and Rosie the Riveter in the United States. Women drove tractors, made ships and aeroplanes and generally replaced the men who had gone to war. Yet by 1944 in America and 1945 in Britain, as the men came home from war, women were told to return to being housewives. But women did not just return to their previous role in marriage; the joint breadwinner was here in a very different form than in the nineteenth century. It was not crippling poverty that drove the necessity to work, but the expectation of what domestically in the home must be present, how to pay the mortgage, what kind of holiday must be provided, and the need to escape from domesticity. Women struggled with the new situation of an increased workload, but the result in many cases was latchkey children. Today one third of school children over twelve come home to an empty house.

But this changing role of women is only a small part of the picture. The emphasis on relationships is another part. In fact, it is a key factor in understanding present day marriage. It would be naïve to think that this emphasis has existed for very long. Before the end of the eighteenth century, and even up to the present in some societies, knowing one's fiancé was not necessary for marriage. Instead, relationships were slowly built up after marriage. People married to have children and companionship. The expectation of life was much shorter than today, and the almost total lack of leisure time meant a very different concept of life. Today, with a longer lifespan and more leisure time, there is time to explore more deeply the experience of relationship in marriage. These, together with the emphasis on sexual relations, means the depth of a relationship and the ability to problem solve are crucial elements for any marriage. Thus, there have been two sexual revolutions in recent times. The first sexual revolution was the change from courting a partner chosen by one's parents to courting someone that one liked. Since the 1960s, this romanticism has been stripped away to get at the sexual core of relationships so that eroticism has been presented as the crucial dimension of human relationships. This was the second sexual revolution with its expectation that sex was enjoyable for both partners.[11] The female orgasm was the subject of women's magazines. The result is the disposability of relationships with an emphasis on their intensity.

The role of this intensity can be seen from the way people view long-term commitment. Timothy Radcliffe tells the story of a student coming up to solemn vows as a

Dominican. His Provincial asked him, 'Can you really promise to be faithful until death?' The student said: 'It depends upon what you mean. If you mean: Will I be faithful no matter what you ask of me, even if it demands my life? Then the answer is: yes. But if you mean: Will I go on being a Dominican until the day that I die? Well I do not know. Who knows who I will become?'[12] It is not the commitment now, this is intense, but what that commitment will be in the future that is the problem.

The same applies to marriage. If the couple's priority is personal fulfilment, when difficulties occur the solution may be divorce because the crisis is perceived as being incompatible with maintaining the personal relationship at the heart of their marriage. Those who work on the idea that love can only be genuine and lasting when it is flawlessly lived, and think that if this is not the case, love is absent, have an unrealistic idea of conjugal love. Human love is always flawed. Unlike our ancestors we expect to control our lives. We feel change more acutely, partially because we live longer and partially because of the way life is changing so rapidly. When difficulties occur, we cannot cope with them, nor overcome them, nor fit them into our development. We think that when the depth of relationship vanishes so does the relationship because we fail to understand purification is necessary for progress, and forgiveness is at the heart of marriage.[13]

Even more crucial is the fear that when people change, the person one married no longer exists. As Radcliffe says: 'if you ever have to see or counsel people whose marriage is on the rocks they will say "I am not the same person who married Jane or Edward ... that person does not exist any more. So how can I be sure my marriage will last?"' What is happening is that couples are celebrating in their marriage vows the depth of their current commitment, not its extension through time. They are living only for now, and are in grave danger of losing the sense of the permanence of their relationship. It is a reflection of modern life that divides life into groups and separate pieces. The problem is that when our lives do not make sense, we cannot see beyond our group. Life lived for the moment has no future.

One result has been that many couples have tried to avoid the disposability of relationships by living together before marriage to see how things work out. They are oblivious to the studies that show that marriage after living together has a higher divorce rate because the difficulties involved are avoided rather than solved.[14] The problem is that living together accepts the breakdown of the relationship as a distinct possibility and therefore after marriage true bonding is more difficult to achieve and may never really take place. This attitude is evident, for example, in the lack of buying things together. What occurs is that the attitudes, issues and patterns the couples take into cohabitation are carried on into marriage. So, when marriage takes place, externally little changes and thus the necessary internal changes do not take place. The result is that couples who have cohabitated before marriage tend to have a different attitude to commitment and permanence. Also they tend to have more conflict and are more prone to domestic violence than non-cohabiting couples. The reason is that they still have to learn to live for the future, not just for the present.

Beneath this lies the problem of the 'privatization' of marriage. This conceives society as a collection of isolated family units. What has caused this concept is rather complex. It is a myth to present the kinless conjugal family as a result of the Industrial Revolution. Families in Europe were not just organized in clans or highly extended, but always included a large percentage of nuclear families consisting of parents and children only.[15] Yet the 'stem' family where the eldest child inherited from their father was the most common form of family life.[16] The kinless family was an anomaly. The nuclear family today is different from the past because of its inward-looking attitude. Home is a protected place, an emotional fortress into which the modern family has withdrawn. The modern

family is based on the mother–infant relationship; domesticity is the basis of the nuclear family. Yet even that is
under attack. The demands of employers necessitating
mobility to move not only from one part of the country to
another but also from one country to another, and the
demands of a higher standard of living have changed
family life. The difficulty of finding work, the desire to be
independent, and the general idea that a family is an
enclosed unit have all contributed to this phenomenon. It
is further complicated by the fact the wife has to work as
well as the husband, and each grown-up child wishes to
be separate, which is reflected in the demand for one- or
two- bedroom flats. The same phenomenon can occur in
marriage where both husband and wife can almost live
separate lives. The privatization of marriage has occurred.

The privatized nuclear family conceives family in a very
narrow sense that creates many difficulties. The absence of
parents or relatives nearby, as Giblin observes, means the
modern family has no buffers to deal with change, so the
stress of contemporary culture, out of touch with the
family's deeper needs and wants, leads to marital conflict
because of the multiple levels couples are asked to operate
on at the same time. There is no one nearby to look after
the children if necessary. There is no shoulder to cry on.
Work absorbs everything during the week and the
weekend is spent catching up on various duties.[17] Moreover, when parents grow old and frail the problem of how
to care for them becomes acute. Finally, when the children
leave home, there is a need to re-learn marriage, for the
modern model of family involves a cyclic relationship:
beginning with the partners, passing through having children and once again returning to a one-to-one relationship.[18] This privatized view of society leaves much to be
desired.

Another part of the same scene is the phenomenon of
one-parent families. In one sense these are not new as
there have always been one-parent families caused by the
early death or departure of one of the partners. What is

new is the choice of women to be a one-parent family, rather than marry the father of their child. This may be an eminently sensible decision when the man in question is taken into consideration. But it is a very different thing to promote one-parent families as an ideal as feminism has done. Feminists see the two-parent family as an intimate environment that is unequal and destructive because it perpetuates the patriarchal society. They see marriage as a trap where a fixed form dictates the way men and woman organize their lives. They argue that women should be free to live in an intimate relationship with whosoever they choose, and thus feminism promotes one-parent families as one of several options for a woman. Sadly, this totally ignores the experience of one-parent families who even with preferential help in housing and social support find the experience totally different from the ideal painted by those who promote it.

Taking this feminist stance a step further is the reaction against what is called 'procreationism'. Gudorf sees the assumption that sex is naturally orientated toward creation of life as the most serious enduring obstacle to a new sexual ethic. Her reasons for the rejection of procreationism are that it limits sex to the marital act and calls all other sexual relationships foreplay, it gives no value to same sex relationships or any sexual relationship where children are not a possibility, and views contraception as killing children.[19] Similarly, marriage contracts, particularly among rich divorcees, exclude children. Curiously, Gudorf's new reproductive ethic is based on the danger of overpopulation so that one child is the ideal; an experiment that already has had disastrous consequences in China with the Little Emperor or Empress syndrome, or has caused similar problems in Italy and the UK with the declining birth-rate. Basically Gudorf is part of a movement that primarily sees sexual intercourse and relationships as being simply for pleasure, and so views marriage in the same light. In this, she is challenging the Augustinian approach that sexual pleasure must be combined with the possibility of procreation. The phenomenon of reducing sex to entertainment is part of the same scene. Sexual pleasure primarily for oneself is a further step on the path of living for the moment.

Thus the disposability of relationships is both the cause and the result of the pressures affecting modern marriage. The emphasis on the externals of love, the intensity of a relationship and the inability to foster mature relationships lead to living together, one-parent families, and the difficulty of making permanent promises to another. The nuclear family has always been with us, but the privatized family is a new and in social terms a dangerous phenomenon.

The Multiplicity of Relationships

Part of the modern reality is the multiplicity of relationships, whether permanent or successive. Permanent multiple relationships in marriage either take the form of polygamy or polyandry, or keeping a mistress. This is not confined to certain races or civilizations, even though it is often identified with pre-Christian civilizations. As a cultural phenomenon, it arises from a seldom-understood folk culture. As so much of the West is a multicultural society, it is worth examining the origins of such phenomena. In an African context permanent multiple relationships follow certain traditional notions of which the most basic is an attempt to recapture, at least in part, the lost gift of immortality.[20] Children are really the physical continuation of their parents so that they do not simply continue a lineage, but immortalize their parents in a direct and personal way. In many African societies ancestors are believed to be reincarnated in their descendants.[21] Thus, fertility becomes central to marriage as offspring guarantee the ancestors continued life. The high incidence of infertility in Africa was a danger to such a belief, so infertile marriages are deliberately broken by the man's family, often by his grandmother, or the answer is found in polygamy. Yet the sending away of a wife is disaster for a woman, whom nobody else will marry and whose only choice is often prostitution. Hence polygamy was a loving response to the first wife who is not sent away and whose status was enhanced by the second wife. Not only that, but security in old age, a guarantee of a fitting burial for parents,[22] and the need for a reliable labour and defence force for the family reinforced such a decision. It the past, polygamy was a religious and social necessity so that the family might live.

In modern urban Africa this reason for polygamy is no more than a folk memory.[23] The complex systems of marriage do not exist so there are no rules determining which kinship group a person should marry. The result is that marriage is modelled on European forms of marriage.[24] Polygamy still exists, but for different reasons. The phenomenon of a 'wife' for home, or 'inside wife' and a 'wife' for the office, 'outside wife', is often no more than mistress keeping. But it can have another meaning. The 'inside' wife is frequently an elite woman living in the 'official' residence, monogamous, adhering to a Western ideal of marriage. The 'outside' wife is more difficult to define. Karanja defines such an 'outside' wife as: 'a woman with whom the man has had sexual relations for several years, is financially maintained during this rela-tionship and whose children are acknowledged'. So, it could be a second marriage according to native law and custom with no legal status, or it could be a second marriage because of status, i.e. the need for a modern educated wife. It most cases the second wife will not be recognized as a wife in the traditional polygamous sense, as the first wife has had no participation in choosing this woman.[25] However, the practice of the rich and powerful having many wives is a different matter. As Steady has shown, polygamy is an important factor in the acquisition of wealth and power. In a rural society this came about through having sufficient workers for the work.[26] In urban societies a large family meant influence, and a greater basis for wealth due to the trading ability of the women. Polygamy here is a matter of prestige where power is demonstrated in the number of women a man may keep, and the number of descendents this power may bring.[27] All this is summed up in a long-running Nigerian advert for Guinness that read, 'Guinness gives power'.

It is important to underline that the reasons underlying urban polygamy are different on the part of men and women. The man seeks primarily the status of fatherhood; the woman primarily seeks children and the status of being a wife. The woman will use children as a bargaining point either to persuade a man to marry her because she is fertile, or to make sure a man appreciates her during marriage. Children both make the union and are the union. This is why African multiple unions are often permanent rather than disposable. However, this is not true of Muslim marriages. In Kenya, 73 per cent of Muslim marriages end in divorce. The reason for this instability is the easy repudiation according to Islamic law and the too easy conditions under which marriage is contracted.[28]

Another reason for multiple relationships in an African urban society is the tendency for men to look outside marriage for satisfaction through a concubine, because with her the man goes out for a drink, to eat, dance and have sex. The man here is far more extrovert in his behaviour than with his wife. Yet sex is not the prime reason for keeping a concubine even though this is how the relationship began. Companionship makes this relationship. At a deeper level the man is seeking his lost adolescence, attempting to leave for a while his family responsibilities, and live once again courtship. Divorce can also be part of the same phenomenon where one partner is traded in for another even after a marriage that has lasted for many years. A restless search for new experiences and pleasures arises where the love found in courtship is sought in place of the true conjugal love of marriage. Multiple relationships in these cases are ties without family.

A similar problem can be seen in Caribbean relationships. While there is a long-standing tradition of Christian
marriage, even in the most difficult circumstances, and
monogamy is truly valued, there is a problem of multiple
relationships. These multiple relationships arise from
common-law marriages, which often are no more than
passing unions, a successive monogamy.[29] Some see this
as a legacy of slavery or a social class subculture, though
Davenport doubts such a cause. Whatever the reason, the
main family unit here is a household group, a domestic
group occupying a single dwelling and sharing a common
food supply. Very often such a group contains no conjugal
pair.[30] Instead, the mother is the key to such a grouping as
can be seen in the classic work *My Mother who Fathered
Me*.[31] Davenport says, 'the household is organized according to kinship, sexual behaviour, and marriage with the
aim of maintaining an independent social unit. Although
this household will change with time, the basis remains
constant.'[32]

But because of the system of households, family is
vague, so a common phrase is 'He is some family to me',
or 'He is near family' while 'She is far family'. Likewise,
the relationship between child and father is vague, even
though the child will bear his name. It is common to find
children who have the most casual relationship with their
fathers. In contrast, the mother is the centre of relationships. The result is multiple relationships before marriage,
where the male plays a minor role in family life, and the
relationships between partners and father and children
are weak. The family centre is the woman, or perhaps
more exactly the women, because often the group consists
of grandmother, mother and sister(s). Although this
system does not prevent stable marriages, the relationship
between the partners is very different from traditional
European relationships. The matriarchal basis of family
means children with different fathers, which in some cases
leads to the exclusion of men, so that when they are
teenagers, the men effectively form a separate group with

a propensity for the whole process to repeat itself.

All these facts point to many more different causes for multiple relationships than is usually underlined. The reason for multiplicity may be immature relations with the other sex, or it may be pride. But above all, the cause is seeking for companionship and sexual relationship without the responsibility for a family. The relevance of relationships is the key to this phenomenon.

The Economics of Relationships

One of the many reasons for living together without marrying is the conviction that it is cheaper for two to live together than one. This is particularly true when accommodation is taken into consideration, but it also underlines an economic attitude that profoundly affects relationships. Our culture has developed a profound concern for and belief in economics, so much so that we define life in terms of value for money, success and efficiency.[33] Bauman says that economics is behind the movement to a more pleasurable life, based on the economic cycle.[34] Economics is the new science that seeks to control life. The result is that relationships are seen in the light of 'Are they worth it?'. The time they take up, the effort they demand, and the often-fleeting results, mean that the long-term commitment to marital love comes at too high a price. Not only that, love is also being expressed in material gifts where the cost of the gift measures the amount of love. Pre-marital contracts on the division of goods, if the marriage should end in divorce, are another sign of the same attitude of value for money. But this attitude can only lead to disaster, as love cannot be understood in economic terms.

Therefore, amid the isolation of nuclear and one-parent families and the culture of economics, the major problem marriage faces today concerns the relevance of relationships because it is not only their disposability or multi-plicity, but also their durability that is in question. Perma-nence has being replaced by intensity so that relationships are lived for this moment. The result is that marriage has become privatized, a concern of the couple alone. This is not only shown in the reluctance to marry at all, but is also most clear in the modern emphasis on relationships. Feel-ings come before commitment, to the extent that if feelings change, the commitment changes. Thus, people live for the moment.

Finding Meaning in the Marital Relationship

The phenomena of the disposability, the multiplicity and the economics of relationships eat away at the traditional understanding of marriage. This presents the Church with the greatest difficulty in revealing the true meaning of marriage, as a hedonistic search for excitement and self-fulfilment often contradicts love orientated toward the future.[35] But it is the phenomenon of living for the moment that negates any true idea of growth in love or family. Family involves responsibilities that require long-term commitment. So, when living for the moment is combined with ignorance of the teaching of the Church as regards the theology of marriage, the problem is multi-plied. Add to this the perception that divorce follows marriage, and one can understand why marriage is seen as a serious risk and the idea of family is obscured.

Furthermore, the Church's explanations about marriage in recent years have been largely ignored because the impression people have of the Church's position is itself a problem. Marriage is a complex domain where civil and canon law, moral and sacramental theology intersect. Marriage is both a civil and religious reality. Failure to appreciate this double reality bedevils explanations regarding the sacrament of marriage because the Church since the advent of the 1918 Code of Canon Law has only been presenting marriage as a legal reality. A theology of marital relationships was imprisoned within the concept of a contract so that there was no real concept of a personal love that is both orientated toward the future, as well as being lived in the present. Insistence on the permanence of the bond presented a static concept of marriage. Furthermore, as the insistence on lived relationships grew, this static concept of love had no meaning for married couples beyond the ceremony on their marriage day.

It was just as problematic for the clergy. Marriage was seen as a contract so that the forms the priest had to fill in for a marriage only presented marriage from a canonical point of view. This is very clear when the couple are asked to swear they know of no impediment to their marriage. It is even clearer in seminary training that allotted a great deal of time to the canonical presentation of marriage, and almost none to the theology of marriage. But marriage presented as an institution does not provide inspiration. When this is combined with marital sexuality being seen as a danger, rather than a gift, so that fear of sin is inculcated, rather than ways of relating to each other, it is not surprising that practising Christians see their marriage as no different to pagan marriage, except for a blessing. Christian marriage to a great extent has lost its spiritual significance because marriage is conceived as being under the reign of sin, rather than under the reign of grace.

While the answer has been that marriage is a special kind of contract, which is holy, this has been an obstacle to the theology of marriage.[36] The origin of this approach goes back to the Roman concept of marriage as an exchange of consent. However, to image marriage as an exchange of exclusive sexual rights over another's body, as Duns Scotus did, is to ignore a rich patrimony of theology.[37] To insist, as Cardinal Gaspari did in the 1918 Code of Canon Law, that contract was the only way to conceive marriage was an error.[38] In 1932 he went even further when he wrote: 'marriage *in fieri* (what brings it about) is the act of creating a marital contract accurately manifesting internal consent

on the part of the persons bound by no invalidating impediments. Marriage *in facto esse* (what is brought about) is the
abiding marital contract itself with its attendant natural
rights and obligations.'[39] Consequently, Gaspari saw the
essence of marriage as sexual rights and duties and the
covenental bond between the spouses was ignored.

This interpretation was entirely of Cardinal Gaspari's
own creation. In 1933 Gaspari was challenged over his
reductionist position. Although he soon admitted that the
term 'contract' regarding marriage did not appear in
Roman or Gallic law, he found his critics temerarious and
misguided because marriage comes about by the consent
of two parties to exclusive sexual rights. Further studies
underlined the extent of Gaspari's creation. Navarrete
found that the documents of the Church and canon law
contain hardly anything about the ends of marriage as
goals until the formulation by Gaspari of Canon 1013.[40]
Even more curious is that the first draft of this canon
makes no such claim.[41] Likewise, Fellhauer examined
Gaspari's use of eight sources to support the right to
sexual relations as the sole object of consent. Of these, six
make no mention of this right and the other two deal with
the marriages of Joseph and Mary, and Jacob and Leah.[42]
Thus, the absolutist form of the contract of marriage was
Gaspari's own creation.

Although Gaspari's view of marriage was to be very
influential, this was not the only opinion. Long before,
Sanchez had emphasized that the union of marriage was
the perseverance in the sharing of life.[43] In addition, St
Thomas Aquinas held that consent brought marriage into
existence, but he considered the essential element was the
bond that unites the spouses. Likewise, in 1912 F. X.
Wernz said: 'If marriage is considered as to what brings it
about, it can be defined as the lawful and undivided
contract of a man and a wife for the generation and education of offspring. If on the other hand marriage is taken as
the *bond* of a permanent society, as in common speech and
even that proper to theologians and canonists, it is defined

as the lawful and undivided *union* of man and wife for the generation and education of offspring, or, more briefly, the undivided conjugal or *marital society* of man and wife.'[44]

But the presentation of marriage was not the only obstacle to understanding the Church's theology of marriage. Its teaching on sexuality was perceived as wholly negative in outlook. Great changes have taken place in the last fifty years. Longevity, leisure and the social phenomenon of the contraceptive pill, have substantially changed the arena of sexual ethics. The possibility of separating sexual pleasure from reproduction means that marriage is now seen in the light of interpersonal union and satisfaction. Another sexual revolution had taken place. In the past, birth control largely concerned the man, but the contraceptive pill gave women control over conception. This revolution in birth control challenged, not in theory, but in fact, the guiding principle of Christian sexual morality that the primary purpose or good of sexuality was the procreation and education of children.

For centuries all sexual activity, from the rituals of dating and courtship to the full expression of sexual intercourse, was judged in the light of this primary end. The prospect of separating the procreational purpose of sexual intercourse from the mutual support of the partners meant that human beings could, and would, understand, experience and live, sexuality in a new and different way. This separation is now well established in society, so much so that contraception is seen as the norm and a failure to take precautions is blamed on a lack of sexual education. Secular society has taken the ability to control conception to mean sexual intercourse is a major instrument of pleasure. The result is that sexual intercourse is now emphasized as a form of recreation. Thus, the meaning of marriage was undermined. As the old contractual basis of marriage was swept away, the Church found great difficulty in answering why a code of ethics that prohibited sexual intercourse before marriage was important.

This was the scene the Church faced in the 1960s just before Vatican II. Yet a different approach had already begun. Dietrich von Hildebrand and Herman Domms had proposed a renewed emphasis on personal relationships.[45] They rejected a 'purely biological approach' because the intention to propagate by itself could not unite the heart and the spirit, which the marital act expresses. In addition, Pius XI in 1930 in *Casti Connubii* spoke of a specific kind of love, *caritas*, which is the essence of marriage, and held marriage was *traditio personae*, the giving over of persons. In 1963 Vatican II took this a step further, when it rejected the canonical approach of the preparatory text: 'Concerning Marriage, Chastity and Virginity', and instead focused attention onto the *Letter to the Ephesians* which emphasizes the marriage covenant in the light of the relationship between Christ and His Church. Thus, marriage was no longer to be viewed as being under the reign of sin, but instead it should be considered within the gospel of grace.

The term 'contract' was replaced by the term 'covenant'. Vatican II saw marriage, as a community of life and love, in a new light – the relationship of the spouses. Hence marital love was not a quality or virtue of marriage; it was the expression of the divine presence in marriage. So, the essence of marriage goes beyond the partners expressing their love for each other. At one level emotional love becomes conjugal love, because emotional love has become true physical and practical commitment. At another level conjugal love has the element of family in it. Family as expressed in the new family the couple are; and family in the union of two families that they represent. But in Christian thought the presence of Christ in marriage means that there is an even deeper level that gives life to marriage and shows us God's design. As *Lumen Gentium* said: 'Christian spouses, in virtue of the sacrament of matrimony, signify and partake of the mystery of that unity and fruitful love which exists between Christ and His Church (Eph. 5.32).'[46]

Yet this vision of marriage has hardly filtered down to the ordinary Christian. In spite of Vatican II giving a spiritual perspective of marriage, this spiritual perspective is often masked by a retreat into canon law: so much so that marriage as a covenant has been hidden in some English translations of *Gaudium et Spes* ever since.[47] The canonical view of marriage as an institution meant the Christian ideal of marriage was meaningless to the ordinary Christian as it bore no relation to their experience of life. This is why the theology of marriage needs to show that the permanence of the sacrament, the presence of Christ, and the sacredness of conjugal love are brought to the fore. There are long forgotten truths that need to be brought into the light again. In brief, there is a necessity to explain the phrase of Vatican II that authentic married love is caught up in divine love. Otherwise, the waspish remark of Nietzsche will remain in so many people's perception of the position of the Church: 'Christianity gave Eros poison to drink; he did not die of it, but degenerated into vice.'

The Way Forward

Critics say Christian marriage is old-fashioned, a leftover from the past, unsuitable for the future. This is reflected in the different ways of understanding the present climate in which marriage finds itself. Some see this as a concerted attack on the Christian ideal of the family. Others find that the real difference today is the changed attitude of women to marriage; marriage is now between equal partners with a very different ideal in mind. Again others would see the emphasis on relationships, which have fundamentally changed the ideal of marriage. Others call for a new sexual ethic, which would see sex as naturally meant for pleasure. When the factors present in today's society are borne in mind some have concluded that family is incarnated in a culture that does not wish to support it. Thus the negative solution some propose to these scenarios is to reject the emphasis on relationships and the equality of the spouses, and re-emphasize the patriarchal family ideal. Not only is this untenable socially and theologically, but it has missed the point.

The major problem faced by couples getting married today is to understand their life together in a community of relationship. The current climate of intense but not durable relationships makes this even more difficult; and those who see their own marriage as some form of contract make the problem worse. There is, as Martinez says, 'a lack of a credible presentation of the inner meaning and all embracing view of the sacramental experience of human marriage'.[48] While Martinez tends to search for this expression in liturgy, the real problem is much deeper. *The Times* of London reported recently that, 'marriage means nothing to many modern parents'.[49] Herein lies the real difficulty. People have lost or are very confused about the meaning of marriage. The huge number of marriages that fail, together with the experience of divorce, multiple fathers and the practice of living together have had a disastrous effect on the idea of marriage. If marriage has lost its meaning, the solution cannot be to condemn the numerous problems of modern marriage, nor to expect psychology to answer the problems found today. Rather, it is necessary to fill the void ordinary Christians feel and give meaning to the sacramental nature of marriage, which embraces the need for companionship, mutual support and physical love making and give this human need a spiritual dimension.

Even from the preceding analysis, necessarily incomplete, it is evident that the void can be seen in the instability of marriage or the multiplicity of relationships. However, these are only the signs and symptom of disease, not the disease itself. The problem is how to express love. Marriage requires a constant exchange of love expressed in numerous gestures and acts. It is within this love that the void exists, as is evident from the disposability of relationships. Obviously, it is possible to argue that instability in love is natural, a part of being human. Of course in one sense this is true. Yet disposable relationships or multiple relationships do not belong to the essence of love. Love as the force and energy behind relationships desires completeness, not passing attachments. Love abhors emptiness. Love brings fulfilment as a person and motivates life. The discovery of empty space in the house of love is deeply disturbing. The void, that some experience in the discovery of these empty rooms, threatens to leave them less a person. It leaves a person with less of a framework for telling his or her own story. Motivation diminishes so much that marriage either becomes a convenience, remaining together for the sake of the children, or leads to divorce.

Love is not mere attraction; to mature, love needs a spiritual dimension that gives it the values that inspire it. The ideals that were there on the day the couple first made a commitment to each other may be made more realistic as time passes, but they are also deformed by the battering life gives them. They can be lost and a void is created inside the marriage. It is these ideals that need a spiritual dimension to remain alive. This does not mean that a spiritual dimension can solve all the problems a marriage faces. Nor does it provide instant answers to the difficulties a relationship faces. The point is that a spiritual dimension inspires and keeps true love alive because it is a positive force for good. It only exists because God gives His love to us. Or to be more correct we can love because we share in the divine love. So, a Christian outlook says conjugal love flows from Christ so that marriage is the grammar that God uses to express his love and faithfulness.[50] St Paul speaks of a mysterious force operating inside the union; even if one of the partners is a believer that makes the partner holy and the children holy.[51] Hence the whole family is part of a new creation. Thus the core of belief concerning marriage is that marriage is not a human creation, but a divine creation, a monogamous creation in contrast to the polygamy of men,[52] and it has been handed down incorrupt from generation to generation.

Its scriptural foundation is 'two in one flesh' which Paul taught means that marriage is based on the perfection of love as found in the love of Christ for his church. Love is not simply a quality or virtue of marriage; it is the expression of the divine presence in marriage. What is essential in marriage goes beyond the partners expressing their love for each other. Emotional love becomes conjugal love when emotional love has become true commitment. True commitment becomes family; family as expressed in the new family the couple are; and family in the union of two families that they represent. But there is an even deeper level that gives life to marriage and shows us God's design. This is the presence of Christ in marriage. Marriage as a community of life and love sees the spouses in a new light – their relationship.

Relationships are the key to the further exploration of the meaning of marriage. They express the hidden forces that move the spouses. They give meaning to the marriage and allow the person to tell their story in partnership with another. They do not remove the humanness of Christian marriage, which will have many moments of stress. Rather, they allow the stress to be superseded and healed once again with love, because they emphasize love as a gift of self, not merely the receiver of love. Hence, the bio-social-anthropo-psycho-spiritual model of marriage can only find its completeness in the spiritual element. Or put in another way, philosophically each of us sees everything in three dimensions, time-present, time-past and time-future. From birth to death is a physical, psychological and social passage through space and time. But these dimensions can only speak about time-present and time-past. Time-future is beyond them. Hence as theology deals with matters eternal as well as temporal the missing dimension of space-time is spiritual.[53] Likewise, the missing dimension in Christian marriage is theological.

It is this element that needs exploring. Already it is obvious that this is not an easy task. There is a built-in resistance to exploring this dimension. It is evident in past and present attitudes in the Church. It can be seen in the consumerism of today. Yet a return to the sources is necessary so that it is possible to see why God invented marriage and understand what makes marriage. Such a search must first explore the reason for adopting once again the ancient concept that marriage is a covenant of life and love. Then by examining the key text of Ephesians the true meaning of the sacrament of marriage can be seen in all its glory. As St Paul said: 'This is a great mystery' (Eph. 5.33).

Notes

1   According to Holland and Henriot *'social analysis can be defined as the effort to obtain a more complete picture of a social situation by exploring its historical and structural relationship'* (original emphasis). Holland J. and Henriot P., *Social Analysis: Linking Faith and Justice*, Orbis Books, Maryknoll, 1984, p. 14.

2   Holland and Henriot call this a 'pastoral cycle'. Ibid., pp. 15–18.

3   See for example, Home Office, *Marriage Matters: A consultative Document by the Working Party on Marriage Guidance*, HMSO, London, 1979, p. 14.

4   Martinez G., *Worship: Wedding to Marriage*, Pastoral Press, Washington DC, 1993, p. 27.

5   Canon 1055 first uses the term covenant, but then uses the term contract. It is the latter word that is used in all the other canons on marriage.

6   Orsy L., 'Faith, Sacrament, Contract and Christian Marriage: Disputed Questions', *Theological Studies*, vol. 43 (1982), pp. 378–398.

7   *Gaudium et Spes*, n. 48.

8   Orsy L., 'Married Persons: God's Chosen People' in *Christian Marriage Today*, ed. K. Demmer and A. Brenninkmeijer-Werhahn, Catholic University of America Press, Washington, 1997, p. 39.

9   Dominian J., *An Outline of Contemporary Christian Marriage*,

Liverpool Institute of Socio-Religious Studies, Liverpool, 1976, p. 50.

10 *The Toronto Star*, Saturday 8 July 1995, A22.

11 Shorter E., *The Making of the Modern Family*, Fontana, Glasgow, 1976, p. 86.

12 Radcliffe T., *Making Promises Till Death*, Priests and People, July 1992.

13 Statement of the French Bishops Commission on the Family, 'The Divorced and Remarried within the Christian Community' in *Catholic International*, vol. 3 n. 18, 868.

14 The facts are that over half of marriages are preceded by cohabitation. The average cohabiting household stays together for just over one year. Men are more often serial cohabiters than women. The lower the standard of education and religious practice the more likely they are to cohabit. While there is more than one form of cohabitation, the reasons for its occurrence are the changing values of family and a decline in the importance of marriage. To this must be added declining confidence in religious and social institutions and the delay of marriage for economic reasons. Less than half of cohabitating couples ever marry. NCCB Marriage and Family Committee, 'Marriage Preparation and Cohabiting Couples: Information Report', *Origins*, vol. 29, Washington, 1999, 14.

15 Shorter E., *The Making of the Modern Family*, Fontana, London, 1977, p. 38.

16 Ibid., p. 39.

17 Giblin P., 'Marital Conflict and Marital Spirituality', in *Clinical Handbook of Pastoral Counselling*, ed. R. Wicks and P. Parsons, Paulist Press, 1993, pp. 33–327.

18 Dominian J., *Marriage, Faith and Love*, Darton, Longman & Todd, London, 1981, p. 32.

19 Gudorf C. E., *Body, Sex and Pleasure*, Pilgrim Press, Cleveland, 1994, pp. 29–50.

20 Mbiti J. S., *African Religions and Philosophy*, Anchor, New York, 1970, pp. 92–99. Also Parrinder G., *African Mythology*, Hamlyn, London, 1967, pp. 54–63.

21 Mbiti, *African Religions*, pp. 164–166.

22 Mbiti J. S., *Introduction to African Religion*, Heinemann, London, 1975, p. 108.

23 Experts date this change from the late 1960s. Obviously

those flowing into the cities from the countryside may still retain the old ideas.

24   Traditionally the first wife chose the second wife. Parkin D. and Nyamwaya D. (eds), *Transformations of African Marriages*, Manchester University Press, Manchester, 1987, p. 2.

25   Karanja Wambui Wa, 'Outside Wives and Inside Wives in Nigeria: A Study of Changing Perceptions of Marriage' in *Transformations of African Marriages*, pp. 248–261.

26   Steady F. C., 'Polygamy and the Household Economy in a fishing village in Sierra Leone' in *Transformations of African Marriages*, pp. 211–230.

27   Little K., *African Women in Towns*, Cambridge University Press, Cambridge, 1973, p. 151.

28   Le Guennec-Coppens F., 'L'instabilite conjugale et ses consequences dans la societe Swahili de Lamu Kenya' in *Transformations of African Marriages*, pp. 232–245.

29   Davenport says the phrases used for these relationships are 'boy friend', 'girl friend' and 'sweet-heart'. Common-law marriage is rarely used as a description. Davenport W., in *The Family System in Jamaica, Marriage, Family and Residence*, ed. O. Bhannan and J. Middleton, The Natural History Press, Garden City, New York, 1968, p. 255.

30   Soloen N. L., 'Household and Family in the Caribbean: Some definition and Concepts' in M. M. Horowitz, *Peoples and Cultures of the Caribbean*, The Natural History Press, Garden City, New York, 1971, pp. 404–405.

31   Clarke E., *My Mother Who Fathered Me*, George Allen & Unwin, London, 1966.

32   Davenport in *The Family System in Jamaica*, pp. 247–284.

33   Collier J. and Esteban R., *From Complicity to Encounter: The Church and the Culture of Economism*, Trinity Press International, Harrisburg, Pennsylvania, 1998, pp. 10–11.

34   Bauman Z. quoted in an essay by Jaqui Stewart, 'Ethics and the Community: Some work in progress', presented to the Association of the Teachers of Moral Theology, Leeds, November 2002.

35   *Familiaris Consortio* section 81 states: each of these elements presents the church with arduous pastoral problems.

36   This is not a new opinion. Bishop Beck in 1959 wrote that: 'Catholics as well as non-Catholics are coloured by the

teaching that marriage is a contract ... [which] uncon-
sciously weakens the notion of a permanent and indissoluble union.' He goes on to blame working mothers, credit
cards and birth control. Beck G. A., 'The Contemporary
Crisis' in *The Meaning of Christian Marriage*, Dublin, Gill &
Son Ltd, 1963, p. 6.

37   Scotus defined marriage as an indissoluble bond between
a man and a woman arising from the reciprocal exchange
of authority over one another's bodies for the procreation
and proper nurture of children. *IV Sent. Dist. 30* q. 2.

38   1917 Code: Canon 1013. Gaspari, as the principle author of
the 1917 Code of Canon Law, insisted that marriage is a
contract whose primary end is the procreation and nurture
of children; its secondary end is mutual help and the rem-
edying of concupiscence. The essential properties of
marriage are unity and indissolubility, which acquire a
unique firmness in Christian marriage by reason of its
sacramental character.

39   Gaspari P., *Tractatus*, p. 12.

40   Navarette U., 'Structura Iuridica Matrimonii Secundum
Concillium Vaticanum II', in *Periodica* vol. 56, 1967,
357–383. Gaspari bases himself on Augustine who did not
speak of ends but of goods.

41   The end of marriage is not only the procreation and
nurture of children, but also mutual help and remedy for
concupiscence.

42   Quoted in Mackin T., *What is Marriage?*, Paulist Press, New
York, 1982, p. 213.

43   Likewise, Thomas Sanchez (1550–1610) pointed out that it
was the bond that was the essence of marriage. Following
its traditional meaning of an institution, he said marriage
had the following elements: mutual consent giving rise to
an external contract, which gives each the right to the
other's body, the obligation to render the marriage debt
and to consummate the marriage. But none of these were
the essential element because they were what brought
marriage into effect. So he emphasized the union of
marriage to the extent that he defined marriage as perse-
vering in a single sharing of life whose goal is mutual habi-
tation. Sanchez T., *De Sancto Matrimonii Sacramento
Disputationum, Liber Secundus, De Essentia et Consensu*

Matrimonii, Venetiis, 1726, 91.6, 1, n. 8.

44   Quoted from Mackin, *What is Marriage?*, p. 204.

45   von Hildebrand D., *Reinheit und Jungfräulichkeit*, translated as *In defense of purity*, Sheed & Ward, New York, 1935.

46   *Lumen Gentium* n. 11.

47   For example Flannery A. (ed.), *Vatican II: The Conciliar and Post Conciliar Documents*, Dominican Publication, Dublin, 1975.

48   Martinez G., *Worship: Wedding to Marriage*, The Pastoral Press, Washington, 1993, p. viii.

49   *The Times*, Friday 28 June 2002.

50   Kasper W., *Theology of Christian Marriage*, Seabury, New York, 1980, p. 27.

51   1 Cor. 7.14. Conzelmann in his commentary points out the mass of interpretations of this verse, stating the decisive idea is not an ontological definition of the state of the non-Christian members of the household, but the assertion that no alien power plays any part in the Christian's dealings with them. Through the believing partner, the marriage between a pagan and a Christian is withdrawn from the control of the powers of the world. Conzelmann H., *I Corinthians*, Hermeneia, Fortress Press, Philadelphia, 1975, p. 122.

52   This is clear not only from the story of Adam and Eve, but is reinforced by the picture of God as the bridegroom that took one wife, Israel.

53   Ouspensky, P. D., *A New Model of the Universe*, London, Arkana, 1984. He says: 'The six-pointed star which represented the world in ancient symbolism is in reality the representation of space-time or the "period of dimensions", i.e. of the three space-dimensions and the three-time dimensions in their perfect union, where every point of space includes the whole of time and every moment of time includes the whole of space; where *everything* is *everywhere* and *always*' (p. 445). I am indebted to Professor Millard for bringing to my attention this insight.

Chapter Two

Renewing the Theology of Christian Marriage at Vatican II

If marriage is a covenant of life and love, it is difficult to understand why the decision at Vatican II that Christian marriage is a covenant is being concealed. Yet it is a curious fact that 'marriage is a covenant' has been covered up in many English translations. It is not just the blatant mistranslation of the most popular edition of the documents of Vatican II that consistently translates the Latin *foedus* (covenant) as 'contract' that indicates this.[1] Even in a later statement of Paul VI, when he talks of the covenant of marriage, this is translated as a marriage pact. Is this just reactionary pique, or a more serious attempt to reject the theology of marriage that *Gaudium et Spes* adopted? The answer is not easy. It would be wrong to say it is simply a matter of terminology. The answer goes beyond such a simple solution. Rather, the answer lies in the concept of marriage, a concept that is made more complex by its double reality of being at the same time both a personal and a public relationship.

Rather than anticipate a proper examination of the problem, it suffices for the present to point out the pastoral consequences of viewing marriage as a contract or a covenant. Marriage as a contract means that the sacrament is confined to the wedding day and envisages a static view of marriage as a sacrament, only the contract continues throughout life. The church wedding confers a blessing on the union of the couple giving grace to lead a married life. Obviously the couple must be properly prepared to receive the sacrament and shoulder the responsibilities marriage entails. After that it is up to the couple to fulfil, in so far as they can, their marriage vows.

Marriage as a covenant presents a very different picture. Whilst it is obvious that proper preparation for a marriage is essential, and that an adequate understanding of what marriage entails is very necessary, marriage as a covenant envisages the sacrament continuing throughout life so that the sacrament is not static, but dynamic. The sacrament is constantly being renewed. This is because a covenant is a personal exchange, rather than simply an exchange of rights. Or in the words of *Casti Connubii*, marriage is *traditio personae*, a giving of the person, rather than only granting to each other exclusive sexual rights. Many married couples would be shocked to think that marriage could be reduced to a contract about sex; although the rich do reduce marriage to a contract over money when they make pre-marriage agreements over property. Palmer is correct when he points out:

> Contract is used of things, of property or of personal belongings. When persons are involved, it is not the person who is hired or contracted for, but his services ... [While] a covenant is seen as a relationship of mutual trust and fidelity. Hence to speak of a covenant of fidelity is redundant. Fidelity is of the essence of covenant. Contracts can be broken by mutual agreement, by failure to live up to the terms of the contract, by civil intervention. Covenants are not broken; they are violated when there is a breach of faith on the part of either of the covenantors.[2]

Thus, in a marital covenant the giving of the person

creates a new unity in a permanent relationship. Thus, a covenant is as expansive and as all embracing as a contract is restrictive and limiting. Obviously, the pastoral implications are wide reaching.

Prior to Vatican II for almost four hundred years marriage was conceived as a contract. This canonical concept changed the Roman concept of marriage from a marital society brought about by consent, to marriage as consent to exclusive cohabitation and carnal union. The Thomistic concept of the union of marriage as a union of souls and bodies, a community of domestic intimacy, became with Duns Scotus the mutual gift of bodies with a view to intercourse.[3] It is thus that marriage became a contract involving exclusive sexual rights. While there was always some uneasiness about the reduction of the marital consent to simply exclusive sexual rights, which can be seen in the insistence that the consent was to a marital society as well as the mutual gift of bodies, the 1917 Code of Canon Law opted for sexual rights.[4] In that code, marital consent was the perpetual and exclusive right over the body, as ordered to acts suited of themselves to the generation of children.[5] Canons 1082 §1 and 2, 1086 §2, and 1111 are all concerned with the procreation of children as an essential part of the contract. Only canon 1013 §1 mentions the secondary end of marriage as mutual help and allaying concupiscence (sexual lust). This position was further emphasized by the Holy Office in 1944 and again in 1951, condemning those that deny that procreation constitutes the primary end of marriage, and hold that the secondary ends are equally principal and independent.[6] Conjugal love never gets a mention; the emphasis is on sexual duties. The marital community came in second place.[7]

Only with Pius XI did a broader view come about. Although *Casti Connubii* quotes canon 1081 as regards the specific marital right, Pius XI presents marriage as a communion, a community or a society for the whole of life caused by the interior conforming of the spouses to each other.[8] He describes the peculiar and unique character of the marital contract, which denotes both the indissolubility of the matrimonial bond and the consecration of the contract by Christ. It was Christ who elevated marriage to the rank of a sign, which is the cause of grace.[9] The reason for this is found in the mystical signification of Christian wedlock, because it signifies that most perfect union which subsists between Christ and the Church.[10] It is this concept, together with Pius XI describing the love that exists in both relationships as charity[11] that becomes the springboard for the replacement of 'contract' by 'covenant' that took place at Vatican II. So, although some saw the change as a considerable revolution in theology, the seeds of such a development are in *Casti Connubii* in 1930.

The Formation of *Gaudium et Spes* in Vatican II: the Zurich Text

To assess correctly how such a development took place, it is necessary to trace the formation of the text of *Gaudium et Spes* in Vatican II. *Gaudium et Spes* was not foreseen in the pre-council documents. With the acceptance of the concept that the Council must speak not only to the Church '*ad intra*', but also to the world '*ad extra*', the idea of a new document concerning the Church in the Modern World was born. The necessity for a document of this kind came out of the wishes of John XXIII to address modern problems in a different way than had been the recent custom of Rome. The previous Roman method was theoretical and legalistic, where timeless principles expressed in medieval terms were seen as the only way to approach a problem. To the outside world, the Church appeared as a castle repelling all enquiries with words it alone understood.[12] Terminology was not the only problem. What lay behind this terminology was a rigorous logic that did not admit new ideas. So the new document required a new methodology.

The inspiration behind this new methodology was Mgr Pavan, whose role in drawing up John XXIII's encyclical *Pacem in Terris* was well known. Accepted by the influential conservative Fr Tromp, John XXIII's famous phrase 'the signs of the times' became a way of discerning the saving will of God.[13] This meant beginning not from principles, but from the reality in which people lived.[14] It appealed both to diocesan bishops who faced the problems of modern life, and theologians who wanted another kind of theological tool that had been used by Christ himself. John XXIII believed God wrote history, and so understanding events would lead not only to better pastoral strategies, but also to placing God once again in our history. The spirit of the age of the twentieth century was purely secular and had succeeded in separating religion from life, even to the extent that the Church believed that sacraments were administered only to individuals. Religion was a private affair. *Pacem in Terris* rejected this thesis, and so would Vatican II.

Yet the use of this new method was not without difficulty. To begin, a text had to be produced that was not too theological or lacking in reference to contemporary problems, nor too excessively sociological. These tensions can be seen later in Liberation Theology's use of this new method.[15] Many influential voices rejected the approach, including Karl Rahner, arguing that the Council should proceed theologically, basing its doctrinal conclusions on revealed truth. It needed the pressure of debate in the Council sessions and the interest of the press to convince the Council Fathers that this method was the way to be a spiritual force in the world.[16] This is the background to *Gaudium et Spes*. Only when these facts are taken into account can the debate that centred around the formation of that part of the document on marriage be understood.

What clearly illustrates the differences between the old and the new approach is the preparatory text on marriage. Just before the beginning of Vatican II, a text entitled 'Concerning Marriage, Chastity and Virginity' had been circulated to the bishops.[17] In many ways it presented few problems, if a negative approach to marriage and sexuality was acceptable. The outlook and terminology emphasized that the unique end of marriage was the procreation and education of children, even if the marriage was not fruitful.[18] Only in very second place came the notion of mutual help and solace for the partners in domestic life: both of these were seen as the way the consequences of concupiscence could be avoided.[19] Hence, marital consent could not exclude procreation, and was described as the unique and exclusive right over each other's body. From this the conclusion was drawn that unity and indissolubility belonged to the essence of marriage.[20]

Such a schema offered no real theology of marriage, apart from the statement that 'marriage is not a human invention but part of the divine creation restored by Christ and elevated to the dignity of a sacrament'; nor did it face modern marital problems. Furthermore, it totally omitted the approach of Pius XI's encyclical *Casti Connubii*, for the debate on whether love was the essence of marriage, which had occupied theologians since then, was ignored. In fact, its main concern, as is evident in the errors it proposed to reject, was to bring back a canon prepared for Vatican I in 1870, but never discussed, which insisted that it was impossible to separate the contract of marriage and the sacrament.[21] Thus, the proposal was out of touch with the reality of modern life, so the text was rightly seen as incapable of dealing with the problems facing the Church and not worthy of discussion in the Council itself.

A completely new approach was required, even though the sub-commission formed to elaborate the new text had to deal perpetually with drafts in the spirit of the rejected schema.[22] However, as the Council was not expected to last for long, the Co-ordinating Commission proposed to include as many of the preparatory texts as possible in two parts. First, a theoretical section that would present principles, and later, a more pastoral section with some concrete application of these principles. So, Fr Labourdette drew up a compromise text. However, the passages that spoke of mutual love in marriage were suppressed. The reason given for this was the need to base doctrinal statements on what were called 'more objective' norms.[23] Fr Häring records that he was advised to say nothing by a moderate conservative as the text would give the Council a very salutary shock.[24] In fact, as John XXIII died before there could be any examination of this text, the text was never debated.

After the lay theologians defeated efforts at the Mixed Commission[25] to omit the chapter on marriage, developments were guided by two main starting points: the biblical insight of humankind being made in the image of God, and marriage being a reflection of the relationship between Christ and his Church was one starting point. The other starting point was the discernment of the signs of the times in relation to marriage.[26] The latter was mainly caused by the appearance, in the meantime, of the encyclical *Pacem in Terris*. To take these points forward, at the working session of the sub-commission in Zurich, a one-page document on marriage was drawn up, which was accepted by a very large majority of the Central Commission and presented, plus an appendix, to the Fathers at the third session of the Council.[27]

The new document, after speaking of the right of a child to be born not only into a well-ordered family (*sana familia*), but also the right to be educated according to the spiritual, social and economic situation of that family, underlines the nature of family life. Conjugal life is not only concerned with procreation and mutual help, but also with mutual sanctification so that children can find a holy saving model in family life. This model exists because a Christian family participates in the covenant of love between Christ and His Church (Eph. 5.32). Marriage is not merely an instrument of procreation, but of its nature is an indissoluble covenant between persons, for the greatest good of the children and the true love of the partners. If there are no children, this does not take away the fundamental value and indissolubility of the marriage. Nevertheless, such is the innate character of conjugal love that marriage of its nature is ordained to the procreation and education of children.[28] This approach was a definitive turning point for a theology of marriage at Vatican II.

The presentation did not please some Fathers as can be seen from the remark of Cardinal Heenan of Westminster: 'Beware of experts bearing addenda'.[29] In fact Archbishop Felici, the Secretary General, announced that the addenda were private documents with no official standing, but was forced to retract at the direction of the Moderators that they were conciliar documents, but would not be debated. However, this did not stop many comments being made on the appendix.

The appendix that had disturbed Cardinal Heenan was a development of *Casti Connubii* with which it soon became clear that he, and a certain number of Fathers, was not familiar. The appendix begins with six signs of the times:

- the ignorance and separation from the religious basis of marriage and the family among Christians;
- the conviction in the minds of both men and women that personal relationships bring about happiness and stability in marriage;
- the absence of the social conditions to promote the unity and indissolubility of marriage;
- the need for responsible parenthood because of the pressures coming from population control and modern life;
- the new dangers arising from modern teaching regarding marriage facing the young;
- the pressure on the ideal of marriage generated by culture, economic and social conditions.

Whilst these problems reflected many of the bishop's concerns, for Cardinal Heenan the omission of the problems of mixed marriages and contraception were grave errors. This caused a stunning attack by Heenan who said the document was 'unworthy of a general council ... a set of platitudes that reads like a sermon'. The instruction not to debate the addenda would be fatal, and to leave the text to be interpreted by experts would be worse: 'I fear specialists when they are left to explain what the bishops mean.' There followed a fierce attack on the experts who had drawn up the document, and in particular Fr Bernard Häring, and a call for a new commission with 'real' experts to draw up the text.[30] The general impression of the speech was summed up by Bishop Wright of Pittsburgh: 'It is clear that the archbishop felt very deeply and personally about what he had to say – whatever he had to say.' In fact, the attack on the Zurich text was a minority opinion, for the Fathers overwhelmingly approved the direction taken by 1579 votes to 296.

The real surprise was that the text did not reflect the current canon law. Perhaps this was to be expected, as it had ignored the debate over the theology of marriage since the publication in 1926 of Von Hildebrand's *Reinheit und Jungfraulichkeit,* which proposed marriage as a community of love. In fact, canon law took its approach from Duns Scotus, who saw marital consent as the exclusive sexual rights of each other's body and hence defined marriage as a contract. This new departure of a covenant of love caused Cardinal Döpfner of Munich to comment, 'the theology here is as new as the problems themselves'.

Cardinal Léger of Montreal went further, saying the renewal of theology in this area depended on the theologians addressing the recent discoveries in biology, psychology and sociology. He continued: 'Many theologians think that the difficulties that are met today ... are rooted in an unsatisfactory exposition of the ends of the institution. A certain pessimistic and negative attitude towards human love has prevailed, which cannot be attributed either to Scripture or Tradition, but to philosophies of the last centuries, which has obscured the importance and legitimacy of conjugal love in marriage.'[31] This perceptive comment underlined the problems of the past approaches. Marriage was conceived in the inappropriate terms of scholastic philosophy and Augustinian theology. He was certain that the authors of the present schema had got off on the right foot.[32] The schema says: 'The divine vocation of marriage which is holy and sanctifies the partners, in that where conjugal love dwells domestic life is renewed, because conjugal love brings about faithfulness, unity and indissolubility in marriage, as well as a true and holy responsibility in the procreation and education of children, taking into account the condition the family finds itself in.'[33]

This is a radically different programme and approach from what went before, because it lays to rest the Augustinian attitude to marriage. St Augustine saw marriage as being tainted by lust, so that sexual acts could only be justified if they were ordered towards having children. Instead, here conjugal love is recognized as bringing about faithfulness, unity and indissolubility. Furthermore, responsible parenthood is a product of this love. Going even further in its brief description of the conjugal vocation, it sees procreation as the fruit of 'one flesh' and a co-operation in creation. 'God saw it was not for humans to be alone' (Gen. 2.18; Matt. 19.4). 'He created them from the beginning male and female and joined them in a covenant of love and blessed them: Increase and multiply and fill the earth' (Gen. 1.18). They are called to a vocation in 'one flesh' (Gen. 2.24; Eph. 5.31). It is an indivisible and indissoluble union joined together through which in the co-operation of human generation He is glorified.[34]

So, matrimony in its origin, nature and end is declared sacred.[35] It is significant that man and woman are joined in a 'covenant of love' where co-operation in procreation glorifies God. Even more significant is the use of the phrase 'covenant of love' and the reference to Ephesians 5.31 as an explanation of 'one flesh'. Furthermore, whilst marital consent in its essence intends this covenant of unity, indissolubility and love to be at the service of life,[36]

the validity of this consent does not depend on a particular level of perfection of love, provided that the consent is
free and does not positively exclude unity, indissolubility
and fecundity. Cardinal Léger commented that it shows a
renewal of the ends of marriage. He said: 'They have taken
care to emphasize the mutual love of husband and wife.
We notice with satisfaction that they have avoided the
complex of problems, which introduces an opposition
between a primary and secondary end of marriage.'[37]

Others, however, were very dissatisfied in this regard,
demanding a return to declaring procreation as the
primary end of marriage. Among these Cardinal Ruffini
demanded a return to the true doctrine of the Church as
found in *Casti Connubii* and the speech of Pius XII to
midwives. Obviously, he had not read *Casti Connubii* very
closely. As well as emphasizing the primary end of
marriage as being the procreation of children, Cardinal
Browne suggested a distinction between the 'love of
friendship' which desires to promote the welfare of others,
and the 'love of concupiscence' which aims at gaining a
good for oneself. The first assured the balance and joy of
family life when the second was in danger of coming in
conflict with the first. As Nowell commented: 'One could
see what he means, but surely the point is that in a happy
and successful marriage the two should become inextric-
ably intertwined.'[38]

Cardinal Léger also found the schema inadequate
because it failed to present conjugal love and mutual help
as an end of marriage, and in no way tackled the problem
of the expression of love in marriage. He wanted conjugal
love, where both body and soul are involved, as an end in
itself of marriage, something good in itself and which has
needs and laws of its own. Just stating that marriage is a
state was inadequate. It must be affirmed that the intimate
union of husband and wife had an end in love as well.
And this end is the *finis operis*, legitimate in itself, even if it
is not directed towards procreation. Although he claimed
this is no more than confirming the principles that the

Church has approved of for many centuries in its treatment of sterile marriages, it must have been revolutionary to those who heard him.

In fact these desires were partially met, as can be seen in the section dealing with love (*amor et caritas*). Quoting St Thomas, it states that the contract between Christians is not the sacrament itself, but the sign of holy things that sanctify humankind so that the whole of married life bears witness to the new and eternal covenant between Christ and His Church. This sign is achieved by perfecting natural love, so conferring indissoluble unity, with the result that the sacrament causes growth by perfecting the partners.[39] The growth comes about through the Spirit, who perfects human love so that the partners must in a special way portray and participate in the pure and abundantly fruitful union of Christ and His Church.[40] To make abundantly clear that this growth in love is the effect of the sacrament, the document speaks of the enlarging of the spouses' hearts because Christ, the Word incarnate, lives in their marriage and causes it to flourish. It is in this way that 'the intimate personal community of marriage that is brought about by love (*caritas*) is sanctified by the sacrament'.[41]

The text insists marriage is a school of love, and it is this love that prompts the couple to desire and receive children and care for them. Likewise, from the very nature of conjugal love flows conjugal chastity because the covenant of love demands such a sign. Hence marriage is a covenant of love both in the order of salvation and in the order of creation. Joined to the love of Christ for his Church, the covenant of love between the spouses is eschatological. Joined to each other in one flesh, they take part in creation bringing forth new life. Moreover, the extraordinary faithfulness of Christ in his love for the Church is the sign for the spouses, whose vocation is to show this sign before the world through their fidelity. Conjugal love is of its nature irrevocably faithful; faithfulness made stronger because it is made holy by Christ.[42]

Yet the analysis of conjugal love cannot be left there. Its practical expression cannot be omitted. The proposed text said:

> Marriage is not a mere instrument of procreation, but of its nature is an indissoluble bond between persons; especially because the good of the offspring demands love, the spouses truly love one another. If there is no offspring, marriage is not deprived of its fundamental value and indissolubility. Nevertheless the nature of conjugal love is such that marriage is by its nature ordained to procreation and education. Yet responsible parenthood will require them to judge whether to have a child at this time according to the educational and economic conditions, the health also of mind and body, and in addition the good of the family, the Church and the needs of society.[43]

This really provoked a reaction. Cardinal Ruffini described this as 'hard, obscure and ambiguous' and asked that the text be revised according to the teaching of the Magisterium. Likewise, Cardinal Ottaviani was not pleased, especially as he was the eleventh of twelve children: 'My parents never doubted Providence.' Cardinal Browne said 'true' experts were studying the problem. On the other side, Cardinals Suenens and Alfrink said this was not a formula for moral laxity. Instead, there is a moral conflict in performing one and the same act. The biological end may be in conflict with the situation of the family, and the duty to preserve the fidelity of marriage. Both stressed there must not be a hasty decision. In a memorable phrase Suenens said: 'I beg of you my brother bishops, let us avoid a new "Galileo affair". One is enough for the Church ... The truth – both natural and supernatural – will set you free.' Long applause followed his speech.[44]

Behind this conflict lay another issue. It is clear from the intervention of Cardinal Browne and others, including the

intended interventions of Bishop Pearson of Lancaster and
Bishop Holland of Salford, that some thought the Church
could not go back on four hundred years of tradition
expressed in the term 'contract' as found in *Casti Connubii*.
The foundation of this 'all or nothing' school of thought is
that if the Church had been wrong in its teaching for four
hundred years then the Church had failed. This was
impossible. Therefore nothing could change. Some held
the fallacy here was the Church equals the Roman Curia
and those agreeing with them.[45] Rather, there was a
failure to distinguish the philosophical concepts used to
express dogma, and the dogma itself. Or even more
exactly, the failure to realize that the expression of the past
now concealed rather than illuminated the truth. This is a
point several Fathers made in the course of the debate. In
fact, the Council changed previous expressions regarding
marriage, even contradicting statements of the Holy
Office. As Cardinal Ottaviani was to admit to Pope Paul
VI: 'I was always in the minority.'

The primacy of children in marriage was carefully
nuanced in *Casti Connubii*. Speaking of conjugal love it
taught: 'This mutual inward moulding of husband and
wife, this determined effort to perfect each other, can in a
very real sense, as the Roman catechism teaches us, be said
to be the chief reason and purpose of marriage, provided
marriage be looked at not in the restricted sense as instituted for the proper conception and education of the child,
but more widely as the sharing of the whole and the
mutual interchange and partnership thereof.' This was
because the Roman catechism placed mutual help before
the bearing of children.[46] So, from a contractual view of
marriage, its primary purpose was the procreation and
education of children.[47] But from a covenantal view the
purpose of marriage was conjugal love. Bishop Reuss of
Mainz said this highlighted the true significance of conjugal life.[48]

However, the reaction in the Council and the reaction of
the press need careful balancing against the intention of

the writers of this document. The document had no intention of promoting childless marriage, or putting careers in place of childbearing. When the text is seen as a whole, certain features stand out. Neither promoting conjugal love, nor carefully not speaking of the prime end of marriage as children, indicated a diminution of the importance of children in family life. Instead what was being presented was the centrality of conjugal love in marriage. A point that could easily be overlooked, further underlines this. Pius XI in *Casti Connubii* had distinguished between *amor* and *caritas*. *Amor* had meant sexual intimacy, while *caritas* expressed the deep love between partners. No such distinction is made here. Instead *caritas* signifies conjugal love as a whole. This removed the theological problem concerning the essence of marriage. The central point of the proposed schema is conjugal love.

The official reaction was to close the debate on the next day and a hold a standing vote that approved the direction taken by the schema. But although the debate was curtailed, in some way the question of responsible parenthood was a distraction from the real innovation: marriage was a covenant and community of love. Without this, the question of responsible parenthood had no real basis. The fact that conjugal love was central to marriage meant responsible parenthood could be an expression of true love. Later drafts would clarify this point. The stage was now set for a more extended document on the covenant of marriage.

Towards a Definitive Text: the Aricca Text and its Amendments

Following the suggestion that the addenda be reinserted in the main text, the previous concept of conjugal love quietly returned to the body of the schema without serious opposition.[49] Thus, the schema presented on 21 September 1965 was longer and quite different from that which the

Fathers had seen previously. Sadly, some of thrust of the former version was lost in this new text. For example, the 'signs of the times' regarding marriage were the same as the first draft, but expressed in obscure language more removed from the lived experience of couples. Technical terms were now used to express problems, such as referring to marriage as an institution and deviant forms of this as polygamy and other false forms of marriage. Marriage, it stated, was damaged by eroticism, hedonism and egoism, and constrained by economic, social and demographic changes.[50] However, this obscure language was corrected in future drafts and the technical terms were mostly removed. Instead, words such as polygamy, divorce, so-called free love, self-love, worship of pleasure, and illicit practices against human generation finally replaced the technical terms.

The next section on 'The Sanctity of Marriage and the Family' is quite a different matter. Here the concept of marriage as a covenant is expanded and clarified:

> The conjugal community has been established by the Creator and qualified by His laws. It is rooted in the conjugal covenant of irrevocable personal consent … Thus, a man and woman, who by the marriage covenant of conjugal love, are not two, but one flesh, render mutual help and service to each other through an intimate union of their persons and their actions. Through this union they will experience the meaning of their oneness and attain to it with growing perfection day by day. This intimate union, the very nature of conjugal love, imposes total fidelity on the spouses and argues for an unbreakable oneness between them.[51]

The notes issued for this section are very interesting. The fact that there is no mention of a 'contract' of marriage is explained in the following way. Following the vote of the Fathers, the clearer term 'irrevocable personal consent' is used. An additional reason for using the biblical term 'covenant' is the difficulties the Eastern Church has with the term 'contract'. The use of the term 'covenant' strengthens the concept of the indissolubility of marriage, otherwise in the absence of the required love, the marriage would become null.[52]

The reasons for these assertions occur further on in the text. Just as in the past there was a faithful covenant of love between God and his people, so now the Saviour marries the Church, and the spouses in the same way marry each other. Therefore, this covenant is the inbuilt foundation of the sacrament of marriage.[53] The result is that there is a growth of the covenant during marriage. 'Due to the unity of body and soul found in mutual help and service the partners sense an increase and fulfilment of their unity.'[54] Not only that, but because through the marriage covenant they participate in the divine covenant of Christ and His Church, through their conjugal love this love becomes salvific. This important insight into the saving qualities of marriage expresses the continuance of the sacrament; Christian marriage is much more than a wedding day ceremony. At the same time the sacrament is participated in at each act of service and love.[55] Therefore, the Christian family within marriage images and partici- pates in the covenant of love of Christ and the Church, making present the life of the Saviour of the world.[56]

The reaction to this approach was generally favourable. Cardinal Colombo of Milan said the doctrine expressed had solid foundations and was very useful in pastoral practice. Cardinal Conway of Armagh said it was a good synthesis of Catholic doctrine, and Cardinal Léger said it was better than the previous text. But this was not the opinion of everyone. Archbishop Munoyerro said: 'It was inopportune to omit the term "contract of marriage" because it is agreed to both by canonists and theologians and occurs in pontifical documents ... The term contract expresses much better the strength of the union and pact that is ordered to a specific end.'[57] This obviously was not a lone voice because 190 Fathers asked for the insertion of the word 'contract' for 'covenant'. The Central Commission rejected this because the relationship between Christ and His Church was not a contract. As marriage participates in this relationship, it cannot be a contract. Furthermore, historically, the marriage contract was between two families rather than two spouses. Just as telling was the reply that the term 'contract' obscured the genuine nature of marriage because people consider a contract as something that can be determined by the parties themselves, and can later be broken by mutual consent. Yet Christian tradition has always seen marriage as founded by the Creator, who gave it its own particular rules, and as Christ witnesses, from the beginning marriage was seen as permanent and unbreakable. Finally, a contract concerns things, services and rights rather than persons, which was contrary to the vision of the encyclical *Casti Connubii* that described marriage as giving of the person to each other, *traditio personae*. It was this that caused the rejection of the request of thirty-four Fathers to return to a more juridical concept of marriage as 'the mutual transfer of specific rights and duties'. The 190 Fathers who wanted to return to impersonal definition of the code of 'an exclusive and perpetual right over the body for those acts that are proper to the generation of children' were reminded that language like this was neither pastoral nor conducive to discussion with the world.[58]

The text also speaks of Christ having blessed this many-faceted love, as it comes from the fountain of divine love, and structured as it is on the model of His union with the Church. There were few objections to this, except for one Father who wanted the blessing to be on the contract rather than on conjugal love; and 148 Fathers who wanted to speak of the blessing only in regard to fruitful union. But the Commission could quote the Council of Trent to repel such moves and insisted on the covenant of love that makes Christ present in the spouses through the sacrament of matrimony. In a profound insight the Council of Trent had said: 'Christ abides with the spouses thereafter.'[59] This would not exist if the blessing were on their contract.[60]

In the middle of all this debate occurs a statement that flows from understanding Christian marriage as a covenant. This statement on the purpose of marriage drew objections from Cardinal Ruffini, Bishop De Orbegozo of Peru, and other South American and African bishops. The proposed text said: 'For God Himself furnishes by his loving plan the various goods and ends of marriage which all have a decisive effect on the continuation of the human race, on the individual happiness of the family both on earth and for eternity and on the stability, peace and prosperity of human society as a whole. This generous and authentic conjugal love in some way cannot exist outside a legitimate union and inevitably animates the institution of marriage which is ordained to the procreation and education of children through which the apex of marriage is completed and crowned.'[61]

The problem was what is really meant by goods and ends, *bonis ac finibus,* in this text. The objectors found the meaning vague, omitting both the clear teaching of *Casti Connubii* that children are the prime purpose of marriage and a condemnation by the Holy Office on anyone who taught otherwise. However, the text makes no mention of this. Procreation is said to belong to the institution of marriage. Furthermore, the Commission refused a request to make procreation the primary end of marriage on the grounds that the hierarchy of values can be regarded from various points of view.[62] Another possibility was these goods are to be understood in the Augustinian way of goods flowing from marriage – fidelity, children and bond. As no reference is made to the classic text from Augustine, this is most unlikely. Häring says they are simply the wealth with which God endowed marriage itself in view of the perpetuation of the human race and the temporal and eternal well being of the partners and the children. Hence, he translates *bonis ac finibus* as benefits and purposes, a line that future translators will follow.

But the text did not remain like this. The difficulty was that on one side sterile marriages had to be defended as real marriages,[63] and on the other side procreation and education of children were not incidental to marriage. Cardinal Ruffini said the solution was to return to the concept of primary and secondary ends of marriage. But a vast majority of Fathers did not want to make such distinctions. The solution was to replace the second part of the text with: 'By their very nature, the institution of matrimony itself and conjugal love are ordained for the procreation and education of children, and find in them their ultimate crown.' Inappropriately there is now a reference to the classic text of Augustine after the first part even though the text clearly states procreation belongs to the institution of marriage.[64] As a footnote in Abbott's translation of *Gaudium et Spes* reminds us: 'Here as elsewhere when the question arises the Council sedulously avoids the terminology of primary and secondary ends of marriage. It insists on the natural ordering of marriage and conjugal love to procreation.'[65] So, from the covenant of marriage flows conjugal love that naturally leads to procreation.

The practical consequence of understanding marriage as a covenant is spelt out in the next section on conjugal love. Conjugal love necessarily brings out the personal dimension of marriage,[66] described as:

> eminently human, bringing special gifts of healing and perfecting, exalting the gifts of grace and charity. Such love, merging the human with the divine, leads the spouses to a free and mutual gift of themselves, a gift proving itself by gentle affection and by deed, pervading the services and sacrifices of daily conjugal life.[67] Indeed, by its generous activity it grows better and grows greater. Moreover, this love is uniquely expressed and perfected through the marital act. These actions within marriage by which the couple are united intimately and chastely are noble and worthy ones.

Expressed in a manner that is truly human, these actions signify and promote mutual self-giving.[68]

This beautiful exposition of conjugal love, which emphasizes the personal dimension of marriage and declares the marriage act good, raised few objections. Instead, there were those like Cardinal Léger who wanted to go further. Léger said the chief defect was that it did not give a proper explanation of the aim of marriage. 'It is not enough for the faithful to find the text affirming the purpose of marriage was procreation and education of children. We should declare clearly that marriage is not merely a means of procreation but likewise a community of love. We should distinguish between the species and the individual.' Yet further on the text states:

> Such is marriage and conjugal love that inherent in them is the procreation and education of children. Hence, while not making the other purposes of marriage of less account, the true practice of conjugal love and the whole meaning of family life which results from it, have this aim so that the couple should be ready with stout hearts to co-operate with the love of the Creator and Saviour who then will enlarge and enrich His own family day by day. Marriage, though rightly ordered to children, was not merely instituted for procreation, but the nature of an indissoluble covenant between persons and the good of children demand that in return conjugal love rightly ordered grows and matures.[69]

Obviously Léger did not find this clear enough. However, there is a problem with following Léger's suggestion. The reason behind this formulation is a desire in no way to return to primary and secondary ends of marriage – children and the mutual growth of the partners. Marriage is a community of love, but not only a community of love. This was to cause an important change to the Aricca text's definition of marriage where 'conjugal community' is changed later to read 'the intimate partnership of life and love'. [70]

His fellow Canadian Bishop De Roo of Victoria, speaking on behalf of twenty-three bishops and many lay people, also found the text did not go far enough. Writing at the time, Nowell said: 'If St Jerome, whose feast it was that day, had heard this speech the irascible doctor would have reacted angrily to De Roo's theme of the goodness of conjugal love.'[71] De Roo said:

> Whilst the schema underlined the goodness of married love, it failed to express the gift of the vocation of marriage. Instead of warning of the dangers of human love, it would be better to offer a positive vision of that love. Conjugal love can only be understood from the unique union that marital intimacy brings. The spouses are called not only to give physical life to their children, but also to be a source of life for the whole family that is not possible with only one act of generosity, but calls for a constant renewal of this gift. Constant signs of affection are needed to conserve the conjugal vocation. Conjugal love must be seen within its context otherwise it loses its genuine significance. Conjugal love is a profound spiritual experience that throws light for them on their mutual irrevocable union giving birth through its links to the Creator to life and happiness. Generating new life, providing new members for the Mystical Body of Christ means they become an instrument in the redemption of humanity and the progress of the world. So the creative function of conjugal love goes beyond the family as they construct the temporal community in which everyone can find their destiny. Moreover, a family founded on true conjugal love testifies to joy and love to the world. Thus, knowing and living the richness of conjugal love is useful not only to the Church but the whole of society.[72]

This was an important theological contribution to the

theology of conjugal love, speaking as it does of the 'domestic church'. As was evident in other speeches, it was an aspect of marriage that many bishops had left out of their own theology of marriage.[73] Whilst St Jerome in his asceticism and his exultation of virginity would have reacted angrily against this statement, Bishop de Roo's speech was to confirm the basis for declaring marriage a community of life and love.

By now the direction the Council was taking is clear. 'Marriage may be ordered to procreation but it is not a mere instrument of procreation, but because of the indissoluble covenant between the parties and the good of children, it also demands that the mutual love of the couple is rightly ordered to grow and mature.'[74] So, the Council logically concluded that:

> The spouses know that in building and leading the family, it cannot be left to one's own will, but they must follow their conscience rightly informed by the laws of God and determine the number of children according to the gift of God and what true love indicates. In this matter, the couple vigilant and docile towards God, make a prudent judgement taking into account ordinary advice concerning their state of health both physical and mental, the signs of the times and their material and intellectual state of life. Finally, they will consult the interests of the family, of temporal society and the needs of the Church.[75]

Already, this text had been altered from the previous text, but some were strenuously opposed to it, objecting to the couple determining the number of their children, and the vague answer given by the regulation of births.[76] Cardinal Ottaviani said the principle of responsible parenthood was incompatible with the faith. Cardinal Heenan again was not pleased with the text, calling it 'tame'. He said it contained 'practically nothing that would help married couples in their intimate problems. The difficulties were sketched, but little more'. Cardinal Rossi of São Paolo, Brazil agreed and thought it was better to remain silent. 'Is it not more prudent than running the risk of affirming what might be contradicted tomorrow? ... The indeterminate and imprecise statements in the schema on this question do not suffice at all.'[77]

However, this was mere sniping: the real bombshell was the arrival of four amendments (*modi*) from 'higher authority'. Xavier Rynne describes the scene with journalistic verve.

> When the modi were read, to the consternation of the sub-commission members, there was a look of triumph on the face of the American Jesuit Father John Ford and the Franciscan Father Ermenegildo Lio, advocates of an intransigent position on the subject of birth control, whilst Cardinal Browne is alleged to have said: '*Christus ipse locus est* – Christ Himself has spoken' ... The four modi were to be inserted in the text at specific crucial points with a view to exploding the idea that conjugal love enjoyed equal status with procreation as the ends of marriage and reasserting Pius XI's doctrine of *Casti Connubii* banning all and every type of artificial contraception unequivocally.[78]

The amendments would have changed the whole tenor of the accepted text, undermined its theological vision and made the Special Papal Commission on Family Planning redundant.

It was quickly evident that Ford and Lio – both of whom had been previously excluded from the sub-commission on the orders of the president, Archbishop Dearden of Detroit for their intransigent views – were the authors of these amendments.[79] However, it was to be equally clear on the next day, after a fruitless forty-five-minute discussion on whether the Commission was the proper organ to discuss them, that these amendments were approved of by the Pope. A second letter from the Secretary of State made clear that the Pope considered the amendments of great importance, the method of formulation was not obligatory, certain things could be added provided the sense was retained, and the Pope himself would decide later whether the Commission's decisions were acceptable.[80] Some including Cardinal Léger were aghast at this second letter, and felt their hands had been tied. But the majority on the Commission now set to work in the light of the fact that the method of formulation was not obligatory.[81]

The first amendment asked that the phrase 'contraceptive practices' be added after the words 'so-called free love' with a reference to *Casti Connubii*. After a great deal of discussion, it was decided to insert 'illicit practices against human generation' after the phrase 'excessive self-love' so the text read: 'Married love is often profaned by excessive self-love, the worship of pleasure and illicit practices against human generation'. This change was not so easily accepted because some felt the new text was much weaker. The vote was 22 to 13 with two blank ballots.[82] When it came to where the footnote to *Casti Connubii* was to go no exact place could be agreed on. Abbot Butler, auxiliary bishop of Westminster, suggested it should be placed so as to indicate it was at the request of the ordinary magisterium i.e. the Pope. This was rejected. Likewise, the suggestion of Cardinal Garrone that it be added so as to bring out the Pope's statement to the Cardinals the year before that *Casti Connubii* was binding as of now was also rejected. The upshot was it was agreed that the reference should appear at some other place in the text.

The second amendment asked that 'also (*etiam*)' be omitted in the phrase: 'Hence, the true practice of conjugal love and the whole meaning of family life which results from it, also (*etiam*) have this aim: that the couple be ready with stout hearts to co-operate with the love of the Creator and Saviour, who through them will enlarge and enrich his own family day by day.' And the words: 'Children are the supreme gift of marriage and contribute very substantially to the welfare of their parents' were to be inserted in its place. This would have had the effect of reasserting procreation as the primary end of marriage. This problem was more easily solved. Following the suggestion of Canon Heylen, *etiam* was omitted, but the phrase was inserted in the text after the statement 'marriage and conjugal love are by their nature ordained toward the begetting and educating of children' and followed by an additional phrase that 'while not making the other purposes of matrimony less account'. This effectively removed any possibility of concluding that procreation is the primary end of marriage.

The fourth amendment was taken next which required that the following words: 'but if the spouses are to overcome their difficulties, it is altogether necessary for them to practise the virtue of conjugal chastity sincerely' be added. At Cardinal Colombo's suggestion, it was agreed almost unanimously to suggest the wording, 'Such a goal cannot be achieved unless the virtue of conjugal chastity is sincerely practised.'

The third amendment asked that the phrase 'Relying on these principles, sons of the Church may not undertake methods of birth control which have been or may be found blameworthy by the magisterium' with a footnote to the *Casti Connubii* and Pius XII's Allocution to the Italian midwives to be inserted in place of the words 'methods of birth control considered blameworthy'. The difficulty with this new text was that it wished to bind consciences in the future so the words 'have been or may be' were replaced by the present tense 'are'. To this, at the suggestion of Archbishop Dearden, a long footnote was added including the suggestions of the amendment, adding: 'Certain questions, which need further investigation, have been handed over at the command of the supreme pontiff to a commission for the study of population, family and births, in order that, after it fulfils its function, the supreme pontiff may pass judgment. With the doctrine of the magisterium in this state, this holy synod does not intend to propose immediately concrete solutions.'[83]

Immediately, Fr Ford went to the Pope in a last ditch attempt to reassert the original wording. Paul VI would have none of this and passed the amended text without comment the same day. So after 464 amendments the text was finally decided. The final vote was 2047 for and 155 against. The difficulties could be seen in the fact that the second highest number against any part of the constitution *Gaudium et Spes* occurred on the text regarding marriage.

Marriage is a Covenant

The change from regarding marriage as a contract to regarding marriage as a covenant in *Gaudium et Spes* was very significant. The Church's identification of its sacrament of marriage with law was pastorally and theologically disastrous. Couples who live together without benefit of law or sacrament frequently argue that marriage is just a matter of law. Those who have seen their parents go through the legal agonies of divorce, think of marriage as a legal entanglement having nothing to do with the love they feel for each other.[84] The law is a barrier, so much so that Webber asks if law and marriage were completely separated so that a church marriage was purely a spiritual affair, would people begin to see Christian marriage as it really is?[85]

Obviously, the Fathers at Vatican II saw these obstacles. The Central Commission said 'The term "contract" obscured the genuine nature of marriage because a contract concerns things, services and rights rather than persons, which was contrary to the vision of the encyclical *Casti Connubii* that described marriage as giving of the person to each other.' The construction that Cardinal Gaspari created around the sacrament was likewise rejected; the Central Commission said: 'Historically the marriage contract was between two families rather than two spouses.' Finally, and most tellingly, as marriage was an image of the relationship between Christ and His Church, marriage could not be a contract, as Christ had no contract with His Church. So, a purely legal view of marriage had obscured rather than revealed the reality that God intended.

These points were not all the Fathers at Vatican II had in mind when they replaced contract by covenant. The crucial interventions of Cardinal Léger and Bishop de Roo during the debate over the formulation of the section on marriage in *Gaudium et Spes*, pointed to conjugal love as the expression of the essence of marriage. The insistence on this idea can be seen from the answer to the objection that if conjugal love is the essence of marriage, then marriage could be dissolved if this is extinguished. The response was: First, the love meant here is not just emotional; second, the unity that this love brings is permanent. Marriage is not subject to human decisions about the presence or absence of love as the text clearly says: '... established by the Creator and endowed with its own intrinsic laws'. The word covenant expresses this love because it underlines the permanent relationship that marriage is,[86] an indissoluble covenant between persons.[87] Thus, marriage as a community of love flows naturally from conceiving marriage as a covenant. That marital covenants naturally form an unbreakable bond is underlined clearly in the biblical vision of two in one flesh.[88]

The richness of a marriage covenant becomes even clearer if the marriage covenant is compared to the biblical notion of covenant. Significantly, they correspond exactly. The biblical idea of covenant, where self-revelation, self-gift and self-sacrifice without counting the cost are emphasized, is an exact expression of the unique union of conjugal love. Even a summary glance at the Bible shows that self-revelation is present, both in the original covenant between Yahweh and the people of Israel, which began with Yahweh's self-revelation as their God, and in the new covenant through Jesus. God was not just an idea; they knew Him through His signs and His wonderful works.[89] Likewise, as the covenant came into being, as God took Israel to be His people, and Jesus took our flesh, they were self-gifts of the very being of God. In both cases, they included self-sacrifice, as the love of God is real. Marriage is a covenant, because it symbolizes the covenant between Christ and His Church, so similar conditions are found there. Self-revelation between the couple makes the relationship; self-gift is the essence of love, the basis of marriage; self-sacrifice is the result, as every married couple knows marriage demands sacrifice. Hence, conjugal love must be seen within its marital/covenantal context, otherwise it loses its genuine significance.

However, the biblical concept of covenant goes much further than self-revelation, self-gift and self-sacrifice. The living out of the covenant always takes place in a personal history that can be seen in the history of Israel, and in the history of Jesus. The covenant is a daily reality. Covenant is our story. In this story we can trace the meaning of our lives: not just a personal story, but also a family story, because the other essential element of the marital covenant is family.

This concept of the covenant as a daily reality is most wonderfully seen in the life of the prophet Hosea. In a passage that carries so many references to the marriage of God to Israel, Hosea is told by Yahweh to marry Gomer, a harlot.[90] She bears him two children named *Lo-ruhama*; she no longer holds the love of her parents, and *Lo-ammi*, not my people, showing tragically the state of the family of Israel and Hosea's family. Gomer leaves him for another. However, Hosea is told to take back the adulteress Gomer contrary to Lev. 21.7 so as to show the loving care and lasting union of Yahweh's marriage to Israel. The scene ends with what might be described as a cry from Hosea: it is true the covenant always remains. Hosea's message-by-action portrays his story as Yahweh's story. His family is Yahweh's family. As a covenantal story, it places human history as a symbol of divine history, something John

XXIII believed in and wished to be portrayed in 'his council'.

Thus marriage as a covenantal story of conjugal love is not static; rather it is dynamic. A remark of a bride-to-be puts this concept in everyday terms. 'I could not love my fiancé more, but everyone tells me I will.' Love grows or dies; the two-in-oneness changes throughout life. So the Council wrote: 'a man and a woman, who by the marriage covenant of conjugal love "are no longer two, but one flesh" render mutual service to each other through an intimate union of their persons and of their actions, and experience and grow in the meaning of their oneness, day by day.'[91] This growth does not only belong to the intimate relationship, because the two-in-oneness is meant to be at the service of life,[92] but also gives life to the marriage and may bring forth new life in children. It is this vision of covenant and love that gives meaning to sexuality.

Thus the argument over the renewal of the concept of marriage took place on two fronts. The main advance had been the replacement of the term 'contract' by 'covenant'. This was not a mere argument about words, as some lawyers were later to try and argue, but about changing basic concepts. The marriage contract was based on exclusive sexual rights; the marriage covenant was based on exclusive conjugal love. This covenant of love is what is meant in Ephesians 5.31 by 'one flesh'. [93] That the change is about content and not context is made even clearer by the teaching of Ephesians that marriage is a sign of the eternal covenant between Christ and His Church. Thus, the marriage covenant could grow because the sacrament causes growth. Contracts cannot grow; they can only be replaced. In addition, stating marriage was a state of life was inadequate. The intimate union of husband and wife goes beyond that to understand marriage as a school of love both in the order of salvation and the order of creation, because the love of Christ for His Church is both liberation and creation of new life. The second advance is conceiving marriage as a school of love that prompts the couple to receive children and care for them. Therefore, new life flows from the marriage, rather than being the cause or the justification for acts of love. This rejection of the Augustinian approach to marriage lay behind the question of responsible parenthood and the acceptance of conjugal love as the essence of marriage.

Hence the Council's understanding of marriage was revealed in the words they used to describe it. They referred to marriage as a community and importantly a community of life and love. Marriage is an intimate partnership on a personal level, and an institution on a public level; thus confirming its double reality of being - a personal and public relationship. But most of all the Council saw the foundation of these terms in their insistence that marriage is a covenant of love. It is this 'conjugal covenant of irrevocable personal consent' that is the vehicle that underpins all these phrases. Once again the English translation of the Latin fails to reveal the true meaning here. It is not 'rooted in' as the English translation states. Instead the Latin *instaurare* means 'formed by' once again underlining the force of a covenant.[94]

The conclusion must be as Mackin comments: 'Nowhere in the chapter is the term "contract" so much as suggested, either in its nominal form *contractus* or in its verbal form *contrahere*. This cannot have been the consequence of an oversight. An assembly of over 2400 bishops, hundreds of them canonists by education and avocation, cannot without deciding to do so have discarded the word contract and its concept.'[95] In spite of the constant sniping of a minority, the Council underlined the centrality of the community of love as a lived reality, and totally failed to mention marriage as a contract. Hence, it is incorrect to translate *foedus* as contract for it is contrary to the expressed wishes of Vatican II and makes nonsense of the section on conjugal love by breaking the logical connection between the various sections.

Thus the change of terminology illustrates the true nature of marriage – self-giving that pervades the whole of the couple's lives. This is the Council's interpretation of 'two in one flesh'. Covenant was chosen because it showed the theological basis of marriage. Founded on conjugal love, covenant necessarily brings out the personal dimension of marriage, yet describes the merging of the human with the divine so that love grows, a love that is uniquely expressed and perfected through marital acts. It means that Christian marriage enjoys an enduring presence of Christ throughout married life. So, conjugal love is a profound physical and spiritual experience that throws light for them on their mutual irrevocable union, giving birth through its links to the Creator to life and happiness. Through their creation children express this love and find in that love their own salvation. A notion of contract cannot support any of these insights. Truly, the rejection by the Council of the notion of marriage as a contract and the adoption of the notion of marriage as a covenant is the starting point for a renewal of the theology of marriage.

Notes

1　For example Flannery A. (ed.), *Vatican II: The Conciliar and Post Conciliar Documents*, Dominican Publications, Dublin, 1975.

2　Palmer, Paul F., SJ, *Theological Studies*, vol. 33, 1972, pp. 617–665.

3　Stankiewicz A., 'The Canonical Significance of Marital Communion' in *Vatican II Assessment and Perspectives Twenty Five Years After*, vol II. ed. R. Latourelle, Paulist Press, New York, 1989, pp. 202–203.

4　For example Peter of Ledesma held that consent to a marital society as well as consent to the mutual gift of bodies was needed. *Tractatus de magna matrimonii sacramento*, Venice, 1595, q. 48, a. 1, p. 292.

5　...ius in corpus, perpetuum et exclusivum, in ordine ad actus per se aptos ad prolis generationem. Canon 1081.2.

6　*Canon Law Digest*, vol. 3, 1953, pp. 401–404.

7　Stankiewicz, *The Canonical Significance*, p. 205, where he points out that Cardinal Gasparri, the craftsman of the code, clearly holds this.

8   *Casti Connubii* n. 6.

9   Ibid., nn. 8, 31.

10 Ibid., n. 35.

11 Ibid., nn. 23–25.

12 John XXIII opening address to the Council.

13 Moeller C., 'History of the Constitution' in *Commentary on the Documents of Vatican II*, ed. H. Vorgrimler, Burns & Oates, London, 1969, p. 3.

14 The Relator for the Zurich text, Bishop Emilio Guano, makes this very clear when he outlines the idea and structure of the text. *Congregatio Generalis* CV. II [42], 45.

15 Holland J. and Henriot P., *Social Analysis: Linking Faith and Justice,* Center of Concern, Washington, 1983, examines the limits and elements of social analysis.

16 McGrath M., 'Social Teaching since the Council: A Response from Latin America' in *Vatican II by those who were there,* ed. A. Stacpoole, Geoffrey Chapman, London, 1986, p. 328.

17 The Latin title was *De Castitate, Matrimonio, familia, virginitate.* It formed part of a document prepared by the Theological Preparatory Commission whose members were Mgrs P. Pavan, and A. Ferrari-Toniolo, Frs F. Hurth, G. Grundlach, G. Jarlot, all Jesuits, and A. R. Sigmond OP. The *relator* for marriage questions was E. Lio OFM.

18 ... finis primarius unice est prolis procreatio atque educatio, etiamsi matrimonium particulare fecundum non sit. (11) Appendix – *De Castitate Matrimonio, Familia, Virginitate,* p. 735.

19 Alii autem matrimonii fines obiectivi, ex indole ipsius matrimonii oriundi sed secundarii, sunt mutuum coniugum adiutorium solatiumque in vitae domesticae communione et remedium, quod dicitur concupiscentiae. In matrimonio enim concupiscentia per finem coniugalem recte dirigitur, ideoque rationi subiecta castiati inservit et nobilitatur. Ibid. (11), p. 735.

20 Unitas ergo et indissolubilitas ita sunt cuiusque matrimonii proprieates intrinsecae et essentiales. Ibid. (10), p. 734.

21 'Item damnat errores illos, quibus tenetur matrimonium christianorum vel non esse sacramentum vel ipsum sacra-

mentum esse quid accessorium aut separabile ab ipso contractu.' Ibid. (14), p. 736. There are several references to the proposed canon from Vatican I. Footnotes 8 & 6 give the canons. Canon I: Si quis dixerit, Christum non evexisse matrimonium ad sacramentum dignitatem, et viri ac mulieris coniunctionem haberi inter christianos posse, quae sit verum matrimonium, non autem sacramentum: A.S. Canon II: Si quis dixerit, matrimonii *sacramentum* non esse *ipsum* inter Christianos contractum, qui *consensus* perficitur; aut esse aliquid contractui accessorium et ab eo *separabile*; aut vi contractus mere civilis posse inter christianos verum matrimonium consistere; A.S.

22   For example, Cardinal Léger asked: How is it that the text of the Commission contains new reflections of Father Lio? Likewise, Cardinal Suenens told a confidant: yes, we too have our Father Tromp. Alberigo G. and Komonchak J. A., vol II, *The Formation of the Council's identity, Oct 1962–Sept 1963*, Orbis, Maryknoll, 1997, p. 417

23   Moeller C., 'History of the Constitution', p. 14. This reflected an argument that was only to be resolved in the Fourth Session of the Council.

24   Häring B., 'Fostering the Nobility of Marriage and the Family' in *Commentary on the Documents of Vatican II*, ed. Vorgrimler H., Burns & Oates, London, 1969, p. 229.

25   The Mixed Commission was chaired by Cardinal Octavianni.

26   Moeller, 'History of the Constitution', p. 17 says he was present at a meeting on 15 May 1963 when this was agreed.

27   It was completed on 3 July 1964 and is referred to as the Zurich text. Alberigo and Komonchak, *The Formation of the Council's identity*, pp. 482–483.

28   Matrimonium non est merum procreationis instrumentum, sed ipsa natura foederis indissolubilis inter personas, et maxime bonum prolis exigit, ut coniuges se vere ament; et si proles deficit, matrimonium suo fundamentali valore suaque indissolubilitate non privatur. Attamen talis est amoris coniugalis indoles, ut matrimonium natura sua ordinetur ad prolis procreationem et educationem. *Acta Synodalia* vol. III pars V:132.

29   'Timeo peritos annexa ferentes.'

30   Although the Cardinal did not name him, it is certain it

was Fr Häring who was being shot at. Cf. Rynne X., *The Third Session*, Farrar, Straus and Giroux, New York, 1965, pp. 124ff. See 'Il Concilio Vaticano II Terzo Periodo', *La Civiltà Cattolica*, Roma, 1968, pp. 254–255 for the full text. The outburst was in character but out of line with his previous statements on ecumenism and the laity where he was moderate and forward looking. Later, Cardinal Heenan was reconciled to Fr Häring and invited him to London to address his priests.

31 Cardinal Léger, 112 Congregation, 29 October 1964. Text taken from 'Three Speeches on Marriage', *The Tablet*, 7 November 1964, 1255.

32 Ibid.

33 'In hac vocatione divinitus constituta primo consideranda est matrimonii sanctitas et sanctificans vis; qua perspecta et ratione habita novarum vitae condicionum de amore coniugali et domestico agetur, dein de notis, quae amoris coniugalis veritatem probant de fidelitate nempe coniugum de matrimonii unitate et indissolubilitate, atque de vera et sancta responsibilitate erga prolem concipiendam et educandum; tandem attentionem omnium advertimus ad communionem obligationem renovandi structuras et viate condiciones in mundo, in quo vivit familia.'

34 Videns Deus non esse bonum homini, si sit solus (cf. Gen. 2, 18; Mt. 19, 4), ab initio masculum et feminam creavit eos, amoris foedere coniunxit eos benedixitque eis: 'Crescite et multiplicamini et replete terram' (cf. Gen. 1, 18). Qua benedictione vocavit eos, ut 'in una carne' (cf. Gen. 2, 24; Eph. 5, 31), id est consortio indiviso et indissolubili iuncti Ipsiusque in propagando genere humano cooperatores, Eum glorificant. *Adnexum II De Matrimonio et Familia* 1.

35 Matrimonium origine, natura et finem sacrum est. Ibid. 2.

36 Consensus autem matrimonialis sua essentia intendit huius foederis unitatem, indissolubilitatem et amorem vitae servitio destinatum. Ibid. 4.

37 Léger, 112 Congregation, *The Tablet*, 1256.

38 Nowell R., 'A Delicate Question', *The Tablet*, 7 November 1964, 1255.

39 Matrimonium inter christianos contractum non est igitur sacrum tantum, sed etiam signum rei sacrae quatenus sanctificat homines. Sponsi per valididum consensum

exterius rite manefestum coniunctum Christo se tradunt et a Christo sibi invicem iungitur ut mutuale et libera suorum ipsorum donatione gratiae sacramenti particpes – inquantum obicem non ponunt – tota matrimoniali vita novum et aeternum foedus Christi cum Ecclesia testentur et collaudent ... Gratia autem huius sacramenti docente Concilio Trentino, amor naturals perficvitur, indissolubis unitas confirmatur, sanctificantur coniunges. *Adnexum II De Matrimonio et Familia* 2.

40   Idem, secundum hanc legem ipsa gratia sibi impositum, in Spirito Sancto se invicem amando et in via sanctitatis alter alterius onus speciali modo portando (cf. Gal. 6, 2) purissimam et fecundissimam Christi cum Ecclesia unionem vere representant et participant, et Salvatoris caritatem sibi invicem et filiis aliisque testantur. Cum autem Christus, sacramentorem institutor atque perfector hanc gratiam sua passione promuerit, Eum sequentur crucem cotidie ferendo gaudii Resurrectionis Eius participes; ita in gratia et sanctitate crescunt. Ibid. 2.

41   Deus qui caritas est, ita instituit matrimonium indeque familiam, ut propagatio generis humani fiat in intima personarum communitate, qua mirabilitur amor humanus nacitur et crescit, permanans totam vitam, immo florecit caritas Christiana, quae, Spiritus Sancti Donum, in coniugum corda abundanter diffunditur, et amorem humanum elevat ad ipsum Amorem, unde novas iugitur vires hauriat. Quo vitae consortio, speciali sacramento sanctificato, homines edocentur in regnum amoris Christi, Verbi incarnati, assumi omnem amorem vere humanum, et modo eminente tenerrimum illum amorem qui inter coniuges ac parentes inter et filios viget. Ibid. 4

42   Matrimonium, iam secundum primam Dei intentionem indissolubile, ut sacramentum Novae Legis per Christi gratiam fit signam eximium Eius erga Ecclesiam fidelitas, ita ut coniuges, qui huic vocatione et gratiae cooperantur eiusdem fidelitatis participes fiant et coram mundo eius testes constituantur. Ibid. 5.

43   Matrimonium, quamvis natura sua vitae servitio destinatum, tamen nullo modo considerari debet tamquam merum instrumentum et medium prolis procreandae et nominis sui perpetuandi. Ibid. 5.

44 Of the eight speakers who followed, four spoke in favour of the schema, two against and two raised particular topics.

45 Texts in 'Il Concilio Vaticano II Terzo Periodo', pp. 306–310.

46 Catechism Romanum II cap. VIII, q. 13. It states the ends of marriage are first companionship and mutual assistance; second, the desire for a family, and third as an antidote for lust. *Catechism of the Council of Trent for Parish Priests* issued by Pius V, trans. J. A. McHugh and C. J. Callan, Joseph F. Wagner, New York, 1923, pp. 343–344.

47 *Casti Connubii*, n. 12.

48 'Il Concilio Vaticano II Terzo Periodo', p. 307.

49 *Acta Synodalia* vol. IV pars I:591. R.Tucci wrote that no one had any further intention of dropping the appendix chapters. Moeller in a footnote says this was a very curious episode in the history of the schema. Moeller, op. cit., 44, footnote 56.

50 *Acta Synodalia* vol. IV pars I:478. Aricca text n. 60.

51 Communitas coniugalis a Creatore condita suisque legibus instructa, foedere coniugii seu irrevocabili consensu personali instauratur. *Acta Synodalia* vol. IV pars I:478. Aricca text n. 61.

52 Mentio non fit de 'contractu matrimoniali' sed verbis clarioribus sermo est de 'irrevocabil consensu personali' secundum vota Patrum (cf. 196, 217, 336, 337, 359). Additur terminus biblicus 'foedus' untuitu Orientalium, pro quibus 'contractus' quasdam difficultates facit. Notio instituti matrimonii sequenti phrasi firmatur, ne ullus censeat sese illud arbitrio suo postea dissolvere posse; aut, deficiente amore etiam requisito, matrimonium suum nullum fieri. *Acta Synodalia* vol. IV pars I:536, Historia Textus Praesentis.

53 Exposito fit inde a V.T., ubi foedere inter Deum et populum electum praefiguratur Christus Sponsus Ecclesiae, fundamentum indolis sacramentalis matrimonii. *Acta Synodalia* vol. IV pars I:536, Historia Textus Praesentis.

54 ... intima animorum, corporum atque operum coniunctionem mutuum sibi adiutorium et serbitium paraestant, sensumque suae unitatis experiuntur et semper plenius adispiscentur. *Acta Synodalia* vol. IV pars I:478. Abbott's

72   *The Mystery of Christian Marriage*

comments appear in the notes. Cf. *Acta Synodalia* vol. IV pars VI:484.

55   Amor coniugalis, qui Christiana 'ascesi' dirigitur atque nobilitatur, in divino amore, qui etiam virgines colit, assumitur ac virtute redemptive Christi Ecclesiaeque salvifica actione ditatur, ut efficaciter ad Deum ducat. Quapropter christifideles ad sui status officialis et dignitatem peculiari veluti consacrantur et roborantur sacramento; cuis virtute munus suum coniugale explentes, gradatim ad plenam humanae personae perfectionem mutuam santificationem ideoque communiter ad Dei glorificationem accedunt. *Acta Synodalia* vol. IV pars I:478. The notes state *roborantur* was specifically added to the text and *ideoque* specifically means that glorification is not exterior but expresses the fullness of marriage as well as the sacrament. *Acta Synodalia* vol. IV pars I:536, Historia Textus Praesentis.

56   *Acta Synodalia* vol. IV pars I:479

57   'Il Concilio Vaticano II Quarto Periodo', *La Civiltà Cattolica*, Roma, 1968, p. 129.

58   Häring, 'Fostering the Nobility of Marriage', pp. 232–233.

59   Häring, 'Fostering the Nobility of Marriage', p. 235: 'Moreover, Christ himself who instituted the holy sacraments and brought them to perfection, merited for us by his passion the grace that brings natural love to perfection and strengthens the indissoluble unity and sanctifies the spouses. The Apostle Paul intimates this when he says "Husbands, love your wives, just as Christ loved the Church and delivered himself for her" Eph 5:25.' Cf. DS 1799.

60   Declaration of the Holy Office, 29 March 1944. *Acta Apostolicae Sedis*, vol. 36, p. 103.

61   *Acta Synodalia* vol. IV pars I:478.

62   Häring, 'Fostering the Nobility of Marriage', p. 233 (Responsum 15 and 19b).

63   This is clear from the fact that when ten Fathers asked that the phrase *quasi fastigio* be inserted so that there is no undue stress on procreation because a childless marriage does lack an essential element, it was refused because the term *veluti* was placed there to do exactly this (Responsum 23c).

64   *Acta Synodalia* vol. IV pars VI:484. Some wanted 'fidelity,

children and bond' inserted here. Others wanted 'personal
and spiritual ends' instead. Rather the wording represents
the intrinsic and natural things.

65   Abbott W. M., *The Documents of Vatican II*, Geoffrey
     Chapman, London and Dublin, 1966, p. 250 n. 155.

66   This was further emphasized in the final text, that it
     involves the good of the whole person (emphasis added).
     Gaudium et Spes n. 49.

67   The last phrase will be replaced in the final version by
     'Such love pervades the whole of their lives.' Ibid.

68   Ille autem amor, utpote actus eminenter humanus, cum in
     personam dirigitur ab eaquae terminetur, Corporis anim-
     ique motus peculiari dignitatem ditare eosque tamquam
     elementa ac signa specialia coniugalis amicitate nobilitare
     valet. Hunc amorem Dominus supreme gratiae dono, quo
     christifideles filii Dei vocantur, ornare et elevare dignatus
     est. Talis amor, humana simul et divina conscians, coni-
     uges ad liberum et mutuum sui ipsius Donum, tenero
     affectu et opere probatum conducit; vitae coniugalis
     quotidiana officiis et sacrificia pervadit; immo ipse
     generosa sua operositate perficivitur et crescit ... Haec
     dilectio proprio opere exprimitur et perficivitur. Actus
     proinde, quibus coniuges intime et ordinatim inter se
     uniuntur, honesti sunt et, modo vero humano perpetrati,
     donationem mutuam plenam significant et fovent.

69   Talis est matrimonii et amoris coniugalis indoles, ut ex
     semetipsis ad prolem procreandam simul et educandum
     ordinentur. Unde verus amoris coniugalis cultus totaque
     vitae familiaris ratio inde oriens eo tendunt ut coniuges
     forti animo dispositi sint ad cooperandum cum amore
     Creatoris atque Salvatoris, qui per eos Suam familiam in
     dies dilatat et ditat. Matrimonium autem, licet in prolem
     ordinetur, non est merum procreationis institutum; sed
     natura foederis indissolubilis inter personas bonumque
     prolis exigent, ut mutuus etiam coniugum amor recto
     ordine proficiat et maturescat. *Acta Synodalia* vol. IV pars
     I:480.

70   *Acta Synodalia* vol. IV pars VI:483.

71   Nowell R., 'Marriage and the Family: Continuity and
     Change in the Church's Teaching', *The Tablet*, 9 October
     1965, 1113.

72   'Il Concilio Vaticano II Quarto Periodo', p. 137. The summary from the Italian is my own.

73   As Nowell comments: 'it would be unfair to accuse any of the Council Fathers of having a Patristic attitude towards sex, some of them seemed remarkably suspicious of it'. Nowell, 'Marriage and the Family', 1114.

74   Matrimonium autem, licet in prolem ordinetur, non est merum procreationis institutum; sed natura foederis indissolubilis inter personas bonumque prolis exigent, ut mutuus etiam coniugum amor recto ordine proficiat et maturescat.

75   Sciunt coniuges, in familia condenda et ducenda, non ad arbitrium suum procedere sibi licere, sed conscientia se regi debere quae lege Dei recte informetur, necnon suum esse prolis numerum secundum Dei dona verique amoris indicationem determinare. Qua in re iugi vigilantia et docilitate erga Deum, communi consilio atque conatu prudens iudicium sibi efformabunt, intendentes salutem mentis ac corporis, dignoscentes temporum et staus vitae condiciones tum paedgogicas tum oeconomicas ad denique rationem servantes boni ipsius familiae, societatis temporalis et Ecclesiae necessitatum.

76   For example Bishop Taguchi of Osaka, Japan who said it was inappropriate there because of pagan practice. 'Il Concilio Vaticano II Quarto Periodo', p. 129.

77   'Il Concilio Vaticano II Quarto Periodo', p. 134.

78   Rynne X., *The Fourth Session*, Farrar, Straus and Giroux, New York, 1966, p. 213

79   Canon Heylen is reported to have said of Fr Ford and other conservative theologians: 'They obey the Pope when the Pope obeys them.' Rynne, *The Fourth Session*, p. 213, footnote.

80   Rynne, *The Fourth Session*, pp. 213–215.

81   The details of the whole affair including the letters sent are to be found in 'Il Concilio Vaticano II Quarto Periodo', pp. 486–493.

82   Rynne, *The Fourth Session*, pp. 216–218.

83   *Gaudium et Spes*, footnote 14.

84   This is based on Webber C. L., *Re-Inventing Marriage, A Review and Re-vision*, Morehouse Publishing, Harrisburg, 1994, p. 143, who interestingly poses these questions.

85   Ibid., pp. 144–45.
86   The divine vocation of marriage which is holy and sanctifies the partners, in that where conjugal love dwells domestic life is renewed because conjugal love brings about faithfulness, unity and indissolubility of marriage
87   Matrimonium non est merum procreationis instrumentum, sed ipsa natura foederis indissolubilis inter personas, et maxime bonum prolis exigit, ut coniuges se vere ament; et si proles deficit, matrimonium suo fundamentali valore suaque indissolubilitate non privatur. Attamen talis est amoris coniugalis indoles, ut matrimonium natura sua ordinetur ad prolis procreationem et educationem. Acta Synodalia vol. III pars V:132.
88   *Gaudium et Spes* n. 48.
89   Cf. Eichrodt W., *Theology of the Old Testament*, SCM, London, 1961, p. 37.
90   Authors endlessly debate whether she was a harlot because she represented Israel and its rejection of Yahweh, or whether she in fact was a harlot because she was a worshipper of Baal, or she was just a harlot. Most probably all three meanings are contained in the text.
91   *Gaudium et Spes* n. 48.
92   This Text of *Gaudium et Spes* speaks of marital love being for the greatest good of the children revealing the true love of the partners. See footnote 8.
93   This is clear from the footnote to Ephesians 5.31 in the text of *Gaudium et Spes*.
94   Mackin, T., *What is Marriage?*, New York, Paulist Press, 1982, p. 281 n. 36.
95   Ibid., n. 37.

Chapter Three

Covenant, Conjugal Love and Sexuality

In the midst of our current uncertainty over sexuality, there exists an immense longing for more meaningful and human sexual relationships. Reducing sexual intercourse to casual recreational enjoyment may be pleasurable at the time, but such love disappears as soon as the pleasure is gone. Likewise, reducing marital sexual intercourse simply to procreation is unreal. Sexuality has a much deeper meaning that transcends biology: togetherness, commitment, consolation, celebration, forgiveness, joy are some of the words that describe that meaning. One of the joys of marriage is growing together in a loving relationship, which by its very nature changes as the stages of life pass. Throughout married life, through the procreative period, past the menopause into old age, the meaning changes. Marital sexuality cannot be reduced to procreation.

It is because of the many dimensions of sexuality that there is a real problem in explaining sexuality. It is not just the negative evaluation of the Latin Fathers, or the modern presentation of sexuality as primarily erotic phenomena of a largely genital nature;[1] the traditional philosophical arguments based on biological design have a problem. It is not possible to understand sexuality purely as a biologically based need, which is oriented not only toward procreation, but also toward pleasure. The problem is further exacerbated by the distinction that is made between sexual acts and sexuality. While sexual acts today are considered to be mainly for pleasure, sexuality is a much wider term having symbolic meanings based in psychology and culture.

Though sexuality is one of the most culturally defined and controlled of human gifts, mainly because of its utmost importance to human society, the meaning of sexuality is frequently concealed or deformed by culture as feminism has long been crying out. In addition, the Church is often blamed for a misogynist outlook where sexual pleasure is interpreted as a snare to trap the unwary. The impression given is that if 'sex' were recognized as a good in itself, all these problems would disappear. Yet this is no solution, because sexuality is a vessel that holds a variety of gifts that need direction, and each age tries to direct these gifts for the good of the society. The problem is that this direction has often been manipulative and negative even though it values sexuality.

Due to infertility and infant mortality previous sexual emphasis was on procreation. Today, with the disappearance of many practical problems associated with infant mortality the emphasis has changed. The control of conception, the removal of legal sanctions against abortion, and the apparent need to control population growth, have moved sexuality into personal bonding and pleasure. The Church's response to this sea change was difficult because any change in this area was dangerous. Indeed, some bishops at the Second Vatican Council argued that marriage should continue to be seen as a contract associated with exclusive sexual rights over another's body because marriage was a remedy for sexual desire. This view of marital sexuality occurred because sexuality was corrupted by concupiscence, lust. Thus, sexuality was under the reign of sin because lust is a permanent destabilizing force. The only real justification for sexual activity in marriage was the begetting of children.

Often the blame for this negative view is laid at St Augustine's door, forgetting this view was common among the theologians of his time. Sexuality carried lust, meaning that conjugal love is at permanent risk of derailment.[2] Sexual pleasure could only be justified in the search for conception because intercourse was primarily for achieving this end (*usus*) rather than for enjoyment (*frui*). While Augustine shared this view, it is often forgotten that Augustine also had a positive view of marriage. He saw in the creation of man and woman in Genesis a bond of blood relationship and a bond of friendship. This bond of friendship underlying marriage overrode the importance of procreation.[3] For Augustine, marriage needed faithfulness, children, and in the case of Christians, a sacred bond to be good. Faithfulness was the primary good of marriage. It was many centuries later that children became the primary purpose of marriage.

It was this traditional view that needed refining. Yet, to alter a perception of marriage that had endured for centuries was a difficult undertaking. But right from the beginning of Vatican II, the bishops realized that a new approach was needed that went beyond a contractual understanding of marriage as rights and duties.[4] Conjugal love that expressed unity and permanence had to be shown to be more than a sacred sexual contract ordered to procreation. The solution was to express the personal dimension of marriage. The acceptance in *Gaudium et Spes* that conjugal love is good because it is 'caught up into divine love and is governed and enriched by Christ's redeeming power' means that sexual relations within marriage are not under the reign of sin but under the reign of grace.[5] Hence the Council's answer to the signs of the times was to emphasize the place of love within marriage. Marriage is a covenant not a contract. Marital sex is declared to be good, and the idea of marriage as a remedy for concupiscence died.[6]

But this was only the first step. The relationship between conjugal love and sexuality still needed spelling out. Such an interpretation was difficult because not every marital act is ordered to procreation.[7] The thesis of *Gaudium et Spes* is: while it is clear that children are part of conjugal love,[8] and married couples interpret the love of the Creator,[9] procreation is not the integral sense of conjugal love because marriage is not instituted solely for procreation.[10] This is true because 'the divine law reveals and protects the integral meaning of conjugal love, and impels it toward a truly human fulfilment'.[11] A theology which justifies a marital act only if the intention to procreate is present, is misguided. In its place the bishops developed a positive view of human sexuality and marriage, where the essence of marriage is in the permanent relationship expressed by conjugal love.

Thus, conjugal love can only be understood from the marital covenant. Marriage as a sacrament cannot be understood as a contract because the bond of marital intimacy portrays that marriage is fundamentally a relationship. This relationship is worked out during a marriage as sexual desire is absorbed into married love. There is no longer a distinction between *amor*, sex and *caritas*, love, because marriage as a sign of the love of Christ and His Church is a glimpse and a participation in divine love. Lust has no place here. Sexual intercourse in marriage is a good in itself, and does not need justifying by procreation alone. Conjugal love in itself is sufficient reason.

Sexuality within marriage in its fullest sense is the source of community. The marital covenant means that self-giving is not any one act, or the blessing of fertility, but a dynamic force for the whole community of life.[12] Spouses are called not only to give physical life to their children, but also to be a source of life for the whole family and the community. Just as the original covenant brought about the people of God, the marriage covenant brings about a new concept of being the people of God by partaking in the community. In addition, the community of love which grows within marriage, and from which children may be born and in which children grow up has a spiritual dimension not only of learning about God, but also by experiencing the love of God within marriage. Their family story is a salvation story. This achievement is not possible with only one act of generosity, but calls for a constant renewal of this gift of each other. Thus, sexuality within marriage is not only an integral part of being human; it is also an integral part of love and salvation.

The application of this vision has been very challenging. The idea of marriage as a contract had whittled away the options and clarified the approach to whether a marriage really took place. Replacing such a taut legal approach with the broader approach of a covenant and conjugal love meant many avenues had to be explored again. This proved difficult in the years after Vatican II. It had left sexuality in an ambiguous position, as sexuality was only considered from within marriage, and all expressions of love before marriage were all considered of the same moral wrongness. There was no attempt to answer the question why God made us sexual beings except to say it was for procreation. The role of sexuality in relationships by the bonding of the partners was practically ignored or seen as dangerous. Finding the solution in the concept of conjugal love needed at least one or two generations of theological reflection, whereas an instant answer was expected from *Humanae Vitae*.[13] The danger at this point was to return to the old ways, to try, as Torrance warns, to turn God's covenant into a contract, or reduce conjugal love to procreation.[14]

The method used was to reflect on the meaning of conjugal love, in the sense that discovering the meaning of marital sexuality here would give a sound basis for sexuality as a whole. This approach was not surprising, as in Christian thought sexuality finds its fulfilment in conjugal love. The Second Vatican Council declared marital sexuality a good in itself, not a good dependent on children. Conjugal love exemplified this good, and by examining conjugal love the good of sexuality could be defined and its theology identified. So, to clarify the role of sexuality, it is necessary to explore the inspiration given at Vatican II so that the interrelationship between conjugal love and sexuality becomes clearer. Obviously this is a huge agenda that cannot be satisfied in a single chapter, but the broad outline and the way that the signposts of theological thought point can be indicated. This is the aim of this chapter.

An Anthropology of Sexuality Based on Purpose

The difficulty of interpreting the interrelationship between conjugal love and sexuality is immediately evident even in the formation of *Gaudium et Spes*. The four amendments that appeared at the last moment in its formulation at Vatican II signalled problems ahead, especially as Paul VI had proposed them. The reason why he proposed them is difficult to fathom.[15] He certainly did not write them,[16] and was not wedded to them to such an extent they had to appear exactly as proposed, because he accepted immediately the changes the Commission made and refused to insist on their appearance in their original form. The amendments certainly signified not only a desire to keep the previous position on marriage and contraception based on natural law, but also the need (in the eyes of some) to maintain procreation as the prime purpose of marriage and sexuality.[17] That it was a conservative agenda is obvious from those who wrote the amendments.[18] Certainly in the Pope's mind it was not a ploy to predetermine the question of contraception, as he had not made up his mind at this stage. Maybe the amendments were no more than a desire to clarify the direction marital theology was going, or unease with the imprecision of the new terms.

However, an acceptance of these amendments as written, would have introduced another theology in opposition to the one already adopted. This was impossible, so the amendments were dealt with in such a way that a balance was achieved, but it also meant that different points of view were represented in the text.[19] So, the text in *Gaudium et Spes* 51 can be subject to two readings: either marital sexuality depends on a natural law interpretation of the purpose of the marital act, children, or marital sexuality depends on interpreting the essence of marriage, authentic conjugal love. Later, *Humanae Vitae* combined these two interpretations in the procreative and unitive significances of marital intercourse.

This incident with the four amendments was both the cause of future difficulties and the solution to understanding these difficulties as Fr E. Lio drew up both the amendments and the section on natural law in *Humanae Vitae*.[20] The cause of the insertions was conflicting views of the theology of conjugal love. The second amendment wished to imply and in the mind of Fr Lio insist, that children were the prime 'end' (purpose) of marriage. To achieve this, it asked that 'also (*etiam*)' be omitted in the phrase: 'Hence, the true practice of conjugal love and the whole meaning of family life which results from it, also (*etiam*) have this aim: that the couple be ready with stout hearts to co-operate with the love of the Creator and Saviour, who through them will enlarge and enrich his own family day by day.' At the same time the phrase 'children are really the supreme gift of marriage and contribute very substantially to the welfare of their parents' was to be inserted. To omit '*etiam*' would mean that children were the prime aim of marriage, and this was rejected. But at the same time it was admitted by the Commission that in no way did they intend to put procreation into second place. Instead, they clarified the text by adding the required phrase, at the same time adding: 'while not making the other purposes of marriage of less account'. This effectively removed any possibility of concluding that procreation is the primary end of marriage. The fourth amendment required the clause: 'but if the spouses are to overcome their difficulties, it is altogether necessary for them to practise the virtue of conjugal chastity sincerely' be added to the text.

The agreed wording was: 'Such a goal cannot be achieved unless the virtue of conjugal chastity is sincerely practised'. These changes did not give confused signals.[21]

However, the insertion of the first and third amendments did produce a confused signal. The first wished to return to the natural law approach found in *Casti Connubii*. This is clear from the demand for an explicit reference, which was supposed to be made to that encyclical. Although such an insertion was never made, as the Commission could not agree, it was an indication of future problems. The third amendment sought to insert the phrase 'relying on these principles, sons of the Church may not undertake methods of birth control which have been or may be found blameworthy by the Magisterium' with its attendant footnotes to *Casti Connubii* and Pius XII's *Allocution to Italian Midwives* so as to pre-decide the question of contraception. The Commission refused as the matter had been withdrawn from the Council and placed in the hands of a special commission. Instead, in a crucial text they said:

Hence when there is question of harmonising conjugal love with the responsible transmission of life, the moral aspect of any procedure does not depend solely on sincere intentions or on an evaluation of motives, but must be determined by objective standards. These, based on the nature of the human person and his acts, preserve the full sense of mutual self-giving and human procreation in the context of true love. *Such a goal cannot be achieved unless the virtue of conjugal love is sincerely practised. Relying on these principles, sons of the Church may not undertake methods of birth control which are* found blameworthy by the teaching authority of the Church in its unfolding of divine law.'[22]

In a footnote the Commission added references to *Casti Connubii*, the *Allocution to Italian Midwives*, and Paul VI's *Address to a Group of Cardinals*, 23 June 1964. Paul VI immediately accepted the way his amendments had been used, and dismissed the pleas of Fr Lio. A final attempt to get a rejection of this section of *Gaudium et Spes* by distributing copies of the original amendments to the Fathers at the Council completely failed.[23]

The meaning was clear: conjugal love is to be interpreted by objective standards based on the nature of the human person and his/her acts in the sense that these acts preserve the full sense of mutual self-giving and human procreation in the context of true love. This is the nub of future interpretation in the Church's duty to 'unfold divine law'. But the problem with this text is the reference to *Casti Connubii* and the *Allocution to Italian Midwives*. The method used in these works to unfold divine law is natural law based on biology where reason observing natural processes formulates morality accordingly in a single step. This tradition sees natural law in creation itself, because God as creator made things in a specific way. Humans have their own nature, so natural law describes the obligations flowing from the way things are.[24]

While it is certain that Paul VI used natural law to interpret the meaning of marital sexuality, it is important to ask whether he followed exactly what Lio and Ciappi had drafted.[25] Three points are certain. Paul VI found their draft not pastoral enough, and altered the document in that sense. He clearly stated that the encyclical was his own answer. Moreover, Paul's use of natural law is fundamentally different from its use in *Casti Connubii* and Pius XII's *Allocution to the Italian Midwives*. These both move from a discernment of natural law to moral judgments in a single step. Paul VI proceeds by establishing an objective moral norm from which conclusions can be drawn.[26] In addition, his use of natural law as a method of discernment can also be traced in *Populorum Progresso*. In that encyclical the order of reason produces a view of natural law, which is echoed later in the *Instruction on Respect for Human Life in its Origin and on the Dignity of Procreation*. 'Therefore this law [the natural law] cannot be thought of as simply a set of norms on the biological level; rather it must be defined as the rational order whereby man is called by the Creator to direct and regulate his life and actions and in particular to make use of his own body.'[27] Thus in three important ways *Humanae Vitae* is different from the draft. These differences have to be taken into account in interpreting the encyclical.

Humanae Vitae argues from the natural law by emphasizing the importance of the objective biological order instituted by God.[28] This demands that spouses follow the will of the Creator that is expressed in marriage and married love.[29] These natural laws order the incidence of fertility, provide an infertile period in the woman, and are connected with the procreative and unitive signification of these acts. [30] As the sexual faculties are concerned by their very nature with the generation of life (*genitalium quidem virium qua talium, quoniam hae suapte natura ad vitam humanam progignendam spectant*),[31] direct interruption of the generative process is to be rejected. So, although new life is not the result of each and every act of sexual intercourse, sexual intercourse must retain its natural potential to procreate new life.[32] Therefore, the thesis is that the objective moral order can be discerned in the way nature orders sexuality.

Reactions at the time to this approach varied. Many, such as Marshall, simply denied that intercourse is essentially a procreative act. Rather, 'married couples experience intercourse as an act of union which above all expresses and fosters love in a way nothing else can'.[33] Others such as Selling, objected to the way the argument of *Humanae Vitae* is built on the natural law because it presents an objective natural order, intentionally created by God directing a right order of priorities in stark contrast to *Gaudium et Spes'* basis of the human person.[34] Again, some such as McCormick saw the strength of the argument in its consistency, as *Casti Connubii* used marital love as a motive for sexual intercourse, yet they also saw its weaknesses lying in the preconception that a biological fact rather than a person determines the morality of an act. This is contrary to the guidelines given in *Gaudium et Spes* n. 49 and the reply of the Central Commission, which underlined that the morality of marital acts should be judged solely as to whether the acts are fully envisaged in their total reality. Otherwise biology determines theology. Conjugal love cannot be just one of the inner senses of the marital act.[35] Sexual intercourse expresses this love or it is rape as Paul VI expressly mentions.[36] In brief, by itself, biological interpretations of natural law reduce conjugal love to animal behaviour.

The difficulty of using natural law as a method of inter-pretation can be clearly seen in subsequent documents that make sexual values rest solely on the biological final-ity of the sexual faculty. The 1975 declaration *Persona Humana* and the 1986 letter on *The Pastoral Care of Homo-sexual Persons* seem to see only a set of norms on the biological level as they understand the finality of the faculty determining its morality.[37] Thus, *Persona Humana* writes in 1975: 'when the finality is respected the moral goodness of the act is ensured', meaning physical finality, and the *Observation* of the Sacred Congregation for the Doctrine of the Faith in 1979 holds that *Gaudium et Spes* 51 is speaking of genital acts when it speaks of objective stan-dards based on the nature of the human person and his acts that preserve the full sense of mutual self giving.[38] So, in the application of *Gaudium et Spes*, conjugal love is only seen in a generic sense, while sexual activity is judged in a particular sense through natural law. It is a return to the division of conjugal love as *amor*, procreative love, and *caritas*, personal love of Pius XI in *Casti Connubii*.

The proof for the above is the statement of the Sacred Congregation for the Doctrine of the Faith that the Central Commission at Vatican II answered a proposal to reinstate the hierarchy of ends put forward by 'many Fathers': 'In any case, the primordial importance of procreation and education is shown at least ten times in the text.' The problem is that apart from the fact that a hierarchy of ends was consistently refused, and only one Father asked for an explicit mention of the goods of marriage, there was a request at the same time to explicitly say conjugal acts were of the whole person, not merely based on biology. The reply to this request was 'the text already says this'.[39] Thus, it would seem obtuse to hold biology was the only interpreter of sexual acts, or to reduce marital acts to a genital level of animal reproduction, or to conclude that the prime purpose of intercourse is reproduction. Such a conclusion would be contrary to the express intention of *Gaudium et Spes*.

This illustrates why there have been problems over the reception of *Humanae Vitae*. Its non-reception by many has led some to question the value of the encyclical. Some find the arguments from natural law unacceptable as they totally omit the relational or unitive part of marital acts, or deem them as having no input in discerning the meaning of such acts. Likewise, attempts to emphasize the relationship alone, by using the principle of totality, are just as unacceptable because that viewpoint ignores the reality of the body. In general, the reason for using natural law is that it means moral norms are open to all because they do not depend on belief, but on nature and reason. As regards the procreative aspects of sexuality, natural law was seen as essential because without a biological norm the traditional arguments against non-marital and non-coital sexual behaviour would collapse. Thus theologians who wished to preserve these values would go so far as to hold that natural law is the sole means of interpretation.[40] This fear may be justified in the light of some attempts to not use natural law,[41] but it does not justify automatically rejecting all other approaches, particularly as it had already been demonstrated that marriage could not be adequately interpreted from procreation, because this purpose does not adequately describe sexual relationships throughout a lifetime of marriage.[42] This fatal flaw seriously challenges the neo-scholastic use of natural law as the sole arbiter of morality in this area. However, this does not mean necessarily that the teaching of *Humanae Vitae* was incorrect, only that the tool used to sustain it, natural law, was inadequate for the job.

But this was nothing new; von Hildebrand and Doms had shown many years before that marriage is not adequately interpreted from procreation.[43] Von Hildebrand began by distinguishing between the meaning and the purpose of marriage, claiming that marriage's highest value is not found in achieving a goal outside itself, like prolonging the human race or the Church. Obviously, marriage does serve these goals, but it is the community of persons, the two in one flesh, which gives meaning to marriage.[44] This means that though marriage serves procreation, marital sexual relationships cannot be interpreted properly from this Augustinian point of view.

They were not the first to propose this. Von Hildebrand built on Ebertz, and Linsermann, who in 1878 held that sexual intercourse is subordinate to the higher purpose of marriage, for the higher purpose of marriage is spiritual, otherwise sterile marriage would be forbidden.[45] In 1933 Schwendinger underlined the same point. A sterile marriage, to be a marriage, must have another meaning, which can only be found in the community of persons. He wrote: 'The Me–You community still remains the first thing when one looks at marriage objectively. The first thing that a husband and wife want is not to create a third thing distinct from either. The third person is not what unites them and makes them say we, nor do they fulfil and consummate each other through it. No the first and most obvious characteristic of marriage is the direct union in love between a Me and a You. The object of their desire is the whole person.'[46]

Although reaction at the time these proposals were put forward was divided, and the Church defended the prime purpose of marriage as children, the debate shows that a natural law interpretation of the purpose of marriage is severely deficient. To rely on the procreative meaning of marriage meant that love is excluded from the essence of marriage, which in an age that relies on love as the basis of choosing a partner makes interpreting marriage from reproductive purpose alien to ordinary Christians. In addition, spouses do not find in their marriage a subord-inated-ends structure. As Mackin comments: 'Plato's and Aristotle's utilitarian evaluation of human sexuality which reduce it to a reproductive capacity is foreign to the ordin-ary Christian's idea of marriage.'[47] Thirty years before *Humanae Vitae*, Doms had rejected a reproductive purpose understanding of marriage and insisted on a phrase remarkably evocative of *Gaudium et Spes* that 'human nature transcends that of other animals because it has a spiritual soul'. All this was echoed in Vatican II, which said the essence of marriage is the marital community.

The conclusion must be that to interpret *Humanae Vitae* based only on the purpose of the sexual act is not tenable. This is even the position today of those who are the most ardent defenders of *Humanae Vitae*. Grisez, Boyle, Finnis and May argue that it is the will that counts in moral acts so that to reject the basic good of life is wrong.[48] Likewise, Smith rejects arguments based on biology in that they tend to condense sexuality to a biological purpose. She notes that the same problem is present in those who oppose a natural law interpretation. It is evident in Curran, who bases himself on a physical understanding of sexuality, and Haring in his proposal of an evolutionary vision of nature. Both are wrong for it is not in biology that the value of sexual acts is found.[49] Further analysis is needed.

An Anthropology of Sexuality Based on the Signs of Unity and Procreation

The path for this analysis can already be found in *Humanae Vitae*. The encyclical uses the word *significatio* meaning a sign or indication. This term cannot simply be translated as 'purpose' or 'end'. These terms were deliberately avoided. Instead, the emphasis is on two signs contained within conjugal love: a sign of the union between husband and wife, and a sign of their fruitfulness, children. The unitive significance of the marital act comes about because of the self-giving of the spouses.[50] *Humanae Vitae* emphasizes that conjugal love is essentially self-giving in totality, so much so that if this gift is withdrawn, it debases the marital act.[51] The procreative significance is identified with the generation of life. The language of the body combines both these signs.[52] This means the much quoted phrase: 'Human intelligence discovers in the faculty of procreative life the biological laws which relate to the human person' must be balanced by another phrase. 'Human intelligence also discovers this same faculty has more than a procreative meaning.'[53] Paul VI's intuition is that human sexuality is never a neutral reality because it is always a process of communication, which finds its completion when both signs are present. Conjugal love is the expression of the community of love.

In this Paul VI is accurately reflecting *Gaudium et Spes* 51 when it asks that sexual acts preserve the full sense of mutual self-giving and human procreation in the context of true love, so that this approach is not a new departure. In addition, the sense of the word *significatio* can be found in several discourses of Pius XII, and this teaching was clearly expressed by Josef Fuchs before Vatican II.[54] Yet it was a step beyond *Gaudium et Spes* as it now interpreted conjugal love through these signs. Paul VI deliberately used the term *significatio* as expressing the meaning of conjugal love. He emphasized that the inseparable connection, established by God, which man on his own initiative may not break, means sexual acts always have a double significance. He wrote: 'For its intimate structure, the conjugal act, while most closely uniting husband and wife, also capacities them (*eos idoneos etiam facit*) for the generation of new life, according to laws inscribed in the very being of man and woman. By safeguarding both of these essential aspects, the unitive and procreative, the use of marriage preserves in its fullness the sense of true mutual love and its ordination to man's exalted calling to parent-hood.'[55]

Yet, while the relationship between the unitive and procreative signs is clear, there are problems with whether this is a connection that is always there, or a connection that cannot be broken. The English translation 'intrinsic', based on the 'original' French/Italian version of the encyclical implies the connection is always there. The Latin text of *Humanae Vitae* says this relationship is an indissoluble connection (*nexu indissolubili*), that is it cannot be broken.[56] Each term gives different signals because intrinsic points to the relationship, while indissoluble points to a quality of this relationship.[57] The sense is that it is impossible to separate the two entities, but that is not because they always have to be united as though they composed a kind of compound entity. Both *Gaudium et Spes* and *Humanae Vitae* conceive the two signs of conjugal loving as total self-giving so that any interference with the signs has a disruptive influence and attacks the expression of mutual self-giving.

Even more problematic is the discernment of the exact nature of Paul VI's signs of unity and procreation, and their relationship to the intimacy and fertility of sexuality. The problem is: does sexuality only have the meaning Paul VI ascribes to it? Is sexuality only fully expressed in inter-course? The experience of married couples is that every loving act from touching to intercourse expresses the sexual self and their personal union, and in some circum-stances other acts of affection are just as meaningful as intercourse. Part of the problem here is the assumption that unity and procreation are interchangeable with inti-macy and fertility, because they are all meanings of the conjugal act. This attitude is misguided because intimacy is not the same as unity, and fertility is not the same as procreation. Unity and procreation are what come about, but intimacy and fertility are what bring them about. This is obvious when it is realized that procreation may be seen as more absent than present in the marital act, as only a very small proportion of such acts result in conception.

Some clarity is brought to the problem by making the crucial distinction between a purpose, a consequence and a meaning. A purpose is the object intended or 'end' in scholastic terminology. The consequence is the result, while the meaning is their inner significance. An act of intercourse may have the purpose of conceiving a child, and the consequence of unity and procreation, but the meaning lies in the conjugal love of the couple. If conjugal love is absent, the act is debased as in prostitution or in rape. Clearly Paul VI wanted unity and procreation to be meanings, which leads to the speculation that Paul VI changed the wording in *Humanae Vitae* from ends (purpose) to *significatio* (sign), for the logic proceeds as if they are purposes. Therefore, the Pope underlined that meaning is the key to understanding sexual acts. The problem is, as Doms pointed out thirty years before *Humanae Vitae*, the meaning of the marriage act goes beyond the biological sense of procreation. He concludes that 'the principal and primary purpose of marriage is not the child, but the mutual forming and perfecting of husband and wife in the metaphysical, natural and, above all, supernatural orders'. The meaning is found in the human significance of sexual acts.[58]

If the meaning is found in conjugal love, not in its purpose, then sexuality needs a broader canvas. It needs a more inclusive anthropology, and a theology of sexuality to show its meaning. This does not mean that the direction taken by *Humanae Vitae* was false; rather the opposite is true. The intuition of Paul VI is that human sexuality is never a neutral reality because it is always a process of communication needing further explanation. Thus the analysis of *Humanae Vitae* is incomplete as Paul VI intimated when he said: '*Humanae Vitae* ... is above all the positive presentation of conjugal morality concerning its mission of love and fecundity ... but it is not a complete treatment regarding man in this sphere of marriage, of the family and of moral probity. This is an immense field to which the Magisterium of the Church could and perhaps should return with a fuller, more organic and more synthetic exposition.'[59]

Sexuality as the Language of the Body

The next stage in finding a fuller, more organic and more synthetic exposition is developed in John Paul II's long series of Wednesday audiences from 1979 until 1984, much of which is embedded in *Familiaris Consortio*. The basis is an adequate anthropology – that is, what does it mean to be a human person? This required a closer look at *Gaudium et Spes*. Concerning conjugal love and sexuality, *Gaudium et Spes* teaches two important things. First, there is no true contradiction between the divine intention pertaining to the transmission of life and the fostering of authentic conjugal love.[60] Second, that human procreation is on a completely different level than animal life.[61] The emphasis is on mutual self-giving as the essence of marriage, because marital love is the heart of marriage. Understanding this relationship, the human dimension that makes marriage possible, is one of the keys to the theology of marriage. The other key is the divine relationship that is present in marriage. John Paul II explored both of these keys.

The Council's understanding of the first key was that this love is authentically human,[62] making all bodily expressions of affection fully human. Marital love is not an instinctive erotic response; instead it is a willing gift of the person to another person.[63] In this is found the meaning of sexuality. *Gaudium et Spes* understands marital love in a totally different way than the Augustinian approach of concupiscence. Marital love is not seeking pleasure as an end in itself. Such love disappears as soon as the pleasure is gone. Sexual acts preserve the specific character and dignity of human sexuality. Essential to this dignity is mutual self-giving, underlining Vatican II's description of these acts as 'personal acts'.[64] When the Central Commission was asked to explain a 'personal act' it said: 'These words mean that the acts are not to be judged solely on their biological aspect but as acts proper to the human person and the latter is to be fully envisaged in its total reality.'[65]

This would mean, as Louis Janssens points out, that the human person must be seen in his or her totality, a spirit in a body, where the nature of a person is bound in space and time as well as by its knowledge and appetite. Thus, to adequately understand the human person three things must be taken into account.[66] First, there is the question of relationships. People find their significance in their relationship to others; so much so that it is only in serving others that the real person is found. Second, being an embodied subject gives value to everyone, allowing a person to give value to his or her actions, so no one should be treated as an object. It means that we must respect others as being in charge of their own life. Furthermore, to speak of an embodied subject implies the unity of the person with his or her body. What affects the soul must affect the body and vice versa. This leads to several important consequences. As we have a bodily existence, we must take seriously the limits and potential of the biological order. We may not injure our body, or misuse it. We must respect it as a symbol of our interiority. Furthermore, the embodied person means he or she is part of the material world and so belongs to this moment of time. There is an obligation to take part in the progress of creation, yet there is also a need for awareness that human progress is flawed by human sin so that each discovery has a potential for evil. The spiritual nature of a person is shown in the way a person acts.

Third, each of us lives in this particular place and time on a journey towards our full human development. This does not simply mean a forward development, but what is often described as being in tension with the past and the future. What is important is that being an historical subject means we are becoming, and being called to shape, the future, not simply to settle into a static condition.

The consequence of Janssens' analysis is that conjugal love has a relationship dimension as well as a biological dimension, which together are experienced as a journey towards fulfilment. All dimensions are necessary to interpret sexual acts. It is this personalist and holistic view that Paul VI applies in *Humanae Vitae*, as he says conjugal love is fully human in that it is not just a matter of instinct and sentiment, but also a free act of self-giving, which is total because it implies a special form of friendship, and faithful because it is exclusive until death. Only then does he add that it is fecund, because this love goes beyond the couple to bring forth new life. It is clear for him there is more to the human person than biology. In fact, the human person can only be understood as one who is on a journey. *Humanae Vitae* says: 'The question of the birth of children, like every other question that touches human life, is too large to be resolved by limited criteria, such as provided by biology, psychology, demography or sociology. It is the whole man and the whole complex of responsibilities that must be considered, not only what is natural and limited to this earth, but also what is supernatural and eternal.'[67] This is not surprising since Paul VI specifically says when speaking about *Humanae Vitae* that the basis of his work was a person-based concept to which he added certain pastoral directives.[68]

This insistence on the personal dimension of human sexuality is not new. It is evident in the original statement of Pius XII concerning the use of the infertile period, because he demanded that a serious reason was required for the use of such a natural phenomenon. To use the infertile period without such a reason was wrong. In other words, the method used could not alone determine the morality because that would mean the human element was missing. For conjugal love to be fully human, all explanations of acts of conjugal love have to find their meaning in the human person as well as the act itself. This implies that the act carries the meaning given by that person so it is possible to say the portrayal of the human person in conjugal love is through language, the language of sexuality. This language, as much bodily movements as words, reveals the person and their attraction and feelings toward the other. Of course, like any language, sexual language is culturally determined. The physical potential is expressed in a code that is understood by others. Yet sexuality is never simply biology, or culture. Though sexuality is the way people relate to the world as male or female, it goes beyond this. Barbotin calls it 'the language of being itself'.[69] Through this language self is communicated and intimacy is born.

Therefore John Paul II saw the language of sexuality as a basis for an adequate anthropology. Going further, he saw the language of sexuality as the basis for a renewed metaphysics and a renewed morality as 'objective reality calls man to objective morality'.[70] To achieve this double objective John Paul II followed Scheler, a disciple of Edmund Husserl, and began from human experience. Though he regarded Scheler as inadequate because he emphasized man as feeling value rather than aspiring to value, the Pope showed in his book *The Acting Person* that phenomenology could be integrated with the thought of St Thomas through the transcendence of the human person. This is because phenomenology is a philosophical method that 'aims to make explicit essential features implicit in the "livid-world"'.[71] 'This perception is eidetic [vivid] intuition by which we have knowledge of the essential features in the world. Phenomenology calls such universals essences.'[72] In other words, the person is revealed in the self-giving of sexuality. Thus, there is a connection between the inner world of person and the outer world of everyday life. This unity between the outer and the inner is the nub of John Paul II's method. But he goes much further than modern philosophy that emphasizes the subjective, and says this unity points to an objective reality. West in a crucial phase says: 'His philosophical project has been ... to give proper recognition to the discoveries of phenomenology without renouncing the philosophy of being; to "make room" for subjectivity with a realist philosophy'[73] – Thomism is joined to phenomenology. However, for John Paul II, the essentialist view of Thomism is prior to the external reality of phenomenology, which soon becomes evident in his *The Theology of the Body*. Moreover, *The Theology of the Body* has theological foundation based on scripture. Thus, John Paul II's catechesis is a theological approach based on an anthropology that is an expansion of Paul VI's sign approach, while adding a theological dimension that was not present in Paul's analysis – the body is the original sign of God's own mystery in the world.

The core of his presentation is that sexuality is by no means something purely biological, but concerns the inmost being (*nucleum intimum*) of the human person as such.[74] This inmost being finds its meaning in an 'everlasting vocation to the communion of persons. Man cannot in a certain sense, express this singular language of his personal existence and his vocation without the body. He has already been constituted in such a way from the beginning, in such wise that the most profound words of the spirit – words of love, of giving, of fidelity – demand an adequate language of the body. Without that they cannot be expressed.'[75]

Beginning from Christ's own body that conveyed transcendent spiritual realities, the theology of the body is the original sign of God's own mystery in the world, a nuptial mystery. This is clear in the relationship between God and his people, which is always described in nuptial terms – God is married to Israel. This unique relationship is the basis of *The Theology of the Body*.[76] So, although the divine mystery certainly cannot be reduced to its sign, yet the sign is indispensable in the revelation of the mystery – the sacrament of Christ's person.[77] It is the Incarnation where God became man that allows humankind to participate in this mystery and to express in their humanity the nuptial mystery. All this is summed up in the phrase: 'being two in one flesh'.[78] Therefore anthropology is joined to theology and so to understand conjugal love there is a need for what John Paul II calls an adequate anthropology that understands the language of the body.[79] This is why *Familiaris Consortio* n. 32 presents sexuality as 'the value and task of the whole person, created male and female in the image of God'.

This profound insight into a couples' desire to be one underlines the vocation of marriage as communion that the body expresses. John Paul II finds this in the difference between an unconsummated and a consummated marriage and sees the sacramental sign contained in the vows and in the consummation.[80] It is present in the covenant of Yahweh with His people where the prophets portray the spousal meaning of covenant – fidelity not adultery. This means the human body speaks a divine language so that the 'spousal significance of the body [is] integrally inscribed in the structure of masculinity or femininity of the personal subject'.[81] The body speaks by means of its masculinity and femininity through a personal gift showing the intrinsic nature of sexuality.[82] In other words, an adequate language of the body indicates certain acts of the body have an inherent meaning that should not be violated. Thus the thesis is: men and women only own an action when it is their own and in that ownership they are revealed and they reveal the plan of God.

This movement from sign to language as the basis of interpretation is an interesting development, which calls for an accurate description of the features of sexuality, because the accent is now on the meaning of sexuality. For John Paul II, sexuality involves a man and a woman with a body and the two cannot be divided.[83] Moreover, sexuality is to express the communion of persons and uniting with each other so closely so as to become 'one flesh', they subject their humanity to the blessing of fertility. Self-giving to be a fully human act must be unitive and potentially procreative.[84] So the Pope concludes, for the essential personal element of sexuality to be present, it must be a free gift of self and because of this self-mastery is necessary.[85] So sexuality is a value and task of the whole person.[86] If sexuality is the expression of personal relationships in mutual self-giving, it implies it is a gift to bring about a relationship on the journey towards eternal life as well as a procreative gift.

The basis of this interpretation is that the language of the body reveals an objective dimension, which cannot be in conflict to natural law. The phenomenological perspective reveals a 'fundamental structure (that is, the nature) of marital relations'.[87] The nature of the act is in the very act and this 'fundamental structure of the marriage act constitutes the necessary basis for an adequate reading and discovery of the two significances'.[88] The Pope states this is nothing more than 'reading the language of the body in truth through the ontological dimension ("fundamental structure") and then – as a result – in the subjective and psychological dimension ("significance"). In other words, we are dealing with the norm of the natural law.'[89]

It is now clear that the Pope's methodology is that the language of the body reveals an objective dimension, the fundamental structure or natural law that can be used as a means of interpreting the language of the body. The problem is the language of the body is reduced to a subjective and psychological dimension, which means surely that the essence this language is supposed to display is also incomplete and subject to review. Nor is it possible to condense the marriage act simply to its procreative significance, such an act has a very clear unitive significance. In brief, can the natural law portray both significances and are these the only significances resulting from reading the language of the body? Not only that: a true return to a theological and scriptural basis of sexuality must accept that the language of the body is objective. As Lisa Sowle Cahill says: 'The real problem is that the consequences of adopting a theology of the body have not yet been adequately worked out.'[90] She suggests that self-gift means that the 'interpersonal values are the essence of marriage to which sex and procreation are linked in a firm but subordinate relationship', which is hardly what the Pope holds.[91] For John Paul II procreation is a co-equal relationship along with unity.

While the theological basis of John Paul II's approach cannot be in dispute, however, the way this is used raises several questions. Lisa Sowle Cahill raises the question of the use of scripture, and whether marital experience requires procreation as the completion of conjugal love. She complains that the Pope romanticizes married life. Going further she doubts whether the ideals of unity and self-donation are the same for men and women.[92] Luke Johnson notes all the above and adds the difficulties of the narrowness of the vision that only identifies the body with sexuality, and more importantly the lack of real phenomenology in the presentation. The lack of real phenomenology in the Pope's presentation is evident in his reduction of the signs to a subjective and psychological dimension. Instead John Paul II bases his analysis on scholastic essentialism. Thus, there is little or no contact with human experience in his language of the body.[93]

It is important to note that no one is suggesting that John Paul II is going in the wrong direction with his language of the body. Nor is there any objection to his theological basis, instead the problems lie with interpretation. While occasionally his use of scripture leaves a lot to be desired, his thesis of human love in the divine plan is soundly based. This thesis, which has a long history in tradition, Janet E. Smith argues, does not have a romantic sense as the Pope has primarily in mind the service of one another in marriage. But Smith fails to address the principle criticism concerning the use or absence of phenomenology in its conclusions, and in this sense it is a disembodied theology of the body because it fails to take seriously all the insights that a phenomenology of the body would give.[94] There is a need to attempt to see all the factors that a theology of the body raises.

Towards a Fuller Understanding of Sexuality as a Theology of the Body

John Paul II's method finds his basis in the original sign of God's own mystery in the world, a nuptial mystery as found in Ephesians 5.21–33. The language of the body expresses this mystery and through this language it is possible to discern the essence of sexuality as expressed in natural law. It is in the use of phenomenology and the discernment of the essence of sexuality that questions arise. Instead of the Pope's two signs procreation and unity, recent studies indicate a fourfold dimension of human sexuality: the desirable, the relational, the procreative and the institutional. These interact to give multiple meanings to conjugal love.[95] To this must be added a spiritual dimension. These five dimensions correspond to the traditional categories of procreative, spiritual, and institutional/legal, while leaving the relational and desirable to correspond to the unitive sign. The question is whether the Pope's exposition of the unitive sign sufficiently includes the desirable and relational dimensions.

The essence of Vatican II's understanding of marriage is the gift of the person to the other. Thus, Dominian emphasizes that personal wholeness is the basis of human relations so sustaining, healing and growth are the true signs of conjugal love. To achieve this there must be permanency, continuity and predictability. Thus, as regards sexual behaviour, the framework of moral reference will primarily have little to do with sexual pleasure in itself, but will be concerned with the requirements of authenticating the person in the spouses.[96] This is because conjugal love reveals our humanity, for in loving the accent is on involvement and understanding. It has four dimensions: caring about, caring for, loving another and receiving love. Obviously, all these dimensions depend on the relationship between the couple. Yet these relationships are not just about feeling. A good relationship requires intelligent love. Thus, *caring about* another involves being aware of and paying attention to the needs of the other. This requires attentiveness, and a love that is not egoistic. This love seeks the happiness of the partner. *Caring for* another means assuming responsibility for providing the material necessities in the home, moral and psychological responsibility for conceiving children, parental responsibility in love and the care of the children, maturity of personal conduct in the ordinary affairs of life. *Loving another* requires self-control and temperance, stability and the ability to adapt to changed circumstances, gentleness and kindness of character, willingness and ability for mutual communication and consultation in important matters, objectivity and realism in evaluating events that are part of married life. *Receiving love* is the response to the experience of being loved, the acceptance of the loving embrace. It is at this point that the relationship is strengthened and the gifts of sexuality are received.

Conjugal love sustains emotionally, giving security through recognition, acceptance and the significance each has for the other so that sensitive empathetic communication is achieved with the one who is in touch with our inner world. Just a look at, or touching the other can communicate this conjugal love. It is healing, because love can show the person's real self to the other, exposing painful wounds and leaving them open to healing or further hurt. It is this dimension that makes or breaks both family and community. Healing is present in the mother who picks up her child who has fallen over and kisses the place to make it better. It is present in the husband who sacrifices his own interests and cares for his chronically sick wife; it is present in a family that is kept out of trouble by the good sense of the neighbours. Healing is necessary for community at all levels. Family life is a way, the most common way, to personal and spiritual growth.

Through this sustaining and healing relationship conjugal love grows. Achieving wholeness implies a sensitive availability and a generous response, which affirms both oneself and the other. Thus growth only occurs in a relationship and the greatest growth occurs when we are not overwhelmed either by the need for survival, or the need to heal wounds. Growth depends on permanency, continuity and predictability so that children may have the continuous presence of their parents when they are growing up and spouses might know what is expected of each other. As Dominian says, marriage is a community of life and love as the Council defined.[97]

It is in this experience of unity that is based on desirability and relationship that John Paul II's language of the body is lacking. He underlines that human relationships can only be complete where self-giving is of the whole person; and conjugal love is expressed in a love that is intimate and fertile. He accepts such relationships presuppose respect, permanency, continuity and predictability. He certainly emphasizes the phrase of *Gaudium et Spes* that says: 'marriage is a covenant whose basis is conjugal love that is eminently human, bringing special gifts of healing and perfecting, exalting the gifts of grace and charity'. But he fails to emphasize the human dimension of sexuality where love is joyous and self-giving, sustaining through affirmation and healing through forgiveness, and going beyond procreation. Conjugal love grows beyond the fertile years in a marriage. Love has a wider sense than reproduction.

Yet, his analysis does go beyond human relationships to a divine relationship as expressed in the Epistle to the Ephesians, an area omitted by most who write on sexuality. This divine relationship reveals the Christian as being one body with Christ so that in marriage where two are in one flesh, the relationship participates in the relationship between Christ and his Church. The essence of this divine relationship is love, for Ephesians clearly underlines the personal, total self-giving that love demands both in the total self-sacrifice of Christ for His Church and in the human self-sacrifice that makes marriage. The embodied spirit that this symbolizes, where the flesh becomes a human word, integrates the sexual self.[98] Sexuality is the language of love.

Sexuality as the Language of Love

While the signs form the basis for interpreting the meaning of sexuality in conjugal love, as Dominian mentions the inter-relationship of these signs is crucial as they bring about permanency, continuity and predictability. As an authentic human act, conjugal love indicates four major signs: intimacy, fertility, affirmation and healing. Conjugal love comprises both affection and sensuality. Sensual in that the body as flesh has sensations, desires and pleasures. Affection in as much as this arises from the person capable of love, care, delight that gives meaning to sensuality. Therefore the basis of the offering is the personal gift of one's self. Yet, the same physical act can have a whole range of different meanings from self-gratification to the self-giving of conjugal love. The interaction of factors that brings this about can be illustrated by using Abraham Maslow's hierarchy of human motivation.[99] The basic motivation is physiological needs such as hunger, thirst, shelter and sex. These require an area of safety where there is security and protection from physical and emotional harm, which in turn leads to the key concepts of love and belonging, acceptance and friendship. The next stage is the need for esteem, which externally is status or recognition, and internally is self-respect, reflected in confidence, achievement and freedom. Finally we arrive at self-actualization.

Applying this to the language of sexuality, the first stage is the search for the other where the dynamic is attraction through finding the gifts of another appealing, whether these gifts are beauty, intelligence or power. The person pleases me because I find pleasure in the company of that person. At this stage the relationship is receiving rather than giving. It also has an element of self-deception because mere infatuation is disrespectful because it falsifies the existence of the beloved.[100] As attraction turns into love the next stage is reached where there is a need for the security of knowing that you are loved. This stage is a period of fear, uncertainty and doubt, until each one knows that the person they love also wants to spend their life with them. During this stage mutual recognition grows as each one discovers that the other fulfils their emotional needs and becomes the alter ego. This naturally progresses to the total gift of one's self in marriage, where giving is just as important as receiving. Real love brings about unity, a sense of completion and well being. Intimacy gives affirmation. Love first affirms the other, creating not just a bond, but making the other a new person. Self-actualization has been achieved.

While this describes the various stages of sexual attraction and its culmination in the giving and receiving of each other, there is no way of defining the dynamic taking place by measuring the amount of sexual gratification needed for the stages to progress.[101] This would be a false approach, as the growth of the relationship does not depend on sexual gratification. Instead, the result of sexuality is bonding the couple so that they become one, or in the modern idiom, an item. The growth experienced is in depth because the sexual interaction that is bringing about the various stages is creative love. It is the reason why love heals by reaffirming the relationship, and it is the reason why love brings about a series of new relationships because new life is the sign of this love.

The unity of the couple in the safe area, which we call family, reveals a series of other relationships. As well as constantly renewing the relationship between the couple, love forms new relationships with friends, and family. It is very clear that while a couple do keep in touch with some of their former friends, so often this is only a one-sided relationship. The friends they form as a couple have quite a different character. Likewise, the binding together of two families, which the couple's marital relationship signifies, means new relationships result at another level. Even more significant is that love naturally leads to having one's own children and a relationship with children that is on the same level as the one between the partners, a covenantal relationship. Parental love goes beyond friendship, as the gift of oneself has brought about a child that joins both parents together. Finally, being a family results in another set of relationships as children and parents make new friends. These multiple relationships resulting from creative love show that the movement of intimacy to bond takes place at various levels and brings forth life, and illustrates the inter-relationship between signs as dynamic. At the same time it means that fertility does not belong to a single act, but is part of the whole relationship. Giving of one's person is the heart of love.

Dominian paints a similar picture when he applies the marital community to sexuality. Beginning from the goodness of the gift of sexuality, he says: 'this goodness is intimately related to life itself for human life by definition is a sexual life'. Thus, in contrast to taboos and condemnations that give birth to an inward looking self-centred concept of sex as lust, Christianity portrays sexuality as essential to a marital community, where it only reaches its full meaning in conjugal love. Sexuality is not just a part of life, or a supreme value based on biology and its potentiality for procreation, rather its value lies in the community of life and love.[102] For Dominian 'every act remains a source of continuous procreation in the sense that the life it engenders and enhances in the parents is a supportive continuation of the human life of the children'. As Vatican II says: 'This love (between spouses) is uniquely expressed and perfected through the marital act. The actions within marriage by which the couple are united intimately and chastely are noble and worthy ones. Expressed in a manner which is truly human, these actions signify and promote that mutual self-giving by which spouses enrich each other with a joyful and thankful will.'[103]

Thus sexuality is an all-embracing gift, which, through its signs of intimacy, fertility affirmation and healing transform present relationships and new relationships are made possible. Sexuality is the powerhouse of the covenantal relationship of marriage giving life to a family, to children and to a neighbourhood. It is an essential dimension of being human. Its signs are indications of this power, and their interaction is a sign of the creative and salvational action given to human kind. This is the reason why sexuality finds its meaning in conjugal love. The intuition of Paul VI that human sexuality is never a neutral reality because it is always a process of communication is most exact. As a language, which John Paul II expresses, sexuality aims at union with another, and thereafter expresses this union. It is because it is a relationship-building faculty that has the gifts of intimacy, fertility, affirmation and healing. It presupposes respect, permanency, continuity and predictability. This points to the correctness of a second intuition the Church has always held: that sexuality is intimately connected to family. It is in this sphere that it finds its meaning not only because of biology, but also because in itself it makes possible the relationships that family depends upon, because such relationships demand the complete gift of self.[104] The personal dimension of sexuality is crucial to its proper understanding. If this spiritual dimension is missing, the dimensions of sexuality are incomplete.

The Spiritual Dimension of Sexuality

The gift of sexuality is a gift to the human person. Right from ancient times, sexuality was considered to be a divine gift, or to be more exact a participation in divine life. In pagan society this gift was prized as fertility. Fertility goddesses were a prominent feature of ancient society. But God's original intention was much wider. This is very clear in the creation of humankind in Genesis. God created man and woman, male and female. He made them and named them humankind.[105] To complete the picture, a second version of the creation has been kept which shows man as lonely, a loneliness that the animals cannot fulfil. Man's companion, woman, is a gift from God described in terms specially chosen to emphasize her relationship to him. She is described as an opposite to him, chosen by him, and created from his rib so as to emphasize her position as equal and counterpart to him. This relationship is expressed in the term *basar ehadh*, 'one flesh', emphasizing the humanness, the unity, and sexual union. Adam and Eve are meant for each other and they have one life.

It is immediately clear that the gift of sexuality makes possible a covenantal relationship as their relationship is now described in covenantal terms: 'A man leaves his father and mother and cleaves to his wife and so they become one flesh' (Gen. 2.24). Leaving and cleaving, in Hebrew *asev* and *davaq*, are words used to denote a covenant so that the man abandons his parents to form a new covenant with his wife. This covenant of love means that the power of sex becomes the dynamism of conjugal love giving life to a family, to children and to a neighbourhood. It is an essential dimension of being human. Its signs are indications of this power and their interaction is a sign of the creative and salvational action given to humankind. It is because of this there can be said to be a spirituality of sexuality. The goodness of conjugal love and conjugal sexual acts, the wide diversity of meanings found in conjugal love, the key dimension of life that is given not just for children but for the life of the family and the neighbourhood, all outline the area within which sexuality finds it meaning. The gift of sexuality was good and belonged properly to man and woman.[106] The implication is that it is not sacred acts that make sexuality holy; it is holy in itself by God's act of creation because this goodness comes from the completeness found in the union of flesh not only in a genital sense but also in the completeness of life.[107] It is God's express design.[108]

But this is not all. Going even further, it is clear that the covenant of love is not merely a gift; it is a participation in the divine act of creation, through participating in divine love.[109] The covenant of human love finds its meaning in the way God married Israel, because the covenant between Israel and Yahweh was not an image but a reality vividly expressed in marriage.[110] Isaiah writes: 'Your Maker is your husband' (Isa. 54.5). So powerful was this image that the New Testament takes this a step further, underlining that our capacity to love is a participation in divine love. The essence of Christian marriage is life in Christ, a saving mystery. As Ephesians teaches, the great mystery, the love of Christ for His Church, is 'enfleshed' in Christian marriage, as conjugal love is a participation in divine love, because Christ abides with the spouses. John Paul II notes that excludes any Manichaean or non-personal interpretation of sexuality.[111] In other words, because conjugal love is the essence of marriage, the human reality touches the divine reality of a God who is love. *Gaudium et Spes* underlined this when (n. 48) it taught that the Holy Spirit, the expression of divine love dwells within a Christian marriage. Therefore, a spirituality of sexuality must have the mystery of divine love at its heart.

This is why sexuality is, as *Humanae Vitae* calls it, *munus*, a gift, [112] in the sense in which Vatican II constantly used the word *munus*.[113] It pervades the whole of life. Sexuality is a gift through which not only life and love are given, but also where community and relationships are formed. This aspect is the basis of the fundamental idea that sexuality finds its meaning in family and community. Self-revelation, self-gift and self-sacrifice are always taken as the basis of family, yet these characteristics are also the basis of creative love and give sexuality part of its meaning. Sexuality finds the rest of its meaning in the fact that family is the story of the covenant of marriage so that family is a living presence of the divine.

The divine presence is clearly indicated in Ephesians where the husband and wife portray the love of Christ for His Church, and is found in the biblical account of the covenant which concludes with blessings: the blessing of the divine presence on the way, the blessing of food and drink, good health, old age, and land, are all family blessings (Exod. 23.20–33). Likewise, the banquet that follows seals the covenant with Yahweh where the people are invited to eat with God because they are family. Thus, marriage as a covenant both creates and sustains family, because God is family and the human family is a symbol of His family. This is why moves at Vatican II to make the marriage blessing, a blessing of the contract, or a fertility blessing were rejected. Instead, the couple are blessed as a family. *Gaudium et Spes* spoke of the couple being sealed by mutual faithfulness and made holy by the sacrament, because Christ the Lord abundantly blesses this many faceted love, welling up as it does from the fountain of divine love and structured, as it is, on the model of His union with the Church.

Behind this idea of conjugal love lies a profound conviction that marriage was recreated in God's own image. John Paul II commenting on Ephesians' description of this recreation says it is: 'a spiritually mature form of that mutual attraction – man's attraction to femininity and woman's attraction to masculinity, which is revealed for the first time in Genesis'.[114] Nelson describes the image of the expulsion of Adam and Eve from the Garden of Eden as experiencing the loss of order and the breakdown of all relationships. This experience St Paul describes as the groaning of creation until it is made whole again in Christ. Humankind experiences this as the possibility to be made whole by love. The new commandment of love is a sign of this recreation through the restoration of relationships. The marriage relationship is restored as Ephesians 5.20–33 teaches by basing married love on the love Christ has for His Church.

Thus sexuality takes on a new dimension where self-giving is not only physical but also mental and spiritual. Love is killed by self-seeking. The gift of self is life-giving. Conjugal love is a profound spiritual experience that throws light on a couple's mutual irrevocable union giving birth through its links to the Creator to life and happiness. Therefore, sexuality has a deep spiritual meaning found in a covenantal relationship based on self-giving. Its holiness comes from within itself, as it is a God-given gift. It is a participation in divine creation and divine love; the covenant of love founded a community of life and love, where love was not just natural and right but as the Fathers of the Church had taught, a remnant of paradise. This gives real value to marital relationships and allows a society that emphasizes the depth of relationship to find a sound basis for self-giving. This is the reason why sexuality cannot mainly find its meaning in procreation, an opinion long opposed by the Eastern Church. Sexuality finds its meaning in its participation in a divine force of life and love.

Thus, painting on a broader canvas reveals the necessity of understanding the human sexual person as the bearer of a wonderful gift. This gift is orientated towards relationship and creation. As a relationship gift it makes and sustains the covenantal relationships of conjugal love through intimacy, fertility, affirmation and healing. As a creational gift it brings about family and new life. The need for family to sustain human life is why God created sexuality. Purely philosophical interpretations in this area greatly impoverish the depth of human sexuality as well as providing no spiritual dimension. Sexuality as the language of being itself goes beyond biology as it expresses the human person's deepest feelings. It is in this inmost being that men and women participate in the love of God.

Notes

1 Nelson J. B., *Embodiment: An Approach to Sexuality and Christian Theology*, Augsberg Publishing House, Minneapolis, 1979, p. 17.

2 Otten W., *Theological Studies* 59(1998), 399, n. 28.

3 Augustine, *On the Good of Marriage* 1.1, 2.2. Otten, ibid., p. 398, n. 27 quotes as regards sterile or elderly marriages that Augustine holds 'This does not seem to me to be a good

solely because of the procreation of children, but also because of the natural companionship between the two sexes.' This view seems to be a response to Jovian and Jerome in their dispute about whether virginity was greater than marriage. Jovian held that virginity added to one's public commitment rather than seeing it as a state of paradisiacal purity. Jerome defended virginity with a typical aggressiveness so that he completely demolished marriage. Augustine's more moderate views must be read in this context. See Otten p. 395.

4   The comment was that the old approach was incapable of dealing with the problems facing the Church.

5   *Gaudium et Spes* n. 48.

6   This is admitted even by the most conservative theologians.

7   *Acta Synodalia* vol. IV pars VI:490–491 Responsum 56. The blunt response was that 'not every act is ordered to procreation', or 'this is incompatible with the doctrine adopted'.

8   This is true because the text was changed to read: 'By their very nature, the institution of marriage itself *and conjugal love* are ordained for the procreation and education of children, and find in them their ultimate crown.' *Gaudium et Spes* n. 48 (emphasis added).

9   'Married couples should regard it as their proper mission to transmit human life and to educate their children; they should realise that they are thereby co-operating with the love of God the Creator and are, in a certain sense, its interpreters. This involves the fulfilment of their role with a sense of human and Christian responsibility and the formation of correct judgments through docile respect for God and the common reflection and effort; it also involves a consideration of their own good and the good of their children already born or yet to come, an ability to read the signs of the times and their own situation on the material and spiritual level, and finally an estimation of the good of the family, of society and of the Church.' *Gaudium et Spes* n. 50.

10   This is very clear from the famous quotation from St Thomas, which is rarely quoted in full, and therefore often misunderstood. 'Primary' and 'secondary' refer not to the hierarchy of ends, but to the universal inclination to procreate, which humans share with all

animals, and the particular where such acts bring about human care and satisfaction – the good of the spouses. Thomas wrote: 'Marriage is natural because natural reason inclines thereto in two ways: First, in relation to the principal end of marriage, namely the good of the offspring. For nature intends not only the begetting of offspring but also its education and development ... Secondly, in relation to the secondary end of marriage which is the mutual services which married persons render one another in household matters ... Wherefore, nature inculcates that society of man and woman that consists in marriage.' But the following paragraph gives the proper meaning of 'primary' and 'secondary': 'Man's nature inclines to a thing in two ways. In one way, because that thing is becoming to the generic nature, and this is common to all animals; in another way because it is becoming to the nature of difference whereby the human species insofar as it is rational overflows the genus ... Accordingly man's nature inclines to marriage on the part of the specific differences as regards the second end.' *Summa Theologica*, Supplement q. 41, v. 3. *The Summa of St Thomas* (translation prepared by the Fathers of the English Dominican Province), Benziger Bros., New York, 1948, p. 2711.

11 *Gaudium et Spes* n. 48.

12 This crucial point is made clear in the rejection of either blessing a contract or a fruitful union. The text of Trent is most significant here. Häring B., 'Fostering the Nobility of Marriage and the Family' in *Commentary on the Documents of Vatican II*, ed. H. Vorgrimler, Burns & Oates, London, 1969, pp. 233–234.

13 Selling J., *The Meaning of Human Sexuality*, Louvain Studies 23(1998) 31–35.

14 'The sin of the human heart in all ages – was to try and turn God's covenant into a contract.' Torrance J. B., *Covenant or Contract? A Study of the Theological Background of Worship in Seventeenth-Century Scotland*, The Scottish Journal of Theology, vol. 23, no. 1, February 1970, 56.

15 Cf. Turbanti G., *Un Concilio per Il Mondo Moderno*, Società Editrice il Mulino, Bologna, 2000, p. 756.

16 Fr Lio claimed he wrote these modi even though Fr Ford

was later to claim their authorship.

17   Zalba wrote to Dell'Acqua on 16 November complaining about the excessive value given to physical love so that procreation became subordinate. Cf. Turbanti, *Un Concilio per Il Mondo Moderno*, p. 745.

18   Fr E. Lio and Fr R. Gagnebet, the authors, were considered intransigents by the rest of the Commission. Cardinal Ottaviani put Fr Lio there. Ford was also instrumental in putting forward the amendments.

19   Under the Council rules, when a theology had been adopted through a positive vote (in this case an overwhelming acceptance), it was not possible to make a fundamental change at the last moment. Grootaers J. and Selling J. A., *The 1980 Synod of Bishops 'On the Role of the Family'*, Leuven University Press, Leuven, 1983, p. 185, n. 21.

20   Hebblethwaite P., *Paul VI: The First Modern Pope*, Harper-Collins, London, 1993, pp. 517, 525–526. Hebblethwaite, a noted biographer of modern popes, says, 'The *De Castitate* of Fr Ermenegildo Lio OFM rejected by the Council had eventually prevailed. Fr Lio wrote articles that his *De Castitate* can be considered as a dress-rehearsal or sketch for *Humanae Vitae*.' However, Turbanti stresses the role of Fr Ford particularly in the first amendment. Cf. Turbanti, *Un Concilio per Il Mondo Moderno*, Il Mulino, Bologna, 2000, p. 748.

21   Rynne X., *The Fourth Session*, Farrar, Straus and Giroux, New York, 1966, pp. 216–218.

22   *Gaudium et Spes* n. 51 (amendment in italics).

23   Rynne recounts a story from the Council rumour mill that Fr Ford went to Paul VI to protest at what happened to the amendments. The Pope is said to have replied: 'You, as a moral theologian, tell me there is only one way to look at this matter. On the other hand, Bishop Reuss is also a moral theologian and he tells me just the opposite. Go to him and argue the matter out. When you two moralists reach an agreement, come back to me with the answer.' Rynne, *The Fourth Session*, pp. 223–224.

24   'Natural Law is the demand of creation, experienced in the lives of human persons and promulgated through the light of human reason.' O'Connell T., *Principles for a Catholic Morality* Harper & Row, San Francisco (revised edn) 1990, p. 135.

25 This is clear not only from *Humanae Vitae* n. 4 but also because by 17 June 1967 a version of the encyclical based on a draft by Fr G. Martelet already existed built on the impossibility of rejecting *Casti Connubii*. Fr E. Lio and Fr L. Ciappi drew up the draft of chapter two, nn. 7–18 founded on the 'traditional principles' of natural law. Hebblethwaite, *Paul VI*, pp. 488, 517. Fr Martelet always denied he drew up chapter two and Fr Lio wrote how his document *De Castitate* was the basis of *Humanae Vitae*.

26 Coleman perceptively comments that *Humanae Vitae* should be read in such a way as to recall clearly that it is primarily concerned with objective morality: i.e., it is not directly concerned with formal sin, as it is with God's mercy and forgiveness. It is of great significance pastorally to recall that one does not find in *Humanae Vitae* the kind of language one sees in *Casti Connubii*: that those who indulge in such [acts] are branded with the guilt of grave sin. Coleman G., *Human Sexuality: An All-embracing Gift*, Alba House, New York, 1992, p. 113.

27 *Instruction on Respect for Human Life in its Origin and on the Dignity of Procreation*, Congregation for the Doctrine of the Faith, 22 February 1987.

28 The English translation uses the phrase 'paramount importance' which does not appear in the Latin original. That the answer given by Paul VI is his own and neither the minority nor majority opinion of the Commission set up by Vatican II is clear from *Humanae Vitae* n. 6.

29 This is clear from *Humanae Vitae* n. 4 where Paul VI uses the term 'depend upon' (*nititur*) for his description of the relationship between moral theology and natural law. Selling finds the natural law interpretation in *Humanae Vitae* numbers 4, 8, 10, 11, 12, 13 and 16. Cf. Selling J., *Moral Teaching, Traditional Teaching and Humanae Vitae*, Louvain Studies 7(1978) 4, n. 10.

30 Obviously, Paul VI proceeds from a biological fact to an objective moral order, particularly as the Pope uses the term *nititur* meaning 'depends upon' to describe this process. *Huiusmodi doctrina, quae ab Ecclesiae Magisterio saepe exposita est, in nexu indissolubii nititur, a Deo statuto, quem homini sua sponte infringere non licet, inter significa-*

tionem unitatis et significationem procreationis, quae ambae in actu coniugali insunt (n. 12).

31   The key words are *genitalium, suapte natura* and *spectant* which the French text translates as 'generative faculties as such because of their intrinsic ordination to fostering life'. *Humanae Vitae* n. 13.

32   The Latin text is crucial in interpreting Paul VI's mind. The key phrases are: *Porro ea, de qua loquimur, conscia paternitas praecipue aliam eamque intimam secum fert rationem, pertinentem ad ordinem moralem, quem obiectivum vocant, a Deoque statutum, cuis recta conscientia est vera interpres* (n. 10). *Deus enim naturales leges ac tempora fecunditatis ita sapienter disposuit ... Verumtamen Ecclesia, dum homines commonet de observandis praeceptis legis naturalis, quam constanti sua doctrina interpretatur, id docet necessarium esse, ut* quilibet matrimonii usus *ad vitam humanam procreandam per se destinatus permaneat* (n. 11, original emphasis).

33   Marshall J., 'True Meaning of Marriage', *The Tablet*, 4 September 1993.

34   Selling, *Moral Teaching*, 27. The statements are found in *Humanae Vitae* n. 10.

35   McCormick R., *Notes on Moral Theology, 1965 through 1980*, University Press of America, Washington, 1981, n. 219.

36   *Humanae Vitae* n. 13.

37   *Persona Humana*, Declaration on certain questions concerning sexual ethics, Sared Congregation for the Doctrine of the Faith, 29 December 1975, n. 5.

38   Observation on the book *Human Sexuality: New Directions in Catholic American Thought*, Paulist Press, New York, 1977, Sacred Congregation for the Doctrine of the Faith, 13 July 1979, Enchiridion Vaticanum.

39   *Acta Synodalia* vol. IV, pars VI:477, Response 12. The text that should be quoted is the response the commission made concerning personal acts. 'These words mean that the acts are not to be judged solely on their biological aspect but as acts proper to the human person and the latter is to be fully envisaged in its total reality' (Response 104).

40   Grootaers and Selling, *The 1980 Synod of Bishops*, p. 192.

41   McCormick, *Notes on Moral Theology*, p. 739.

42   Mackin T., *The Marital Sacrament*, Paulist Press, New York, 1989, p. 598.

43 von Hildebrand D., *Die Ehe*, 1929, later translated and published as *Marriage*. Doms H., *Von Sinn und Zweck der Ehe*, 1935, translated and published in 1939 as *The Meaning of Marriage*. Cf. Mackin, *The Marital Sacrament*, p. 624, n. 40.

44 Doms calls this *Zweienigkeit* two-in-oneness. Doms H., *The Meaning of Marriage*, Sheed & Ward, London, 1939, p. 85.

45 Mackin T., *What is Marriage?*, Paulist Press, New Jersey, 1982, p. 226.

46 Schwendinger F., quoted in Doms, *The Meaning of Marriage*, pp. 20–21.

47 Mackin, *What is Marriage?* p. 229.

48 The prime text here is Ford J. C., Grisez G., Boyle J., Finnis J. May W. E., *The Teaching of Humanae Vitae: A Defense*, Ignatius Press, San Francisco, 1988. A complete list of their work can be found in Smith J. E., *Humanae Vitae A Generation Later*, Catholic University Press of America, Washington, 1991, p. 340. Part of their argument here is that to argue from a natural fact to a moral value is an 'is/ought' fallacy or a 'fact/value' fallacy.

49 Smith, *Humanae Vitae A Generation Later*, 176–190.

50 Ibid., p. 109.

51 *Humanae Vitae n. 8, The Truth and Meaning of Human Sexuality, Guidelines for Education within the Family*, Pontifical Council for the Family, Catholic Truth Society, London, 2001, n. 11.

52 This is a favourite interpretation of John Paul II.

53 Coleman, *Human Sexuality*, p. 113, makes these vital points very clearly.

54 McCormick gives the following examples, AAS 43 (1951) 850; AAS 48 (1956) 470. Fuchs J., *De castitate et ordine sexuali* (3rd edn), Rome, Gregorian University Press, 1963. The same analysis is present in an earlier addition of Fuch's work (1959). Cf. McCormick, *Notes on Moral Theology*, p. 217.

55 *Humanae Vitae* n. 12. Translation taken from: McCormick, *Notes on Moral Theology*, p. 216.

56 The Oxford dictionary defines 'intrinsic' as inherent, essential, and defines 'indissoluble' as cannot be dissolved, stable, lasting.

57 The Latin speaks of the connection between the unitive and

procreative sign as: 'men of their own will may not infringe' (*quem homini sua sponte infringere non licet*).

58   Doms, *The Meaning of Marriage*, p. 87.

59   *L'Osservatore Romano*, 6 August 1968, 1–2 and 15 August 1968, 1.

60   Also see *Humanae Vitae* n. 13, *Familiaris Consortio* n. 32.

61   Human sexuality and sexual behaviour 'wonderfully exceed the dispositions of lower forms of life'. *Gaudium et Spes* n. 51.

62   The word used is 'eminenter' to underline the reality that human love surpasses and is different from that of animal attraction.

63   This love is expressed most clearly and comes to its fullness in the conduct that is proper to marriage. The acts by which spouses come together intimately and chastely are good and honourable. Expressed in a way that is authentically human they manifest the spouses' mutual self-giving and impel them to it – the self-giving by which they enrich one another with joyful and grateful wills. *Gaudium et Spes* n. 49.

64   The phrase used is *ex personae eiusdemque actuum natura desumptis*. The full text is: 'Where there is a question of harmonising conjugal love and responsible transmission of life, the moral aspect of any procedure does not depend solely on sincere intentions or on an evaluation of motives. It must be determined by objective standards. These objective standards, based on the nature of the human person and his acts, preserve the full sense of mutual self-giving and human procreation in the context of true love.' *Gaudium et Spes* n. 51.

65   ... *ex personae eiusdemque actuum natura desumptis quibus verbis asseritur etiam actus diiudicandos esse non secundum aspectum merum biologicum, sed quatenus illi ad personam humanam intergram et adaequate considerandam pertinent.* Response 104 c & f, *Acta Synodalia* vol. IV, pars VI:502.

66   Janssens L., *Artificial Insemination: Ethical Considerations*, Louvain Studies 8, pp. 3ff.

67   *Humanae Vitae* n. 7.

68   The original says: ... *e abbiamo volentieri seguito la concezione personalistica, propria della doctrina conciliare, circa la società coniugale, dando cosi all'amore, che la genera e che la alimenta, il posto preminente che gli conviene nella valutazione soggettiva*

del matrimonio ... Abbiamo voluto aggiungere all'esposizione dottrinale qualche indicazione practica di carattere pastorale. Acta Apostalicae Sedis, vol. LX, 30 September 1968, 529.

69 Barbotin E., *La sexualité d'un point de vue anthropologique*, Supplement 27(1974) 445–457 quoted in Guindon A., *The Sexual Creators*, University Press of America, London, 1986, p. 26.

70 West C., *The Theology of the Body Explained*, Gracewing, Leominster, 2003, pp. 33–34.

71 Howarth J., 'Phenomenology, Epistemic Issues' in *Concise Routledge Enclyclopedia of Philosophy*, Routledge, London. 2000, p. 671.

72 R.G., 'Phenomenology', *The Oxford Companion to Philosophy*, OUP, Oxford, 1995, p. 659.

73 West, *The Theology of the Body Explained*, p. 41.

74 *Familiaris Consortio* n. 11.

75 John Paul II, *The Theology of the Body: Human Love in the Divine Plan*, Pauline Books, Boston, 1997, p. 359.

76 Ibid., p. 331.

77 West, *The Theology of the Body Explained*, pp. 53–54.

78 John Paul II, *Letter to Families* n. 12.

79 John Paul II, General Audience 28 November 1984.

80 John Paul II, *The Theology of the Body*, pp. 355–356.

81 Ibid., pp. 357–361

82 *Familiaris Consortio* n. 32.

83 John Paul II, *The Theology of the Body*, p. 61.

84 The conjugal act 'signifies' not only love, but also potential fecundity and therefore it cannot be deprived of its full and adequate significance by artificial means. In the conjugal act it is not licit to separate the unitive aspect from the procreative aspect, because both one and the other pertain to the intimate truth of the conjugal act: the one is activated together with the other and in a certain sense the one by means of the other. John Paul II, *Reflections on Humanae Vitae*, St Paul Editions, Boston, 1984, pp. 33–34.

85 Man is precisely a person because he is master of himself and has self-control. Indeed insofar as he is master of himself he can give himself to the other. And it is this dimension – the dimension of the liberty of the gift – which becomes essential and decisive for that 'language of the body' in which man and woman reciprocally express

themselves in the conjugal union. John Paul II, *Reflections on Humanae Vitae*, pp. 32–33.

86   *Familiaris Consortio* n. 32.
87   John Paul II, *The Theology of the Body*, p. 387.
88   Ibid., p. 87.
89   Ibid., p. 388.
90   The inadequacy of the conclusion is clear from Janet E. Smith's reaction in that she cannot see why Lisa Sowle Cahill should conclude in the way she does. Smith, *Humanae Vitae A Generation Later*, p. 259.
91   Sowle Cahill L., 'Catholic Sexual Ethics and the Dignity of the Person: A Double Message', *Theological Studies* 50 (1989) 146. She goes on to state: 'full interpersonal and sexual reciprocity of men and women implies equality in all spheres, and this implies that reproduction must be controlled to permit women as well as men to mesh family life with contributions in other spheres.'
92   Ibid., 145.
93   Johnson L. T., 'A Disembodied "Theology of the Body"', *Commonweal*, 26 January, 2001. pp 11–17.
94   Smith, *Humanae Vitae A Generation Later*, pp. 258–259.
95   Nijs P., *De eenzame Samenpelers*, Nederlandschhe Boekhandel, Antwerp, 1976 (3 vols). Quoted by Selling, *The Meaning of Human Sexuality*.
96   Dominian J., *Proposals for a New Sexual Ethic*, Darton, Longman & Todd, London, 1977, p. 37. Also *Marriage, Faith and Love*, Darton, Longman & Todd, London, 1981, pp 49–107.
97   *Acta Synodalia* vol. IV pars I:473–8. Modi generales ad NUM. 51–56 (nunc 47–52). 1 & 2.
98   Guindon, *The Sexual Creators*, p. 23.
99   The main works of Maslow are *Toward a Psychology of Being*, 1968, *Motivation and Personality*, 1954, *The Further Reaches of Human Nature*, 1971.
100 Tyrrell T., *Urgent Longings, Reflections on the Experience of Infatuation, Human Intimacy and Contemplative Love*, quoted in Guindon, *The Sexual Creators*, p. 31.
101 This is in line with the general theory of Maslow, who does not provide a measure for the required amount of gratification for each stage to progress.
102 Dominian, *Proposals for a New Sexual Ethic*, pp. 73–76.

103 *Gaudium et Spes* n. 48.
104 John Paul II says the total self-giving would be a lie if it were not the sign and the fruit of a total personal self-giving in which the whole person including the temporal dimension, is present; if the person were to withhold something or reserve the possibility of deciding otherwise in the future, by this very fact he or she would not be giving totally. In other words sexual language is the sign of a personal relationship that must be true. *Familiaris Consortio* n. 11.
105 The Hebrew 'adam' humankind occurs throughout the Old Testament with a marked concentration in Genesis. It is not only used in contrast to God, but also in contrast to the animals. Gen. 1.22, 28; 2.7, 18–24.
106 This is both in the statement 'increase and multiply' and in the concept of 'blessings' which as Westerman says is the power of fertility. Westerman C., *Genesis 1–11: A commentary*, Rowman and Littlefield, London, 1995, p. 140.
107 Gen 4.1, 17, 25; Num. 31.17–18 etc. The key word here is the term 'knowing' which denoted sexual intercourse, and a personal relationship. Hosea uses the same term for Yahweh's relationship with Israel: Hos. 4.1, 6; 6.3, 6; 13.4.
108 Ezekiel continues this theme applying it to human marriage. Ezek. 23.48–49.
109 Kittel G. (ed.), *Theological Dictionary of the New Testament* vol. 1, Eerdmans, Grand Rapids, 1978, p. 654.
110 Hos. 2.19, Isa. 54.4–5, Ezek. 16.7ff. *The Anchor Bible Dictionary* vol. 4, K–N, Doubleday, New York, 1992, p. 570; *Interpreters Dictionary of the Bible* K–Q, Abingdon Press, New York, 1962, pp. 285–286.
111 'We must recognise the logic of this marvelous text which radically frees our thinking from the elements of Manichaeism or from non-personalistic consideration of the body ... It brings the language of the body, contained in the sacramental sign of matrimony, nearer to the dimension of real sanctity' John Paul II, *The Theology of the Body*, p. 378.
112 Smith translates this as mission because this gives sexuality a positive sense, claiming the original is the Italian 'dovere' which translates as 'duty'. Smith, *Humanae Vitae A Generation Later*, pp. 136ff.

113 Classically *munus* can be used positively as a gift, i.e. the gift of the Spirit, or negatively as a bribe. Cf. St Thomas I, q. 39, a. 8; or IIa IIae, q. 78, a. 2, 3; or IIa IIae, q. 100, a. 5.
114 John Paul II, *The Theology of the Body*, p. 379.

Chapter Four

The Mystery of Two in One Flesh

The Second Vatican Council defined marriage as a community of life and love formed by a conjugal covenant. Christian marital love creates a community both human and divine, through the presence of Christ leading the spouses to a free and mutual gift of each other, a gift proving itself by gentle affection and by deed, pervading the services and sacrifices of daily conjugal life. It is this sacramental presence of Christ found in the covenantal vision of Christian marriage that underlines the real difference between getting 'married in church' and getting married in a civil ceremony. The term covenant cannot be a mere agreement or even a solemn promise because it reveals bonds that have a divine dimension. Christ transforms marriages with his presence so much so that marriage enfleshes this presence so that through the love of the partners, the love of Christ becomes real for those who meet a Christian couple.

It might be thought that this approach would have had an immediate effect on the theology of marriage. Yet there is ample room for doubt: Adrian Thatcher would certainly be among those who would question whether marriage as a covenant had been really taken seriously.[1] Thatcher takes three major innovations of *Gaudium et Spes* and finds most of them have been ignored. If marriage is a community, the intimate community of life and love goes beyond the sense of a partnership shared by a couple in a universal institution where married love is authorized. Instead, marriage is a community bound together by love.[2] Married life and married love are inseparable because God made them that way. In a wonderful way married life and married love have themselves become married.[3] In other words, marriage as a covenant means authentic married love is caught up in divine love because marriage is a total life relationship.[4] So, marriage was not just to have children, nor is the meaning of marriage found only in the teaching of St Augustine that marriage brought about fidelity, children and a bond. Marriage is a real community, a covenant and a total life relationship. Most of all Christian marriage enjoys the presence of Christ. In pagan terms, he is the house-god. The presence of the ancestor whose life the family enjoys. But how many of these ideas have been really adopted? Taking canon law as his guide, Thatcher believes the concept of a total life relationship has been adopted in some form, but as canon lawyers do not like abstract notions of love and affection, these concepts has been largely ignored.[5] This is clear from the events that followed the Second Vatican Council.

As the theology of marriage was developed in the pastoral constitution *Gaudium et Spes* some theologians believed that the former Augustinian attitude to marriage continued. It took until the 1970s before it was admitted that the Augustinian theory of concupiscence, marriage as a remedy for carnal lust, was dead as regards marriage. Likewise, the use of neo-scholastic notions of nature was also to bedevil the meaning of what the Council had taught. In fact, some, like Fr Lio,[6] never grasped or accepted the personalist approach, while others went too far. In addition, one of the great difficulties for the Church has been the poor reception *Humanae Vitae* received resulting in the primacy of sexual ethics both in the mind of the faithful and the Magisterium so much so that although every aspect of conjugal life was under discussion throughout the Church, there was little enthusiasm to have a synod on marriage after 1967. Rather, there was an attempt to bury the subject.

Only after the death of Paul VI in 1978, was the role of Christian marriage taken up again in the Synod of 1980. Even this was supposed to be limited to its role in evangelization, catechesis and various other apostolic and ecclesial tasks. But it was soon realized that this was impossible without determining the role of marriage as a sacrament in real life. Thus, the need to begin from the experience of the spouses became the new method to review the question once again. Yet the preparatory Roman document, the *Lineamenta*, hardly took this into account. It was negative, theoretical and manipulative. Negative, because it gave a long list of the problems concerning the institution of marriage resulting from the changing role of the family in modern society – divorce, second marriage etc.[7] But its purpose was not to face these issues. Rather, as Joseph Selling points out,[8] 'instead of outlining topics for discussion or seeking advice from the bishops throughout the world, the author(s) had provided a framework within which answers would be given.[9] As regards Christian marriage, the problem is the threat to Catholic doctrine and morals posed by mixed marriages and the rejection of magisterial teaching especially in the area of sexuality.'[10] The most fundamental difficulty was, 'the lack of a clear concept of the sacrality and sacramentality of marriage'.[11] Leaving aside the numerous misquotations from the Second Vatican Council, which Selling underlines,[12] an agenda was proposed that once again gave eternal answers to questions that were not posed.[13] Thus, the proposed solutions came from a fixed order established by God for marriage.[14]

The serious problem that the answers from above have to face is that even practising Christians have no idea of what the sacrament of marriage is beyond a church ceremony. Furthermore, there is a real taste of Augustinianism in the theology of the *Lineamenta*. Though it does expound the idea that marriage is a covenant based upon love and affection of will, the *Lineamenta* implies: 'this covenant is foreseen in the bond that flows from sexuality, which is called good although disturbed by sin', which is in fact a pre-Vatican II approach to marriage. Furthermore, the union of marriage is said to be total, that is including body and spirit, going beyond the couple themselves 'because from that union will be born children'. As at least 10 per cent of all marriages are infertile, a great number of marriages are childless and incomplete according to this approach, something that *Gaudium et Spes* expressly rejected. So it is not surprising that the *Lineamenta* was frequently criticized and ignored by the Episcopal conferences in their preparation for the Synod.

While many saw the *Lineamenta* as nostalgia for the past, this was not the only roadblock for re-examining the practice of Christian marriage. Some theologians argued that putting marriage forward as a high ideal, which it certainly is in Christian thought, is useless as no one can achieve such perfection. No marriage is without its faults. Instead, it would be better for the Church to return to a contract view of marriage, as this was more readily understandable. People knew what they were doing and the obligations marriage demanded. Divorce, however, is a logical conclusion from seeing marriage as a contract because if I made a contract, I can also end a contract. Describing the marriage contract as having special qualities of unity and indissolubility because the good of society and children demands it, the approach fails when people see their marriage as being neither good for them, society or their children. Moreover, marriage presented as a contract, where the Church places conditions upon it, is seen as constrictive. Perhaps most importantly, marriage as a contract is not what people desire or experience. This view of life removes the power of love from life, and fails to give people an ideal to achieve. As the Little Prince says: 'It is only with the heart that one can see rightly; what is essential is invisible to the eye.'[15] The experience of marriage, though unique to the individuals concerned, has elements and moments in it that surpass human frailty and point to a vision that needs explanation. This is because the transformation that marriage requires of the couple needs a vision of a utopia because utopias are culture-creating where love assumes a human form.

Love, affection and friendship give meaning to marriage as a community. This is not a new idea. Scholastic theology in the twelfth century spoke of marital affection, mutual assistance or human solace as one of the ends of marriage.[16] In their terms, if the object of consent was the conjugal society, as Peter Lombard held, the intermingling of the spouses was necessary at all levels. So, marriage was more than an institution, or an external society. The Second Vatican Council defined marriage as a community of life and love, and saw the spouses in a new light – their relationship. Love is not a quality or virtue of marriage; it is the expression of the divine presence in marriage. *Gaudium et Spes* speaks of Christ having blessed this many-faceted love as it comes from the fountain of divine love and structured as it is on the model of His union with the Church. This key phrase is based on the Council of Trent that said: 'Christ abides with the spouses thereafter.'

Marriage goes beyond the partners expressing their love for each other. Anyone who has had experience with preparing couples for marriage knows there is a difference between love in courtship and conjugal love. In marriage emotional love has to become true commitment. Even more important is the fact that conjugal love has the element of family in it. Family as expressed in the new family the couple become, and family in the union of the two families they represent. This is only one dimension of two in one flesh, where love is made flesh. Another dimension demands that any presentation of marriage must come from the experience of the partners, not from a fixed set of rules placed on the couple from above. Modern thought stops here in its analysis of marriage. Yet to stop at this point is fatal for there is a spiritual dimension that goes beyond an inculturalization of marriage. It is this dimension that gives life to marriage and shows us God's design.

In Christian thought, this is the presence of Christ in marriage. It is the Christian utopia of marriage. As *Lumen Gentium* said: 'Christian spouses, in virtue of the sacrament of matrimony, signify and partake of the mystery of that unity and fruitful love which exists between Christ and His Church (Eph. 5.32). The spouses thereby help each other to attain to holiness in their married life and by the rearing and education of their children. And so, in their state and order of life, they have their own special gift among the people of God (1 Cor. 7.7)'.[17] This is the presence of Christ within Christian marriage because as John Paul II says, basing himself on *Gaudium et Spes* 22, Ephesians 5 reveals – in a particular way – man's lofty vocation where he shares in the experience of the incarnate person.[18] It proclaims a spousal meaning of the body – to love as God loves and this means self-donation. This is the 'great mystery' of Ephesians, which rejects the utilitarian view of the body. Instead, the couple respect each other because they love each other. Their union is a sacramental union in that they are sacrament to each other. All this occurs, John Paul II teaches, because Christ's redemptive love has a spousal nature.[19] This teaching can be found throughout Christian tradition and certainly was one of the important points that were present in the preparatory documents for *Familiaris Consortio*. It is the basis of a sacramental approach to the theology of marriage.

But is the ideal of marriage with Christ present in a Christian marriage a step too far? The majority of Christian marriages today are between those of mixed faiths, and other Christians may not accept this vision of marriage. Yet strangely enough they are far more likely to resonate with this vision than many Catholics. Adrian

Thatcher, a Protestant, wonders whether the Council would have been quite as willing to run with the idea of covenant if more of the Fathers had read Calvin. Calvin in his later years used the idea of covenant not only as expressing the relationship between God and man, but also the relationship between husband and wife.[20] The Protestant sense of biblical theology finds this idea very appealing.[21] Elhrlich says: 'Marriage which is the supreme expression of togetherness of male and female in differentiation and relationship reflects the image of God and represents the covenant by which God has bound himself to his people, his church, to man.'[22]

The recent teaching of the Church, as found in the Catholic Catechism, joins in this approach to marriage. The Catholic Catechism says: 'The Church attaches great importance to Jesus' presence at the wedding feast of Cana. She sees in it the confirmation of the goodness of marriage and the proclamation that thenceforth marriage will be an efficacious sign of Christ's presence.'[23] Later it adds, '... the Christian family is a communion of persons, a sign and image of the communion of the Father and the Son in the Holy Spirit'.[24] But what is the inspiration of these seminal phrases? How does the covenant of marriage lead us to understanding Christian marriage as a sign and image of Christ and the Trinity?

The Mystery of Two in One Flesh

In Africa where a sense of family is very strong, marriage as a covenant produced documents that explored the connection between covenant and family in a very concrete sense. The African Episcopal conference of Tchad spoke of Christian marriage today as *desincarne* because the promotion of the individual, marriage and family life is difficult to achieve. Marriage based on the nuclear family, or where the emphasis is purely on the couple, is not an evangelical model of family life and should not be promoted.[25] Instead, marriage should be incarnated both culturally and religiously in a steady building of the covenant.

So often Europeans totally fail to understand what is being said here. This is not just a rejection of the current Western model of family, or merely a call for an African-ization of the celebration of marriage. It is not just promoting the African concept of an extended family that includes all the relations, nor is it simply insisting on fertil-ity expressed in child-bearing as being essential to marriage. All these elements have been emphasized in the past, as extended families were the rule in Roman society; and child-bearing as a primary end of marriage has been the essence of marriage, when it was considered purely as a contract. Likewise, there has been a debate for centuries over the adoption of Roman customs of marriage particu-larly with the Teutonic peoples. Instead, what is being said here is a call for marriage and married life to be truly Christian in the way that it is experienced every day; or as the Gabonese Episcopal Conference put it; the mystery of marriage must be placed within the mystery of Christ.[26]

This theme is more fully explained in the Bishops' Conference of Zaire position paper. Taking as their focus the African marital covenant in the light of Christ,[27] the bishops present four key concepts. First, God is the source of the family. God is the source from whom all fatherhood comes. He is creative through the family He establishes family, particularly in the procreation of children. In the religious experience of the African people, God is the creating presence, the 'awakener', experienced as the supporting force behind marriage. For the African, the family finds its meaning in relationships that are primarily blood relationships so that their ancestors find expression in each generation, as it is their life that is passed on. It is natural for an African to think an African Christian family would find its meaning in similar rela-tionships where Christ, the ancestor, passes on his life. For the African there is no need for Christ to be born again, in another new incarnation, as an African. The fullness of the divinity, which lives bodily in Christ, is united to every human person because, as a real man, Christ is made of the same stuff as we are. He is of our race and we are of his race.[28] This deeply felt unity of a Christian family to Christ is part of the mystery of Christian life. In other words, from its inception Christian marriage partakes in the salvation won by Christ and passes this gift on to all the members of the family. Marriage in order of creation becomes marriage in the order of salvation.

Second, the notion of family is wider and broader. For the African, the human person is a member not just a piece of a family. He or she is part of a lineage that cannot be broken or ignored, in which they are related to others, both dead and alive. To marry is to enter into this other family world, and to engender children to keep the family alive. Marriage is a covenant because it crosses over family borders and brings new life. A contract could only order relations between the families.[29] Instead, what is being sought here is polarity, a mutual attraction that creates and makes family. So marriage is not a single ceremony, but takes place in stages as the relationship progresses from courtship to full marriage not only of the couple, but also of the two families. The role of mother-in-law, called in some local languages, 'the mother of Twins'[30] and the role of the father-in-law are crucial in this bonding. Getting married in an African context is like playing in an orchestra where each player has their part to bring out the full social score. The heart of this new family is the new house where the husband brings the new wife. This house shows the kind of family that is being formed, as it is their refuge as well as their home. Here he is father; she is mother.[31]

Third, the Christian belief that God is married to his people is the spousal element *par excellence*. This is because the Christian ancestor, God, who gives life through His family, becomes a spouse to us by drawing us to Him. He made us in His own image and likeness, the image and likeness of His love. As the couple are drawn towards each other they are drawn towards God. They become a sacramental epiphany for the marriage relationship goes beyond what they are capable of by themselves because it announces the marriage of Christ to His Church wherein all are reconciled. The bridegroom and bride are one body of which all are members (Eph. 5.30, 1 Cor. 12.12–30).

This leads to the fourth element, namely, the covenant between persons is a sacrament of the Paschal Lamb.[32] The relationship becomes a sign of the Trinity; together they become a grace for each other as they live their love. This love is fruitful in the way it creates vital links between them, and strengthens them against the troubles that will surely come. It is also fruitful in that it brings about new life in a 'domestic church' so the family has a missionary dimension in the community. It is a 'school of social virtues'. Thus, the African family grows as a concrete epiphany of the Church saving humanity.[33]

These elements that are the source of family – a family that includes all relations and the community, a God that is married to His people, and has made the marriage covenant into the sacrament of the Paschal Lamb – illustrate the meaning of a marital covenant in an African context in a very concrete way. Instead of arguing that as God is the source of family and marriage, and therefore has established all the rules that govern marriage, it takes a dynamic view of fatherhood.[34] For the African, marriage has as its model the Trinitarian life of God: the Father (*père surgisseur*) takes all fatherhood to Himself; the Son is the first born of all who are united by His Cross; the Holy Spirit, who comes through the Son, leads us to the Father. Thus the African family offers its members the opportunity to be open to the mystery of salvation accomplished by Christ. From this flows the idea of family. The family that is brought into existence by the marriage covenant find its cohesiveness, first, in the mutual attraction that brought the couple together in the first place, second, in the union of the human families or clans that marriage brings about, and third in the fruitfulness of the marriage in the begetting of children. These ties and the demands made on the couple are brought into existence step by step. This is particularly true as regards oneness, lastingness and fruitfulness. A fact that will lead some to promote that marriage can only exist when all these three elements exist.[35]

Obviously all these elements belong to European Christian marriage, but in the past they were hardly taken into account theologically. Instead, the contractual model envisaged marriage as an institution where procreation was a duty, something which is very clear from its presentation by many European hierarchies in the past. Children were an extension of the Church and the nation.[36] Family was the basic unit of society, and any breakdown in family life wounded society. Patriarchal families were promoted as the ideal. The sacrament of marriage gave a special grace so these ideals could be carried out. Since the Second Vatican Council, where marriage was defined as a covenant, these elements can now find their proper theological place. Theologically, family flows naturally from the marriage covenant, which is why *Gaudium et Spes* refused to use the hierarchy of the ends of marriage. Marriage is not first for procreation and then for strengthening the bond between the partners. Both flow from such a covenant because the model of a biblical concept of a covenant of love is where God is married to His people. Therefore marriage is not merely an instrument of procreation but of its nature an intimate partnership of life and love. In living this covenant, Christian marriage is a partnership where the partners experience the meaning of their oneness and attain to it with growing perfection, day by day, for the good of any children, the true love of the partners, their contribution to the Church and the community. The conjugal covenant of 'two in one flesh' naturally brings about family.

The inspiration for this approach is the biblical conviction that God is the author of marriage. In changing Christian marriage from a natural sacrament to a sacrament of the New Covenant, Christ abides with spouses thereafter in a new family. That is why the essence of Christian marriage is life in Christ, a saving mystery. In other words, because conjugal love is the essence of marriage, the human reality touches the divine reality of a God who is love. It is also why *Gaudium et Spes* teaches that the Holy Spirit, the expression of that life-giving love dwells within a Christian marriage. So in the words of the Dutch theologian Schillebeeckx, marriage is both a human reality and a saving mystery.

Yet conjugal love is a love that cannot remain just between the couple. Bishop de Roo described it as a profound spiritual experience that throws light for them on their mutual irrevocable union, giving birth through its links to the Creator to life and happiness. This is why defining marriage as a community of life and love must go together with conjugal love. As De Lanversin points out the idea of marriage as a community is clearly stressed in *Gaudium et Spes*, and goes beyond the couple progressing from 'I' to 'we', or moving from a juridical level of institution to a psychological level of personal interaction.[37] The community level is a new reality of life-giving love.

This concept is made abundantly clear in the Genesis picture of God's intention from the beginning, where the first marital community is described.[38] 'Therefore, the man leaves his father and mother and cleaves to his wife and they become one flesh.'[39] But a whole new dimension is discovered if this text is looked at more closely. The Hebrew word for 'cleaves' is a covenantal term implying there is a covenant between Adam and Eve. Moreover, becoming 'one flesh', *basar ehadh,* expresses a whole depth of meaning from blood relationship, through the two being of the same kind of being, alter egos, to the concept of physical union. Therefore, 'one flesh' means 'one life' brought about by a covenant.[40] Marriage is incarnated through a covenant; made flesh because this expresses a whole new dimension – conjugal love, the basis of the marital community. The model is 'one flesh' – 'one life'.

The Covenant that brings about the Enfleshment of the Presence of Christ

Covenant brings about one flesh – one life through conjugal love, but not merely on the human dimension of relationship. There is a great mystery, as marriage is made in the image of God, which Ephesians shows. It is presented in a way ancient people would instantly understand. Using house tablets that hung on the wall of nearly every house, containing popular philosophy of the time applied to the duties within the house, describing the husband–wife, parent–child, and master–slave relationships, the author explains the real meaning of marriage as 'one life'. Many of us, at some time, have brought back from holiday one of those tea-towels that have printed on them anything from the rules of cricket written in some confusing way, to one that says: 'the rules of this kitchen are . . .'. These towels are the modern equivalent of a very ancient tradition whereby a clay tablet hung on the wall of Roman and Greek houses giving a moral basis for life. It is one of these tablets that the writer of the Ephesians uses as the basis for his discourse on marriage. Or, to be more exact, it envisages two tablets, one giving the rules for an earthly house which everyone one would recognize, the other giving the rules for the house of God, the Church, that the writer uses. He compares these two tablets so that we might understand the depth of conjugal love showing how the love of Christ for his Church is akin to conjugal love.

It is no surprise that these house tablets were used since Hellenistic Judaism borrowed this scheme of ethical instruction, and Paul and the Apostolic Fathers often quoted them.[41] So it is quite normal that the author of Ephesians would do the same.[42] To make clear what is happening, the author quotes the phrase from Genesis 'the two become one flesh' to underline what he is explaining.[43] This phrase 'two in one flesh' as Jesus says, describes God's intention in creating male and female:

from the beginning He made marriage, the family, a basic unit of human life. The exclamation of Adam when he meets Eve for the first time shows why he rejoiced. 'This is flesh of my flesh and bone of my bones ... this is why a man leaves his father and mother and joins himself to his wife and they become one flesh' (Gen. 2.23–25).

The author of Ephesians does not only use the house tablet to explain Christian marriage. He makes use of many other customs and phrases that would make sense to those who listened to the epistle at the time. The custom of the wife taking a ceremonial bath before marriage, and concepts of Roman marriage are included. Also included is the theme of Ephesians that the great mystery being revealed is God's plan for reconciliation and salvation found in His marriage to the Church. The text, in its intertwining of so many symbols, requires untangling to be fully understandable. However, any explanation must always bear in mind the comparison between the marriage of Christ to his bride the Church: individual Christian marriage is analogous – partly the same and partly different. Direct comparison would be going too far.[44]

An accurate translation of the text of Ephesians, chapter 5, would be: 21. Be subject to each other in reverence to Christ. 22. Wives to their husbands as to the Lord.[45] 23. For the husband is the head of the wife as Christ is also Head of the Church, he, the saviour of the body. 24. So then, as the Church is subject to Christ, let wives be to their husbands in everything. 25. Husbands love your wives as Christ loved the Church and gave himself for her, 26. to make her holy, in that he purified her by cleansing in the water by the Word, 27. to prepare the Church in splendour for himself without spot or wrinkle or any such thing but rather that she might be holy and blameless. 28. In the same way ought husbands to love their wives like their own body. He who loves his wife loves himself. 29. For no one ever hates his own flesh but nourishes it and tends it as Christ his Church; 30. as we are members of his body. 31. 'For this reason a man will leave father and mother and be joined to his wife and the two shall become one flesh.' 32. This is a great mystery; but I interpret it to mean Christ and his Church. 33. At any rate you, too, each individual one of you, should love his wife as himself, but the wife should respect her husband.

There are certain key ideas and key phrases that clarify what this text means. In Ephesians, the relationship between husband and wife takes on a new dimension because they participate in the mystery of Christ.[46] They are not alone in this participation for the Christian community as a whole lives in Christ. This is the first key to understanding this passage. This mystery is expressed in Ephesians 2.14–18 where it teaches that the flesh of Christ brought about the gift of new life so that the Gentiles participate in a new creation and new temple, because they are now members of the household of Christ.[47] The images here are strikingly similar to those used for marriage. Just as marriage is described as being two in one flesh, the reconciliation between Jew and Gentile, and the reconciliation of all creation is brought about by the two becoming one in the flesh of Christ.[48] This is the proclamation of the *Mysterion*, Christ the sacrament.

When this is applied to Christian marriage a whole new ideal of marriage appears as Ephesians intertwines the pagan tablet regarding the relationship between husbands and wives with, as it were, a second tablet concerning the love and relationship Christ has for the Church. The love that Christ has for his Church means that he tends her with care. He wants her to be holy and splendid (v. 27). To achieve this, the image of a cleansing bath is used from which she arises radiant and beautiful, without spot or wrinkle because of the Word (v. 26). So Christ is the saviour of the body. Behind this image lies a Jewish marriage custom, where the woman is prepared for marriage by washing with water. The implication is, Christ marries the Church and through a marriage bath she is saved.[49] Obviously there are overtones of baptism here, but the purpose of the image is to emphasize the saving dimension of marriage, because it speaks of being saved in the 'flesh of Christ'.

This leads us to the concept behind the second key word – flesh. Earthly husbands must love their wives as they love their own flesh because she is one body with him (v. 28). For no one has ever hated his own flesh, but nourishes it and cares for it (v.29). Behind these phrases lies a cultural model of the family. Clearly in the Mediterranean cultural ideal the male cares and tends for the female. But the emphasis here is not so much on caring as on flesh meaning one family, one bloodline, and one body. Just as Christ nourishes the Church, the husband is to nourish his wife, for we are members of one body. Moreover, marriage as one body is akin to the body-church. Hence the continuous love of Christ for his Church is to be reflected in the husband's love for his wife.[50] Instead of the Roman model of marriage, with the notorious infidelity of men in Greco-Roman society, the Church as the bride of Christ is a model for the Christian husband.[51] Rather, the husband is to love his wife, as Christ loved the Church and gives himself up for her. The verb used here in the Greek text is *paradidomi* meaning a relinquishing of oneself, a giving over of oneself for another. This is what Christ does in his love and so should the husband.

The third key to discovering the meaning of the text is the phrase, which is the recurring theme of the whole instruction, to respect one another in reverence to Christ. It is an instruction that is addressed to everyone.[52] For the married, it has a special density. The key word here is the Greek word *hypotassomenoi*. Often it is translated 'be subject to' or 'obey'; yet both of these terms largely miss the point. Rather, because *hypotassomenoi* is a special word, restricted to relationships between friends so as to preserve their friendship, it means to respect or give way to the other. Furthermore, to translate verse 22 as 'wives be subject to your husbands' is incorrect in a second way, because the author did not write it as a command but as a statement 'let wives respect or defer to their husbands'.[53] What is meant is an obliging attitude, a willingness to serve.[54] This special relationship underlines what has happened through the couple being renewed in Christ. Following the fall, wives were described as being subject to their husbands, but it was not so in the beginning. At that point they were equal partners in the vocation to tend the Garden of Eden. The renewal that baptism brings means each is once again an equal partner in marriage.[55] The husband is not depicted as lord over his wife as in a patriarchal understanding.

Similarly, it is not possible to apply verse 23 in a patriarchal sense. While 'head' has a natural connection to a body, its application to Christ in Ephesians as head of the body-church embraces a range of ideas including pre-eminence and source, but not rule. Best argues that the meaning here is that Christ is pre-eminent over the body, rather than the source, because the man is not the source of the wife.[56] It is certain that a comparison is being made between Christ's headship and the husband's headship, but Christ is a collective head, and in a Roman sense the husband was also a collective head in his role of *pater familias*, paternal power. He was the supreme power in the household even over grown-up sons with their own families. All the property of his children belonged to him; he could give any of his female children in marriage.[57] It is this paternal power that Ephesians insists must be based on Christ. Ephesians insists Christ's headship flows from the fact that he is saviour and re-creator of the cosmos, through love. In marriage, the headship flows from love, or as *Familiaris Consortio* says: 'conjugal charity, which flows from conjugal love'. As Tertullian wrote: 'How wonderful the bond between two believers, with a single hope, a single desire, a single observance, a single service! They are both brethren and fellow servants. There is no separation between them in spirit or flesh; in fact they are truly in one flesh, and where flesh is one, one is the spirit.'[58]

So, patriarchal interpretations of this text are cultural and superficial. This is true even if verse 24, 'Let wives be to their husbands in everything', is often presented in a patriarchal sense of the wife obeying her husband in everything. Not only is this a foolish notion, which women have often sensibly ignored throughout the centuries; it also misrepresents the correct meaning. In Roman society marriage was a sharing of everything summed up in the technical term, the whole of life – *omnis vitae*. The difference between a concubine and a marriage lay here. Hence it is only a repetition of what marriage was seen to be. In Roman tradition, marriage itself was a partnership where the virtues of a wife were to organize her house well, safeguard its contents and to respect her husband. The greatest virtue of a Roman wife was discretion.[59] So, in Christian marriage the virtues of holiness and righteousness would lead a wife to respect her husband.

Taking the three key ideas, of partaking in the Mystery of Christ that has renewed everything, of being in one flesh both with Christ and with a wife or husband, and of finding within this relationship mutual respect, Christian marriage in Ephesians takes on a very different appearance: 'This is the great mystery' (v. 32).[60] The marriage covenant has a depth of meaning where enfleshment is not too strong a term to describe its reality. Obviously, while restraint is needed in the application of the analogy of the relationship between Christ and his Church to marriage, there is depth of meaning to be explored. Even though the relationship between Christ and his Church is very different from a marriage relationship, Christ chose his Church, and spouses choose each other. The basis of both is an everlasting covenant of life and love.

However, to reduce the comparison between the two relationships to imitation, in a Platonic sense, misses the point because Ephesians is very careful never to use the word 'because' in comparing the relationship of Christ and his Church, and husband and wife.[61] Instead of comparison, the relationship is within. Best points out that the body is envisaged as growing (Eph. 4.15) and Mackin reinforces this sense of the model of Christ–Church relationship being something to grow into and portray by arguing there is, in Christian marriage, the potential to become images of the Christ–Church relationship.[62] The text therefore, does not mean that every Christian marriage from the beginning is fully an image of Christ's love. Instead, every Christian marriage should grow into this relationship. This is possible because conjugal love has the same properties as the love Christ has for his Church.

Being one body with Christ is one of the basic themes of Pauline theology.[63] In Ephesians this concept is explored in the idea of two in one flesh, not in any dualistic sense of body and soul, but in sense of being one person with the other. It is clear through the analogy of the relationship between Christ and his Church, that there is in Christian marriage, as Schmaus says, an epiphany or showing of the bond between Christ and the Church, full of life.[64] Christian marriage partakes of the nature and the mysterious character of Christ's union with his Church. Scheeben explains this connection by comparing the mystery of the relationship of Christ and his Church with baptism, whereby the baptized become rooted in the Mystical Body of Christ. Baptism, in Paul's mind, makes us wedded to Christ. Christian marriage shows their marriage to Christ in the new light of Christ's marriage to his Church. This is what makes Christian marriage different from any other marriage and why it is inseparable. The union of each in Christ singly is carried over into their marital union with one another.[65] In other words, Christian marriage enfleshes the love of Christ, so that everyone can see Christ's presence in the marriage through the love that is shared by the spouses.[66] It is this enfleshment that makes the relationship of Christian spouses different from that of the non-baptized.

A Covenant that is Creative and Salvific

If Christian marriage means partaking in the mystery of Christ's union with His church, this participation comes about through the Paschal Mystery. Through the restoration brought about by the Paschal Mystery of Christ's death and resurrection, the human relationship in Christian marriage has been changed by the abiding presence of Christ. Here marriage finds its sacramental dimension because for a sacrament to be a sacrament it must participate in the dying and rising of Christ. In marriage, the aspect of this mystery that is present above all is conjugal love that is raised to a higher level where self-sacrifice is its leitmotif participating in the self-sacrifice of Christ.[67] This is the key to answering why marriage is a sacrament and why the Second Vatican Council defined it as a community of love. Likewise, it is the reason why *Gaudium et Spes* saw the essence of marriage as conjugal love, because sharing in this love is the couple's sharing in the Paschal Mystery.[68] This is very clear in the reality of married life. Every marriage has its troughs and peaks and this is the couple's experience of dying and rising. The love that leads to self-sacrifice for their children, paying for education, paying for trips, paying for clothes, is an expression of true love that transforms the lovers. So the Paschal Mystery has a profound effect on conjugal love. Scheeben says that Christ graces the spouses precisely as members of his body, so they may do the work of his body. Together they live the sacrament.

Von Hildebrand expresses the same reality. He says marriage and the sacrament are one and the same reality; so the sacramental reality is the capacity for, or orientation to, imaging the love of Christ. Thus, as every married couple knows, the sacrament does not cause love; it expresses love, because love is a human and divine reality. It is the exchange of love that brings the sacrament of marriage into being, for every sacrament, reality is not only reception but also participation. This is very clear in the experience of love. In marriage the desire to be one with one's love is quite different from friendship, as it is unitive in its fullest sense. In friendship, the recurring theme is the sharing of common tastes, views etc.; in marriage each is wholly for the other as each party seeks to share in the being of the other, not simply in his or her life or thoughts. Its completion is a true knowing in a sexual act. Being in love is a most intense receptivity for the entire charm of the other in its unique individuality as it unfolds.[69]

This is why a contractual view of marriage obscures the sacrament rather than reveals it. If the sacrament of marriage is equated with a contract, the strength of the 'contract' depends on its completion found in consummation. Yet by itself, consummation as a sexual act does not make or even strengthen a marriage. It is not the genital significance that strengthens the bond, but the interpersonal commingling that changes the relationship. Rape within marriage does not constitute consummation.[70] Otherwise the consistent statements of medieval theologians that consummation images the two natures of Christ have no meaning. The essence of marriage is an exchange of persons. In the words of *Gaudium et Spes*, this interpersonal dimension where spouses mutually bestow and accept each other is the sacramental dimension of matrimony. Or, in the words of Ephesians, this dimension is found in service of the other, a mixture of respect and worship as an expression of the mystery, a mystery, because this mutual respect and love is a divine image of the union between Christ and the Church. From this flows the concept of marriage as both a creative image that changes the relationship and gives new life, and a salvific image where the salvation of each depends on the other. The mutual love of the spouses is naturally sacramental.[71]

Christian Marriage in the Order of Creation

With the modern experience of the breakdown of marriage, the claim that Christian marriage is a creative image of the love of Christ for His Church is dismissed as pure theology with no reality. Romantic love is presented at one extreme, love as a myth consummated in great sorrow leading to death; or at the other extreme, is found in the figure of Don Juan who loves only his love and tastes women as one tastes fruit without giving his soul. Don Juan loves no woman in particular, but seeks the feminine of which every woman is an imperfect reflection. Intensity is in both sketches, but passes in different ways. One is an experience of angelic love, the other is limited to the first mornings of love and denies tomorrow. Kierkegaard summed this up when he said, 'It is a woman's misfortune to represent everything in a moment, and to represent nothing more in the next moment without ever truly knowing what she properly signifies as a woman.' Furthermore, a negative vision of marriage that sees marriage as constrictive rather than creative is very common. Victor Eremita wrote: 'Many a genius became a genius through a girl, many a hero became a hero through a girl, many a poet became a poet through a girl, many a saint became a saint through a girl; but who has become a genius, a poet, a hero, or a saint through the influence of his wife? Through her he became a Privy Councillor, a general, a father.' [72]

The lived reality of married love is very different from these sketches. Obviously, it has to be admitted that many marriages are lived imperfectly in the war of the sexes.[73] Jack Dominian, a married man, who was no stranger to the difficulties of married life and human imperfection as a psychologist, points out that the minimum required for a couple to marry is a basic adequate relationship that is physically, psychologically and spiritually compatible.[74] Without this there cannot be a lived experience as a couple. So there must be a capacity for physical union, minimum maturity and freedom to be able to form a psychological union, and the capacity to reflect what life is all about. Many problems stem from difficulties in these areas. However, human love is remarkably resilient, and continues even in the face of many difficulties.

However, there are other factors, which are often over-looked when marriage is seen through jaundiced eyes. Marriage is a community, a family, where the interaction of its members, both parents and children, affects the other. Because of this different kinds of love are proper to different stages of the relationship. In life, couples date their coming together not from their marriage, but from when they first met. It is here their relationship began, and their love began. This is because love is something in itself, before it is something for any other purpose.[75] The stages of the relationship that follow have several stepping-stones. Courtship, engagement, marriage, the early years – usually marked by the coming of children, the middle years – usually marked by the maturing of children and their leaving home, and the later years – usually marked by the role of grandparents. All these stages point to a relationship that is anything but static, and because of these changes difficulties may occur.[76]

The relationship changes take place in four dimensions: physical, emotional, intellectual and spiritual, that affect sexuality, communication, the way a couple look at life and the values they hold. Freud saw these changes as a move from the principle of pleasure to the principle of reality so the original physical attraction changes to a complemen-tariness that suffers stress as the couple seek a way of living together in the different demands that are laid upon them. Furthermore, every couple would agree that through these stages marriage does not simply change in context, but the mutual relationship and mutual help is changed from its very roots. The couple become self-actualizing people who accept themselves and each other. The loving experience makes life both spontaneous and autonomous. This is covenantal love wherein both persons grow. Covenantal love has to be constantly relearned. Knowing how to live together is not learnt once only for life.

Going further, the dynamism of marriage leads naturally to children. With a culture that promotes individualism, even in marriage, today new life is reduced to the biological concerns of child-bearing for women – choice of when or whether to have children with a biological clock ticking away. The desire to have children obviously fulfils a biological scheme if humans are reduced to animals. Humans as persons add another dimension to their biology where they co-operate with the Creator in giving life. Yet, the replies given by couples asked why they had children show that co-operation with the Creator rarely occurs as a motive for procreation. Leaving to one side those who said children just happened, parents see children in many ways as an extension of themselves. It is not just the search for physical traits that point to this, shown in phrases like 'look, he has your nose', there is a desire to continue the family line that is very real in people's minds. The expectations of grandparents often display this. Perhaps this occurs in African culture most clearly, when children are often named after a relative who dies around the time of the birth of a child. Some find in the new child the reincarnation of the one who has just died. Marriage of its nature is very creative in this sense.

Thus the couple discover that marriage is ordered to growth in every sense, growth in their relationship and growth in their family. While this can be a negative experience for some in their inability to cope, for the majority in nearly every way it is self-fulfilling. The claim that marriage is a creative image of the love of Christ for His Church is very real, because Christ's relationship is one of dying and rising. This is what the experience of married life is, because the dimension of dying and rising is found in service of the other, a mixture of respect and worship as an expression of the mystery, a mystery, because this mutual respect and love is a divine image of the union between Christ and the Church.

Christian Marriage in the Order of Salvation

This partnership, where each one completes in some way the other, causes change, pain, and perfection. It is here that marriage goes beyond creation to salvation. As a salvific image, Christian marriage shows the eschatological perspective of the Kingdom, where the salvation that is offered now will find its completion on the Last Day. This image of marriage is found in the Old Testament where marriage always refers to the relationship between Yahweh and His people. The giving of the Law on Mount Sinai was known as the 'Day of Espousals'.[77] Likewise, the New Testament uses the Greek word for marriage – *gamos* nearly always not of human marriage, but the eschatological wedding of Christ and His redeemed.[78]

The secular reality in the Old Testament that becomes a saving mystery is very evident in the life of the prophet Hosea. Israel had fallen away from the worship of the one God to practise the fertility rites of the Canaanite people of the Promised Land. In the Baal-cult fertility was believed to be the result of a marriage between the goddess and the god. Religious prostitution was practised where girls gave themselves to men they did not know for sugared cakes in 'religious marriage' so they would be fertile.[79] Hosea is told by Yahweh to marry such a girl, Gomer (Hos. 2.4) so that the Israelites would understand that God was still married to them. The three children Hosea had by Gomer brings home Israel's unfaithfulness. Their names, especially the names of the youngest children – 'not pitied' and 'not my people' – show what the people of Israel were in the eyes of God. Then Gomer left Hosea, and committing adultery, legally became the wife of someone else. The text speaks of her being stripped bare and becoming a barren forest reflecting her departure from her husband who was obliged to clothe her and give her children. Against the Law, Hosea is ordered to take her back and love her in a lasting union.[80] Even the names of the children are changed, as 'not my people' becomes 'my people'. This prophecy by action showed what the covenant between Israel and Yahweh meant. Israel was the bride of Yahweh. He alone would look after them, clothe them, and make them fertile. This was an everlasting covenant because even adultery did not break it. Yahweh was their husband, their saviour.

This metaphor is first found in the Old Testament where Isaiah paints a picture of a great feast full of all the best food when death is swallowed up forever, and the Lord God will wipe away the tears from every face (Isa. 25.6–9). This theme is taken up in the New Testament where the kingdom of heaven is portrayed as a wedding feast so that those who attend enjoy a bridal relationship with Christ. Christ is frequently called the bridegroom, and John the Baptist is called the friend of the bridegroom, the one who prepared and conducted the wedding ceremonies.[81] The same metaphor is found in Revelation's vision of a new heaven and a new earth (Rev. 21.1–2), where we are part of the holy city of Zion prepared as a bride for her husband. This metaphor of Christ as the bridegroom and the people of God as the bride, which was widespread in early Christianity, makes us look again at the presence of Jesus at the wedding feast of Cana. His presence there goes beyond mere attendance at a feast because the remark of John that this was the first sign, applies not only to water turning into wine, but also to where the event took place, at a wedding feast.[82] Likewise, the parable of the wedding feast as a sign of the Kingdom points beyond mere celebration, for in the words of Ephesians, Christ married his people, the Church, in order to save them and make them holy.[83]

This theme is vividly presented in Matthew's presentation of the wedding feast portraying the eschatological banquet of the kingdom of heaven. Those who are invited give the official excuses not to attend and instead everyone else is invited. (In Luke's version those who are invited are called the chosen.[84]) The one not chosen, the man who got in without a wedding garment, is thrown out. The whole story, full of *double entendre*, points to table fellowship being something more than sharing a meal; it is sharing life, for to be cast out is disaster. It is this theme of sharing life that runs through all the wedding parables. It could be asked what at this point is mysterious because all weddings are about sharing life. But the point is this sharing rises to a new level when Christ participates in it. The kingdom is a family where all its members participate in the life of the Father. Thus, the marriage covenant not only echoes but also presents a great mystery.

The depth of this sharing in the life of Christ is most evident in an Orthodox Church wedding celebration where the couple are crowned, signifying their life in Christ.[85] Their children are called to be 'members of Christ'. Each one of them, in his or her particular personal way, is called to experience the presence of God and reveal Him to the world. The couple are now a 'domestic church'. As Mersch says: 'The marital home is not a domestic church because it is there the children first learn about God. Rather, the marital home is a domestic church because they participate in the Church and their marital acts are acts of the Church.'[86] This is a great mystery – the spouses bring new members of the Church into the world both in their procreation and through their faith, yet at the same time they enflesh the Church. So marriage is salvific in a double sense, both for the partners and for the children.

The Embodiment of Christian Marriage

Perhaps it is now possible to appreciate a little of God's plan when he instituted marriage. Marriage is much more than a one-way relationship between God and humankind. First, marital giving is the unreserved giving of person to person.[87] The giving of gifts, particularly the gift of one's self, is the basis of any marriage and therefore is the basis of a covenant and conjugal love, because consent without the exchange of persons is empty. This giving is characterized by the three traits: presence, depth and permanence. They are the signs of a real marriage. The desire to be together, the depth of the relationship and the permanence of that relationship are a clear indication that a man and a woman are a couple. This is shown by the use of 'we' to describe their partnership, and the need to consult the other before agreeing to any course of action. Thus, it is not surprising that the sacrament of Christian marriage should claim to fundamentally change these three factors through the presence of Christ in marriage. In His presence the spouses should find a new way of being present to each other as well as a new depth of commitment. It is Christ's presence that sustains permanence; it is partaking with Him in the Paschal Mystery of dying and rising that troubles are overcome, and it is his permanent spiritual relationships that sustains our spiritual health.

These points are clear from Ephesians that asked Christian spouses to give way to each other, as the new way of being present to each other, because that is how Christ acted. It is found in the willingness to serve one another. The depth of this relationship is that each are life-giving to the other so much so that each saves the other. This life-giving is in the provision of food because just as Christ feeds the Church with his flesh, so they are to nourish one another – spiritually, physically and psychologically, and they are saved in the flesh of Christ as they relinquish themselves in favour of the other. From this flows the permanence of the relationship. They proclaim the *Mysterion*, Christ the sacrament brought about by the covenant of love they profess. This is why Walter Kasper wrote: 'If marriage represents a special form of being human in Christ that is based on baptism, it is also a special form of sharing in the death and resurrection of Christ. If marital love is seen as existing under the sign of Christ's cross, it must also be seen as being sustained by giving and being given, forgiving and being forgiven and a continuous process of new beginnings.'[88] This is the second reason

why marriage is much more than a mirror of the relationship between God and humankind.

Behind this lies a concept of sacrament as a partaking in
the Paschal Mystery. Each sacrament presents a different
facet of this mystery, yet each sacrament presents the
dying and rising of Christ, together with the gift of the
Spirit. In baptism and the Eucharist these elements are
easy to identify, but in matrimony their presence can be
missed if the sacrament is only considered to be the
exchange of vows and a blessing. When it is appreciated
that the sacrament is a gift of life, for life, dying and rising
become an experience every married person knows. The
full reality of the sacrament becomes even clearer when it
is realized that rising takes place through forgiveness in
the power of the Spirit. Problem solving, a vital ingredient
of any marriage, does not take place through co-existence
where everyone keeps their original position. This only
postpones or covers up the problem. Compromise is
needed. Real problem solving requires moving on to a
new position, not just acceptance that one of you is right
and the other wrong. This can only be achieved through
forgiveness, which is the work of the Spirit. A new way of
looking at life is specifically His gift.

Partaking in the sacrament of marriage is sharing and
brings about salvation. The reason why the marriage
covenant is the reality of salvation, as such, is because
salvation is the definitive acceptance of human beings.
The covenant signifies the acceptance of a unity in love
between God and human beings. It is the sign Christian
marriage should portray to the world. As the spouses
participate in this love through their own covenant of
married love, their marriage is changed. In every way the
Second Vatican Council wished spouses to see the depth
of meaning of that simple phrase of the Council of Trent
that 'Christ abides with the spouses thereafter'. Likewise,
Gaudium et Spes wanted the spouses to see that it is the
covenant of love that makes Christ present in the spouses
through the sacrament of matrimony.

The key to all this is that Christ is the life giver. He is the ancestor, ever present, who passes on his life. This means that the reality of family is likewise essential for his presence because Christ is not present in the individual spouses or individual children, but his presence is within the family as such. Relationships express what a family is, which is another way of saying conjugal love makes, and vivifies, married life. These relationships express love by which the spouses share in the love of God and bring the presence of Christ into their family. In other words, the service of the other, a mixture of respect and worship, is the expression of the mystery, a mystery, because this mutual respect and love is a divine image of the union between Christ and the Church. As *Lumen Gentium* says: 'Christian spouses signify and partake of the mystery of that unity and fruitful love which exists between Christ and His Church.' All this is brought about by the marriage covenant.

The reason why the marriage covenant brings this about is because Christ, who married His Church, did so through the Paschal Mystery of His death and resurrection. It is through taking part in the Paschal Mystery that Christian spouses participate in the sacrament of marriage. Likewise, this is true of the sacrament of marriage. Hence their marriage is embodiment in Christ because they become part of His body, the Church. There is a real enfleshment in marriage, which is unique to that state so to reduce marriage to an institution would not be true. Obviously marriage needs to be expressed in the culture of wherever it is celebrated, and by necessity it is lived out within a certain cultural pattern. Each generation will arrange domestic duties to their own satisfaction. But the Christian depth of marriage shows what new life in Christ really means.

Lastly, Christian marriage is much more than a sign of the relationship between God and humankind because of the love between husband and wife. Husband and wife become one body; it is the same for Christ and the Church.

The marriage of Christ to His Church was a fulfilment, which St Thomas compares to the consummation in marriage. The humanity of Jesus Christ is the means God chose to give Himself to His Church. The Christian couple, 'two in one flesh' find salvation through their flesh, a flesh which Ephesians reminds us, is saved through the flesh of Christ. It is this complete mingling of body and spirit through which each spouse finds salvation in the new life of self-giving. They live in Christ and portray Christ through their love and self-sacrifice. This is the mystery of Christian marriage, two in one flesh.

Notes

1   Thatcher A., *Marriage and Love: Too Much of A 'Breakthrough'?* ITAMS review 8 (2002), 52.
2   This is underlined in the text where in each instance it uses the singular to express this unity. For example it speaks of 'community of life and love <u>has</u> been established by the Creator'. Or again it says: 'By its very nature the institution of marriage and married love <u>is</u> ordered to the procreation and education of children and it is in them that it finds its crowning glory.'
3   Thatcher, *Marriage and Love*, 44.
4   Thatcher is certainly wrong when he asserts that this use of covenant is the first time in Roman Catholic thought. Such usage goes back to the Fathers of the Church.
5   For this Thatcher quotes David Pellhauer and his article *The Consortium omnis vitae as a Juridical Element of Marriage*, Studia Canonica 13 (1979), 19.
6   Fr Lio was a consultant at the Second Vatican Council. Cf. chapter 3.
7   The full list is: divorce, second marriages, trial marriage, illegitimate pregnancy, transitory premarital relationships, ambiguity towards the good of procreation, increasing number of abortions, an uncertain situation of women in society and decrease in the maternal care of children, depressing economic and social factors and increasing materialism among the 'affluent', a breakdown in

parent–child relationships and modern theories of 'self-determination' because of which some parents allow their children to be led astray.

8   Joseph Selling holds the prestigious chair of Moral Theology at the Catholic University of Leuven, Belgium.

9   The only questions asked at the end of this section were 1. What is to be said about the situation of the family in the various regions with reference to pastoral situations? 2. Are there other questions to be considered with respect to this synod?

10 Legal and educational institutions are imposing themselves on Catholics and 'leading to the progressive disintegration of the concept and institution of marriage'.

11 The list is taken from Grootaers J. and Selling J., *The 1980 Synod of Bishops 'On the Role of the Family'*, Bibliotheca Ephemeridum Theologicarium Louvaniensium LXIV, Leuven, 1983, p. 205.

12 Ibid., pp. 208–230.

13 For example ibid., pp. 219, 221 etc.

14 'The family coming from a marriage can mean the partnership of one man and one woman bound together indissolubly by conjugal love in accordance with an order laid down by God.' An 'order laid down by God' will become 'God's will'. In *Familiaris Consortio* it has become 'God's plan'.

15 Antoine de Saint Exupéry, *The Little Prince*, Pan Boooks Ltd, London, 1974, p. 70.

16 The Latin phrases were *maritalis affectio, mutuum adiutorium* and *humanum solatium*.

17 *Lumen Gentium*, n. 11.

18 John Paul II, *Theology of the Body*, Pauline Books, Boston, 1997, p. 306.

19 Ibid., pp. 306–24.

20 Thatcher, *Marriage and Love*, 45

21 Pace Thatcher who holds it is hardly biblical except in the case of Malachi 2 where marriage is undoubtedly an unbreakable covenant. It suffices to say the whole weight of biblical scholarship is against him. Ibid., 45–46.

22 Ehrlich R. J., *The Indissolubility of Marriage as a Theological Problem*, SJT 23/3 (1970), 28.

23 *Catechism of the Catholic Church*, Geoffrey Chapman, London 1994, p. 1613.

24   Ibid., p. 2205.

25   Huguet G. and Bouchard J.-C., *Rapport du Tchad pour la Réunion de L'A.C.E.C.C.T. la Famille et le Marriage*, CET, 1980, p. 6.

26   Conférence Épiscopale Gabonaise, *II Questions Doctrinales posées par l'evangelisation*, E. 1979.

27   Episcopate du Zaire, *Mariage et Famille au Zaire*, Perspective generale.

28   Ibid., 3. It quotes Acts 17.28, Pet. 1.4, 1 John 3.2, Gen. 1.26, Rom. 8.29.

29   The document quotes a Zairean saying: Kifwfwa yii bulanci, bukontsu kabufwafwa (Marriage may die; the brotherhood of the covenant never dies). Episcopate du Zaire, *Mariage et Famille au Zaire*, 18.

30   Ibid., 17.

31   Often this is the way the spouses will address each other showing their dignity and position in life. However, these images of family can be negative as well as positive because the common causes of the breakdown of marriage are family conflicts not between husband and wife but between their two families particularly caused by the in-laws. Sterility is a common cause of disputes as it is a failure to continue the family.

32   This summary can be found in Grootaers and Selling, *The 1980 Synod of Bishops*, p. 33.

33   Episcopate du Zaire, *Mariage et Famille au Zaire*, 31–34.

34   'By way of conclusion, the bishops of Zaire say that God has willed a large family, based upon the model of the Holy Trinity.' Though the Zairian bishops argue from this a large family is the ideal, a step too far as other factors will restrict this fertility, the point being made is that fatherhood promotes life. Grootaers and Selling, *The 1980 Synod of Bishops*, p. 33.

35   This is a detail that canon law fails to take into account. It is not only African theologians that emphasize this point; it is also part of the theme of Kevin Kelly's book *Divorce and Second Marriage: Facing the Challenge*, Collins, London, 1982.

36   For example, the statements of the Anglican, French and German bishops about the duty to beget children for the Fatherland even right up to the Second World War.

37   De Lanversin B., 'Vatican II and Marriage' in *Vatican II Assessment and Perspectives Twenty-five years After*, ed. R. Latourelle, Vol. 11, Paulist Press, New York, 1989, pp. 190ff.

38   Gen. 2.24.

39   Jesus uses this point to correct the scribes' and Pharisees' concept of the dissolvability of marriage. Matt 19.5.

40   'Leaves' is the Hebrew *asev*, a covenantal word that together with the term 'cleaves', *davaq*, another covenantal term, means that the man abandons his parents to form a new covenant with his wife.

41   Lohse gives the following instances of their use Col. 3.18–4.1; 1 Tim. 2.8–15, 6.1–2; Tit. 2.1–10; 1 Pet. 2.13–3.7; Did. 4.9–11; Barn. 19.5–7; 1 Clem. 21.6–9; Pol. Phil. 4.2–6.3. Lohse E., *Colossians and Philemon*, Hermeneia, Fortress Press, Philadelphia, 1971, p. 154.

42   Ibid., p. 155.

43   Paul is not considered the author of Ephesians by a considerable number of scripture experts. Hence the term 'author' has been adopted. However, there is no doubt Ephesians is the product of the Pauline school of theology probably written in Rome between the years AD 80–90.

44   This is not just a general call for placing texts within their context, even the grammar indicates this. Verse 21 where many commentaries begin has no verb, and is a sub clause of the previous verse.

45   English translations often present this verse as 'Wives should regard or obey their husbands as they would the Lord'.

46   Mackin identifies this as a participation in the *mysterion*. But while some authors stress that this passage must be placed within the schema of Ephesians, I cannot find anyone who identifies this with the *mysterion* of Eph. 5.32. Mackin T., *The Marital Sacrament*, Paulist Press, New York, 1989, pp. 70, 74.

47   This is probably based on a hymn similar to that of Col. 1.15–20.

48   This is only time the phrase 'flesh of Christ' is used in Ephesians. Its analogy would be the phrase 'in the body of his flesh' in Col. 1.22.

49   Some have tried to limit this scene to a mystical body of

Christ, but commentators point out this is the only place in Ephesians where Christ is called saviour of the body. But the marriage metaphor being used goes beyond such limitations.

50 Best notes the different tenses that are used in this love. Christ's love is in the aorist tense and so is a continuous love. The husband's love is in the present tense and so he is to love now. Best E., *Ephesians*, T & T Clarke International Critical Commentary, Edinburgh, 1998, p. 541.

51 A great deal of Christological reflection has taken place on these verses. Cf. ibid., pp. 539 ff.

52 The exhortation of respect is directed to all because the participle is masculine even though the original command was applied to women only (cf. Col 3.18).

53 This is because *hypotassesthai* is in the middle voice.

54 Schackenburg R., *The Epistle to the Ephesians*, T & T Clarke, Edinburgh, 1991, p. 245.

55 Mackin T., *What is Marriage?*, Paulist Press, New York, 1982, pp. 64–65. A similar position is found in Lincoln A. T., *Ephesians*, Word Books, Dallas, Texas, 1990, pp. 365–366. MacDonald is concerned this interpretation has a Gnostic background, but accepts the general tenor of the interpretation. MacDonald M.Y., *Sacra Pagina: Colossians Ephesians*, The Liturgical Press, Collegeville, Minnesota, 2000, p. 327.

56 Best, *Ephesians*, p. 535.

57 Treggiari S., *Roman Marriage*, Clarendon Press, Oxford, 1991, pp. 16–17.

58 *Familiaris Consortio* n. 13 quoting Tertullian, *Ad Uxorem*, II, VIII, 6–8: CCL, I 393.

59 The technical term was *sophrosyne*. Cf. Treggiari, *Roman Marriage*, pp. 190–196.

60 It is disputed what the great mystery refers to exactly. Some hold it is only the relationship between Christ and his Church. Others hold it is both this relationship and the marriage relationship. Again some have translated *mysterion*, mystery, as sacrament. Cf. Vulgate and the Eastern Church. They hold this is the key text for marriage as a sacrament. Modern scriptural scholarship denies this.

61 Mackin, *The Marital Sacrament*, p. 72.

62 Ibid., p. 75

63   Best, *Ephesians*, Detached Note IV The Body of Christ, pp. 189–196.
64   Schmaus M., *Katholische Dogmatik* IV/1, Munich, 1952, p. 622. Best makes the point that the headship of Christ is that he is the source of his descendents, the *Stammvater*. Best, *Ephesians*, p. 196.
65   Mackin, *The Marital Sacrament*, p. 595.
66   While some may be surprised by the term 'enfleshes' as going too far, its origin is in the teaching of the Early Church and most clearly stated in John Paul II's *The Theology of the Body*, pp. 314–320.
67   Albert the Great stated that the sacrament of marriage derives its efficacy not only from God *ex opere operato* but also from the recipients *ex opere operantis*.
68   John Paul II expresses the meaning of Ephesians in exactly the same way in *Theology of the Body*, pp. 304–311.
69   von Hildebrand D., *In Defense of Purity*, Helicon Ltd, Dublin, 1962, pp. 67–68. This is a translation of *Reinheit und Jungfraulichkeit*, 1927, a book that was behind *Casti Connubii*.
70   Pace the Holy Office that in 1943 argued that it does.
71   This reflects the universal teaching of the Fathers and the medievals that marriage began in the Garden of Eden and is naturally sacramental.
72   Eremita V., *In Vino Veritas, Stages on Life's Way*, trans. Walter Lowrie, Princeton University Press, 1945, p. 70.
73   Yet the Catechism denies this is due to human nature or from the differences between men and women. Instead it sees sin as the cause of marriage difficulties. *Catechism of the Catholic Church*, p. 1607.
74   Dominian J., *Christian Marriage*, Darton, Longman and Todd, London, 1968, p. 240.
75   Dominian, *Christian Marriage*, p. 240.
76   Dominian J., *Marriage, Faith and Love*, Darton, Longman and Todd, London, 1981. Dominian lists Courtship, The Early Years, The Middle Years and The Later Years.
77   Massyngbaerde Ford, 'Revelation', *The Anchor Bible*, Doubleday & Co., New York, 1975, p. 310.
78   The exceptions are Heb. 13.4 and perhaps John 2.1–11.
79   Schillebeeckx E., *Marriage: Secular Reality and Saving Mystery* vol. I, Sheed & Ward Stagbooks, London, 1965, p. 66.

80 'Go again, love a woman who is beloved of a paramour and is an adulteress; even as Yahweh loves the people of Israel though they turn to other gods and love cakes of raisins. So I bought her for fifteen shekels of silver and a homer and a lecheth of barley' (Hos. 3.1–2). Schillebeeckx comments that this is true if the Law Deut. 24.1 ff. and Lev. 21.7 were in force at that time. Surely they were in force or the action of Hosea has no prophetic meaning. Schillebeeckx, *Marriage*, p. 67.

81 Rev. 8.23, 19.7–9, 21.2,9, 22.17; Matt. 22.2–14, 25.1–12; Mark 2.19; Luke 14.8, 14.16–24; 1 Cor. 11.2–3.

82 Cf. for example *The Catechism of the Catholic Church*, p. 613, that says when speaking of marriage in the Lord: 'The Church attaches great importance to Jesus' presence at the wedding feast of Cana.'

83 Isaiah speaking about it says, 'It will be said on that day, "Lo this is our God; we have waited for him, that he might save us."'

84 Sanders J. A., 'Luke's Great Banquet Parable' in *Essays in Old Testament Ethics*, ed. J. Crenshaw and J. Willis, Ktav Publishing, New York, 1974, p. 258.

85 This is clear from the verses of Psalm 20 which are used. 'You have set upon their heads crowns of precious stones; they asked you for life and you gave it to them.'

86 Mackin comments: 'It gives the spouses a participation in the mystical marriage by which the Son is incarnated in the humanity of Christ, the marriage by which the Church itself becomes reciprocally the body, the flesh of Christ.' Mackin, *The Marital Sacrament*, p. 595

87 Doms H., *The Meaning of Marriage*, Sheed and Ward, London, 1939, pp. 98ff.

88 Kasper W., *Theology of Christian Marriage*, Crossroad, New York, 1986, p. 35.

Chapter Five

The Ecclesiology of the Christian Family: The Domestic Church

At the African synod in 2000 at Rome, the bishops of Africa defined their ideal of the church as being that of a family, the family of God. Although this idea came from the profound sense of family in Africa, it was nothing new. The Early Church took as its model of church the Roman family, and Scripture presented God as taking Israel as His people, His family. Thus, as the term family typifies the relationship between God and His people, it was natural to think of a family called Church. Going even further, the New Testament reveals God Himself to be a family of Father, Son and Holy Spirit. So, the family is the image of the relationship between God and His people. When this is applied to the Church, the Church is the people of God whose life derives from being the family of God.[1] Likewise, individual families are not only an image of Church, but find their deepest life in being part of the community called Church. Calling the Christian family the domestic church has preserved this profound insight.[2] Lost in the Western Church for nearly fifteen hundred years, preserved in the Eastern Church, the idea once again came to the fore in Vatican II and formed the basis of the encyclical *Familiaris Consortio* in 1981.

The reason for such a loss in the West is unclear, but the canonical approach to marriage of the last four hundred years in the West, which spoke of the family as an institution, has been a serious obstacle to revealing the true meaning of a Christian family. Marriage creates a family, a living entity, a way of being, not just a juridical entity, an institution. The concept of a living family has been forgotten by Western theology until recently. Instead, a culturally and theologically static view of marriage has been taught where marriage was both an office and an institution. This led to a superficial view of marriage, which emphasized marriage as a contract applicable to all time. Yet marriage has always evolved just as society evolved. As the pace of life has increased and changes become more frequent, a static view of marriage has become difficult to defend. When this is combined with the modern idea that each marriage is a unique partnership, some argue there is no such thing as a Christian model of marriage. The Church merely blesses whatever form of marriage is prevalent at the time. In many ways this is true, particularly when it is recalled that a marriage blessing was, even by the ninth century, something that was counselled, but not compulsory. But there was a core of Christian belief concerning marriage that was not based on external arrangements, but on a conviction that marriage is a participation in the people of God and through the family salvation is to be achieved.

It is this inner sense of being family, going beyond the way family duties and responsibilities are divided up between husband and wife that is the key to discovering the meaning of the domestic church. This inner sense goes beyond the personal relationship between husband and wife, and flows into all the relationships that make up a family because the personal covenant of the spouses brings about other covenantal relationships between the parents and grandparents, brothers, sisters, uncles, aunts, etc. of the couple, as well as the new covenants they create with their children. These other covenants are not founded on blood relationships, but on the new links a marriage brings about. This is evident in so many ways. The wedding draws together two different family groups not only at the wedding celebration, but also in a permanent relationship. Absence at such a time is seen as a grave dereliction of duty and a rejection of the marriage. Children cement these relationships in a special way. The joy on the face of grandparents as they hold their grandchildren clearly expresses the covenant that binds any family together.

In reality, a family is a knot of relationships that cannot be untied. Conceiving this knot as a web of covenants presents a very different picture of family. A covenant is a mutual gift of persons imposing fidelity and an unbreakable oneness.[3] The acceptance of a new couple into a family joins two families together, forever, throughout life because covenants of their nature imply, though the relationship may substantially change, that the covenant cannot change or be broken. Folk wisdom reminds the partners, you do not just marry the other, but their family as well. The same applies to children. The boomerang effect where those who leave home seem to be constantly returning to live with their parents again is further evidence that the real relationships within a family are covenantal relationships. Vatican II expressed the same truth when it insisted that conjugal love could only be understood from the unique union that marital intimacy brings. The spouses are called not only to give physical life to their children, but also to be a source of life for the whole family.

In addition, the meaning of the familial covenant relationships is crucial to understanding the width and the depth of Christian marriage. Just as the covenant between the spouses is sacramental, so the relationship within families has a special dimension in the plan of God. Marriage is a community, a family, where the interaction of its members, both parents and children, affects the other. This partnership, where each one completes in some way the other, causes joy and pain, and brings about perfection through change. It is here that marriage goes beyond creation to salvation. Christian marriage partakes of the nature and the mysterious character of Christ's union with his Church. It reflects the bond between Christ and the Church, full of life because it is a sacrament.

Yet at the same time, the sacrament of marriage is not separate from married life. The spouses live the sacrament so that the sacrament is not static, but dynamic. It is the exchange of love that brings the sacrament of marriage into being, for every sacramental reality is not only reception, but also participation. In a wonderful way, the sacrament is constantly renewed. When this is applied to the Christian family, a whole new dimension suddenly appears. Family relationships are also sacramental for the family takes part in the marriage. The depth of this sharing in the life of Christ is most evident in an Orthodox Church wedding where the couple are crowned, signifying their life in Christ.[4] Their children are called to be 'members of Christ'. Each one of them, in his or her particular personal way, is called to experience the presence of God and reveal Him to the world. The couple are now a 'domestic church'.

A whole new depth of meaning is discovered where the ecclesiology of marriage becomes clear and the theology of family can be glimpsed. As Mersch says: 'The marital home is not a domestic church because it is there the children first learn about God. Rather, the marital home is a domestic church because they participate in the Church and their marital acts are acts of the Church.'[5] What does this mean and what is the origin of such an idea?

The Origin of the Theology of the Domestic Church

The idea of the domestic Church grew out of the Roman concept of family. For them the key idea of family was blood or work relationship to the *pater familias,* the father. As a Roman family consisted of the whole household including children, even those grown up, slaves, unmarried relatives, freedmen and women, family was often a large number of people. Although they did not necessarily reside together, they formed a single unit. The wife strengthened the family as she continued the bloodline through her children.[6] Children were considered as a kind of insurance policy to protect old age, to act as reinforcements, to prop up the house or form its foundations, or as a pole to which vines may cling.[7] So the pattern of a Roman family was an extended family under a benign patriarch.

The importance of this patriarch cannot be overestimated. Honour was the key value for a family – so much so that the admonition to honour your father and mother was originally addressed to adults regarding their respect for this patriarch. This respect demanded that the wife could not commit adultery for that would stain the family name. Likewise, the sons and daughters showed their respect by caring for the matriarch as she often survived her husband, for the custom was for a man to marry a much younger woman. The basis of this respect was the bloodline of the patriarch. His life transmitted through the family must be kept intact.

In the religious sphere, the patriarchal family was strengthened by the house worship of ancestors and guardian spirits so it was natural that when the patriarch was baptized, all the members of a large household were baptized, and the house became a house church. Even when only one partner was converted to Christianity, most commonly the woman, there was still a house church, but a divided house church. Tertullian writes about the inconveniences of a Christian wife with a pagan husband.[8] 'The pagan husband will not tolerate his wife joining a vigil at daybreak (he will tell her to meet him at the baths), or fasting (he will schedule an important dinner), or visiting the poor for the sake of charity (he will have urgent family business that she must attend with him). Instead she will have to smell the incense of family festivals and go through a door hung with laurels and lanterns for monthly and New Year pagan celebrations.'[9] Yet this did not deter the Christian woman. As can be seen from many early saints, it was the women who finally converted the household.

Yet the difference between an early Christian family and their pagan neighbours had few external signs. Christians frequented the markets, the baths, the shops, even the games, circus or gymnasium, although the latter were frowned upon.[10] However, they were different in that they followed an ethical system inherited from Judaism and found an identity in a heavenly citizenship, a new race.[11] This identity was expressed in a different house church than their pagan neighbours, where the Eucharist, as a family celebration, was the centre of worship.

As the Church came to be seen as one extended family, the Roman family became the model for the Church.[12] Early ecclesiology found its inspiration in the Roman family life. Hence the idea of a domestic church was natural to Roman civilization: in fact the domestic churches were to form the basis of the organization of parishes in Rome. By the fourth century there were twenty-five of these house churches called *tituli* that bore the name of their owners. Archaeological excavations have found the figure of a person with his arms stretched out in prayer beneath the titulus of Bizans on the Celion hill. Likewise, in the church of St Pudenziana, the church is built against the house of Pudens, friend of the apostles, whose doorway still opens into the church.[13] Thus, it is not surprising that the family house church was the *ecclesia* as can be seen in the greeting Paul sends at the end of an epistle: 'Greet Prisca and Aquila, my fellow workers in Christ Jesus ... greet also the church in their house' (Rom. 16.3 and 5).

The source of the domestic church was its role in the community and participation in the Eucharist. Yet changes were to take place with time. At first the domestic church was the community to which others were welcomed. This changed as the house became too small for the community and churches were built. The Roman model of family was only true of a tiny proportion of the population, as most Romans lived in apartments in shabby crowded conditions and lived on the street and ate at the local tavern. As Osiek says: 'the poor ate out, the rich ate in'.[14] The poor did not have a personal house church, so to include them in a worshiping community, the house church had to become a community church. The church building became the gathering point. Yet the idea of a domestic church did not wane, instead the two concepts of Church, a holy building and a family as a holy and sacred place for prayer, worship and ritual coexisted. The house church was not a kind of a house mass that could accommodate a large gathering, but a Christian centre of catechesis and worship, based on a Christian family. The Church was in their house. Within this house the Eucharist constituted the family and the house church. The *agape* or communal meal that Paul refers to before the Eucharist symbolized the community; the Eucharist symbolized the reality of their family in Christ. However, the family celebrations and its yearly cycle of feasts and festivals did gradually become eclipsed by the emergence of a great church building or cathedral and its liturgy.

Throughout this early period it was believed that the return of Christ was imminent. When it became clear this return was delayed, questions arose concerning the role of the house church. The basis of the house church was the belief that Christ entered a couple's life through marriage so that the family and therefore their house church was a sign of His presence and action. As Christians belonged to a heavenly citizenship, a new race, there was a new attitude in the period of waiting for Christ's return. Gnostic heretics, who taught that procreative sex was an abomination because they wished to return to the state of angels who did not marry, were rejected.[15] This struggle to defend the goodness of marriage made the early Fathers of the Church present marriage as a medicinal gift, both prophylactic and therapeutic, preventing spouses from falling into sin and healing them from sin.[16]

Just as problematic was the struggle with the radical Encratities, the self-controllers, who were to damage the ideal of marriage. For them marriage was a second-class calling; celibacy was the real Christian ideal. The theology that supported this position took the Incarnation of the Word of God to mean that the immortal unchanging God had descended into mortal flesh so that it might become immortal, free from decay. So, to be a Christian meant to overcome the frailties of the flesh that tie us to death. Principal among the frailties of the flesh was sexual relations. Thus, celibacy was greater than marriage. Roman Christianity rooted in households resisted this insidious doctrine, which had spread from Persia.

The problem really became serious with the arrival of Marcion in Rome about AD 139. He claimed to renew the vision of St Paul, saying celibacy and virginity were superior to marriage. Even if Clement of Alexandria, and at first, Tertullian, set themselves against this radical renunciation of the world, they did not reject the value of celibacy over marriage, or the vision of a transformed body, but denied this was to be practised now.[17] The solution was chaste sex for procreative purposes, a solution that was to be re-echoed just over a century later. Unfortunately, this left marriage as a second-class calling.

The most extreme proponent of the superiority of celibacy was St Jerome who vented his spleen on Helvidius who dared to say virginity and marriage were equal. Though Helvidius' arguments were probably unsustainable, based as they were on the marriage of Joseph and Mary, Jerome's arguments were worse. He described married life as being filled with the prattling of the noise of the whole household, children clinging to the neck, the computing of expenses so that women could only be holy when they ceased to be married women, imitating the chastity of virgins within the very intimacy of marriage. The proof text for all this was in the parable of the Sower and the seed that fell in good soil and bore fruit, thirty, sixty and a hundred fold (Mark 4.20). This was taken to indicate the result of the varying states of life. The married would bear only thirty fold; the widows would bring forth sixty fold and the virgins one hundred fold. Jovian, who protested against such an exegesis, was roundly condemned.

Jerome's impassioned defence of the superiority of virginity and celibacy was an embarrassment, and Augustine, basing himself on St Ambrose, sought to repair the damage by defending marriage because it produced fidelity, children and a bond.[18] At first sight this reinforced the Roman sense of family, the preservation of the father's name and the father's religion. However, when this is seen within Augustine's theory of concupiscence, another dimension appears. From his point of view fidelity, offspring and bond were the justification for marriage because sexual passion (concupiscence) that disobeyed reason was the result of Original Sin. Augustine found this confirmed in the words of Psalm 51 'behold I was brought forth in iniquity, and in sin did my mother conceive me'. But Christian marriage rescued carnal concupiscence by turning it to a good use through parenthood. So, fidelity, procreation and permanence expressed the essence of marriage.

This position needs examining closely because Augustine has been sometimes misrepresented. Augustine still referred to the Christian family as the domestic church when he said: 'the father carried out the duties of the bishop in his own family'. In addition, Augustine put fidelity in first place.[19] He was reflecting a tradition that saw fidelity as the first essential quality of marriage because it expressed the uniqueness of the relationship found in marital chastity as well as assuring a legitimate heir.[20] In Roman legal writing this relationship was called *coniunctio*, the marital union. Although Western theologians were to seize on offspring as the motivation for marriage,[21] the sacred bond, *sacramentum*,[22] was the essence of marriage and could not be broken,[23] because the sacred bond was the sign of the mystery of Christ in his Church – a mystery that was destroyed by remarriage.[24] So permanence was an essential quality of marriage.[25] Thus, despite the difficulties of defending the sacramentality of marriage, Augustine held marriage was a sign of the mystery of Christ in his Church and defended the concept of marriage as a domestic church.

In Augustine's time, getting married was still a family affair rather than the elaborate ceremonies that were to come into being after the eighth century in the East and even later in the West. Marriage took place in the home. In addition, the poor were not married in the Roman legal sense. Only the rich provided a model of marriage: a fifth-century saint urged the Church to leave the poor alone as they could not marry in the way the Church conceived marriage. The marriage blessing by a priest was recommended, but not compulsory. Thus, the idea of a domestic church was not so much theological, but practical, in the sense that Christian families were seen as a centre of catechesis, not only for the family's children, but also for the whole neighbourhood.

However, it was not a lack of theology that caused the domestic church to disappear in the West, rather it was Augustine's justification of marriage under the regime of sin through children that made marriage into an institution, which began the change. In the East, such an explanation was never accepted.[26] The consequence of Augustine's approach, practically and theologically, was decisive in the centuries that followed. In the West, marriage became a duty; children were its purpose. Inheritance was the driving force. Valid marriage was the prime concern. Thus marriage could be called a contract. It meant that the classical definition of Ulpianus, which formed the basis for the idea of a domestic church, emphasizing the legal union of man and woman and the sharing of life,[27] had now been superseded by the exchange of sexual rights upon which the permanence of marriage depended.[28] Thus, the ancient definition that marriage was a society, a sharing, was put in second place and even thought deficient. Two other ideas came centre stage.[29] First, marriage had a natural goal or end, offspring, through which concupiscence was allayed and the bond between the partners strengthened. Second, marriage was created by consent in a contract that gave exclusive sexual rights to the spouses. These ideas excluded the idea of a domestic church so worship in the home became purely devotional, as is even visible today in popular piety. For example, in Austria the practice of *Herrgottswinkel*, God's corner, and a *hausalter* continues the idea of the domestic church in this way.[30]

However, in the Eastern Church, the concept of *ecclesia*, the community, was both a physical and theological reality. Marriage, as an image of the relationship between Christ and his Church, could not remain purely on a practical level. Beginning from the text of Matthew 19.4, the East held that marriage was a vocation from the beginning, and a vocation of co-being with God and a remnant of paradise.[31] To this they added the very Greek idea, that marriage was an image, a reflection of the relationship between Christ and his Church. This in no way idealized marriage. Instead marriage was both an image and a type, a kind of relationship. Whether the couple are quarrelling or not, they are still an image of a way of life that can rise above human frailty. Thus, marriage was not primarily a remedy against concupiscence, or for the procreation of children, rather it was the kingdom present in the nuptial community itself. This is why Erickson can write: 'Like consecrated virginity... marriage from the beginning points to the kingdom where biological bonds and natural affinity are transcended by the immediacy of a loving personal relationship between Christ and his Church.'[32] This dimension goes beyond Jewish or Roman concepts of marriage. For what is truly new in Christian marriage is

not procreation or consent, but the possibility of the unity
of man and wife being transformed into a new reality in
the reality of the Kingdom of God. This transformation is
the gift of *koinonia* or communion, which is the supreme
gift of the Spirit (John 17.22–23).

The text of Ephesians 5.20–33 is crucial to this position.
Ephesians, commenting on the phrase from Genesis that
the 'two shall become one flesh', says that this should be
understood in the light of the relationship between Christ
and his Church. The crucial point is that this relationship
is not only one of interpersonal love, but also of communion within the Church. Thus, there is a threefold basis for
the domestic church. First, the concept that marriage
creates co-being. According to Gregory of Nyssa, our spiritual nature exists in the likeness of the Creator; it is
similar to what is above. In its own impenetrability it
shows forth the impress of the Inaccessible. Thus, the
faculty of loving is the seal of God's image in man (1 John
3.1). Strictly speaking personhood exists only in God.
Man, the 'image', has a longing to become a person and his
efforts are realized only in as much as the person participates in the image of the divine Other. This is confirmed
by the mystery of Ephesians 5 where marriage reflects the
union between Christ and the Church as an eternal bond.
This mystery is found in the self-revelation and self-determination of the partners. The sacrament is the transform-
ing of human love into a new reality of heavenly grace
where grace has taken flesh in this life.[33] St John Chrysostom says: 'The qualities of love are such that the beloved
and the lover no longer form two beings but one ... They
are not only brought together but they are one.'[34] Thus the
spouses in their unity are, as Chrysostom says, 'an image
of God Himself'.[35] For human love is projected into the
eternal Kingdom of God, so much so, that the unity of
Christian marriage and the eternity of the marriage bond
remain even if one of the partners dies.[36]

The second key concept of image comes about because
marriage, as an icon of a living God, is holy, because as

Clement of Alexandria says: 'It anticipates the Kingdom and already constitutes a little kingdom, its prophetic image.'[37] This emphasis on the nuptial community as the image of the church naturally leads to the concept of a domestic church, because the sacrament has an ecclesial dimension based on the relationship between Christ and the Church (Eph. 5.2). St John Chrysostom underlined the meaning of this in his portrayal of the Christian family. Though he lived in a time of social upheaval, he did not present the family simply as a social bulwark that only gave great benefit to the state,[38] but time and time again he returns to the Patristic theme that salvation is accomplished within the church, because it makes the kingdom of God present in an unbelieving world. The family, as a domestic church, is an essential part of this work.[39]

In a similar way, Gregory of Nazianzus uses the model of the relationship of Christ and his Church to defend the ancient doctrine that the connection between marriage and the Church is the basis of the ecclesiology of marriage.[40] He wrote, meditating on Ephesians: 'It is a beautiful thing for the wife to honour Christ through her husband; it is a beautiful thing also for the husband to not denigrate the church through his wife.'[41] So the domestic church is an image for Christian husbands and wives where the wife, in loving her husband, makes the husband the intermediary for her love of Christ. Likewise, the husband, in loving his wife, loves the Church and through the Church loves Christ.

The third basis of the concept of a domestic church is its salvational aspect. For Chrysostom, parenthood was an office of the community, assigned to parents by God and the church, accompanied by martyrdom. His model for this was Abraham and the self-sacrifice of Hannah. While their self-sacrifice underlines the concept of martyrdom in marriage, it is the family rather than the monastery where the world should see the church. This is because the relationships signified by a married couple mirror the Church. Stavropoulos lists these relationships as: openness of all married couples in the here and now – the relational aspect; openness to God – the salvific aspect; openness to the partners themselves – the conjugal aspect; openness to children and to others – procreative and community aspect.[42] These relationships underline what living in the Church means by *koinonia*, community.

So, the community aspects of Christian marriage go far beyond the prevention of and cure for sexual desires. Through the covenant it is caught up in salvation history; it is a sacrament of the Kingdom.[43] The consecration of the spouses' union becomes communion revealing joy and a new creation. When a Christian's home is transformed into the Church or a church, when its occupants salute each other with a holy kiss, are hospitable to people and remain free of deceit and hypocrisy, then Christ is present.[44] This is because love, hospitality and authenticity are fruits of the presence of Christ, as Chrysostom wrote: 'Let the house be a Church, consisting of men and women ... "For where two," He said, "are gathered together in My Name, there am I in the midst of them" (Matt. 18.20).'[45] Thus marriage stands in the closest relationship to the life of the whole Christian community. It is often referred to as a little church or a domestic church.[46] Salvation comes through the Christian family.

Hence, the Early Church, particularly in the East, had a rich theological basis for the concept of a domestic church. The covenant that brought about co-being, the one flesh, at the same time brought about an image of the relationship between Christ and his Church. This relationship is salvific because the relationship between Christ and his Church is also salvific. Therefore, in two different ways, the relationship that exists between Christ and his Church is the ultimate cause and origin of the unity of marriage, and of the domestic church.[47] Lastly, the domestic church of its nature is the Church, not just a mere image: the family is the little church, the building block of the great Church. Thus, from the house churches of early Christianity, whose centre was the Eucharist, there grew a rich theology of marriage and the family.

The Modern Concept of the Domestic Church

This theological tradition of seeing the family as the domestic church, an expression of the great Church, disappeared in the church in the West from the time of St Augustine until the Second Vatican Council. The reasons for this are unclear. Certainly, conceiving marriage as an institution was unhelpful. More decisive was conceiving Christian marriage as a contract. Although the Eastern Church spoke of a contract of marriage it was only one of three ways marriage could take place and did not refer to the marriage as such, but the betrothal.[48] St Albert the Great also spoke of contract in this sense. It was Duns Scotus' fourteenth-century definition of marriage as a contract, the exclusive right over each other's bodies, that removed any spiritual meaning from marriage, especially if it is remembered that the sole purpose of marriage at that time was considered to be procreation. When this is combined with the idea that the couple gave to each other the sacrament, it privatized the sacrament of marriage so that the priest's role became that of a witness who blessed the marriage.

While the idea of a domestic church was always preserved in the East, its return in the West at the Second Vatican Council is just as mysterious as its departure. At the insistence of only one bishop, Bishop Fiordelli of Prato, did it surface again. After discussing the priesthood of the laity, the draft document on the Church turned to the ecclesiology of the sacraments. Commenting on the section on marriage, Bishop Fiordelli said: 'The draft should be praised as it also includes the married state (in its ecclesiology). However, it is less pleasing in that the draft speaks only of the married, and says nothing about the married state of Christians i.e. the Christian family. But in the Church, the Mystical Body of Christ, they are not only members of the body, but should be considered also as an organic part that communicates this body.'

Describing how there is a diocesan and parochial

community, he laments that nothing is said about the family community as part of the Mystical Body of Christ, because Christ willed that the family be the basic unit of community in the Church by elevating marriage to the dignity of a sacrament. Through this, the family is directly sanctified, becomes a fount of divine life and shows the mystical function of the body. So, following the example of the Fathers, both from the East and the West, the family merits, and can and must be called, a *little church* because through it is communicated the mystical unity and love between Christ and the Church. In other words, the family can be considered as the first and the smallest unit of the Church. Thus, the Church begins from the Christian family, is next seen in the parish and then the diocese.

To emphasize this Fiordelli suggested amendments which stated that the spouses do not simply have their own special gift, but are in a specific state, the most powerful of all the lay states though inferior to the priesthood. The spouses do not just symbolize the mystery and love of Christ for his Church, but communicate this mystery. The family should not be called the 'domestic church', but the 'little church' as this was the way the Fathers spoke of the family. [49]

These comments were accepted. The final text says:

> Christian spouses, in virtue of the sacrament of matrimony, signify and partake of the mystery of that unity and fruitful love which exists between Christ and his Church (Eph. 5.32), help each other to attain to holiness in their married life and in the rearing and education of their children. And so, in their state and order of life, they have their own special gift among the people of God (1 Cor. 7.7) ... The family is, so to speak, the domestic church. [50]

Regretfully, this does not clearly express Bishop Fiordelli's points that marriage communicates the mystery of the relationship between Christ and his Church and that as a domestic church families are a basic part of the Church. Instead what is being expounded here is the special priesthood of the partners in a Christian family.[51] As the official website of the hierarchy in the Philippines says: 'The Second Vatican Council has pointed out how the family, the primary and vital cell of society, shows itself to be the domestic sanctuary of the Church through the mutual affection of its members and the common prayer they offer to God. The Christian family is thus seen to be a domestic church.'[52] The problem here is that the domestic church may be seen only as seed ground for the Church, which is outside the Church.

However, this is not the attitude of *Familiaris Consortio*, the Apostolic Exhortation issued in 1981. It says the family is called to experience a new and original communion brought about by Christ and the Holy Spirit. The Christian family constitutes a specific revelation and realization of ecclesial communion, and for this reason too it can and should be called 'the domestic church'.[53] What is being emphasized here is that the domestic church is not just an image of the love of Christ and His Church, but also that marriage is a participation in the Church as sacrament. Strictly speaking, Christ is the sacrament because his self-communication is not just through words or signs, but because Christ gives his own self. Sacraments are only possible because Christ became man and joined humanity with God. In time, the Church is the basic sacrament because of Christ's love and life, which it communicates through the Holy Spirit. The domestic church is a specific revelation of this sacramental action.[54]

In contrast, Orthodox theology had long since reached this point and developments from the ninth century onwards concentrated on marriage as taking place within the kingdom of God.[55] For the Orthodox, psychology, sociology or law cannot explain Christian marriage because the sacrament is based on the human person as a citizen of heaven. The faculty to love is the seal of God's image in humankind (1 John 3.1). In contrast, Latin theology has concentrated on the bond of marriage conceived in a legal form.[56] Meanwhile, Eastern theology taught that the transformation of marriage into a reality of the kingdom of God transforms procreation and surpasses legalism by the eternal joy of an eternal love.[57] Meyendorff says:

> In the sacrament ... humanity communicates in the supreme reality of the Holy Spirit, without ceasing to be humanity: on the contrary it becomes more human, more authentically human, as it accomplishes the destiny which has been its own from all eternity by the gift of communion, koinonia, which since Pentecost has manifested the Church and is the supreme goal which Christ himself marked out for all mankind in the Church, that they may be one, as we are one (John 17.22–23).[58]

Love in marriage is not just inter-personal, but extends to the whole Christian community and there finds its complete meaning. Erotic love is transformed in the family by the domestic church, because only in Christ's love can the Christian find the reconciliation of man and woman, male and female, Eros and person.[59] The domestic church, as an image of the love Christ has for His Church, re-establishes the wholesome polarity between man and woman and makes this love bear fruit in their love for their children and for others.[60]

The expression of this theology is found particularly in the Orthodox liturgy as an expression of the wedding feast at Cana.[61] The materials involved, water and wine, proclaimed the birth of the Church on the Cross as well as the Eucharistic nature of the Church. Christ revealed his glory in the domestic church of Cana, and according to the Greek Fathers, it is He who presides over every Christian wedding.[62] So the natural bonds of marriage, which are the image of the relationship between Christ and His

Church, are emphasized in the wedding liturgy as a reflection of the love of Christ for His Church.

In the Orthodox marriage service, where the first part is a betrothal service that used to be a separate rite, are two very ancient prayers from the eighth or ninth centuries. The first calls upon God to bless the couple. The second prayer, that takes place just before the betrothal, reflects Christ's betrothal of the Gentile Church connecting this betrothal to the mystery of Christ and his Church.[63] After the crowning that follows next, which is the climax of the betrothal service, comes the procession. Although the crowns are a sign of glory, honour and martyrdom, as every true marriage involves self-sacrifice, as well as a sign of the couple's roles in their home, which the ancient Fathers described as the priesthood of the domestic church, it is the procession where the priest leads the bride and groom around the lectern that emphasiszes that the sacrament does not remain simply at an inter-personal level. For just as the couple take their place in society so too does the sacrament. The procession, three times around the lectern, symbolizes life and eternity, a thirst for paradise. The readings which follow the crowning, from Ephesians 5.20–33 – marriage as an icon of the love of Christ and His Church – and John 2.1–11 – the wedding feast at Cana – emphasize the symbolism of marriage as a domestic church.[64] All this takes place during the Divine Liturgy, for there is no independent marriage rite, and marriage necessarily involves receiving Holy Communion, which was seen as the marriage being sealed by Christ.[65] Thus the Orthodox liturgy emphasizes the ecclesial dimension of marriage in the betrothal, the procession and the communion. It is not surprising that St John Chrysostom says: 'Marriage is a mysterious icon of the Church.'[66]

The Latin Church has no liturgical theology to compare to this, although the two traditions fuse again in the new role that Christian marriage has within the church. *Familiaris Consortio* says: 'It is the love between husband and wife and between the members of the family that is the participation in the prophetic, priestly and kingly mission of Christ and his Church so that the Christian family fulfils its prophetic role by welcoming and announcing the word of God, fulfils its priestly role by being a community in dialogue with God, and fulfils its kingly role by being a community at the service of men.'[67] Marriage then is a sacrament that endures during the life of the couple.[68]

The family's priestly role is theologically most significant because of its connection to the Eucharist. Already it is clear that the Orthodox Church considers that the Eucharist makes the marriage sacramental. Unless the couple partake of communion, the marriage is purely a civil ceremony.[69] In addition, several Orthodox theologians point out that there is a strong connection between the wedding service and the Eucharist, as both have their moments of offering, invocation of the Holy Spirit, communion and thanksgiving. The couple offer themselves, the crowning is accompanied by the invocation of the Spirit, communion is essential, and thanksgiving is made at the end. Without going as far as this, *Familiaris Consortio* says: 'The Christian family's sanctifying role is grounded in Baptism and has its highest expression in the Eucharist, to which Christian marriage is intimately connected.' Likewise, the Second Vatican Council drew attention to the unique relationship between the Eucharist and marriage by requesting, 'marriage normally be celebrated within the Mass'. This brings to mind the Orthodox insistence that marriage cannot be separated from the Eucharist because the Eucharist has always been and remains the norm of ecclesiality.[70] Separation from the Eucharist meant excommunication and if marriage brings about a domestic church, it must be through the Eucharist as well as through marriage.

Today, the Western Church appears to be moving in the same direction. *Familiaris Consortio* says 'the Eucharist is the very source of Christian marriage because it represents Christ's covenant of love with the Church.'[71] The

Eucharist is the fountain of charity. Even more fundamentally the Eucharist is essential to the Church because to grow as Church means to grow in the likeness of Christ. The unity and holiness of Christ are essential characteristics of the Church and so partaking in the Eucharist, the essence of unity and holiness is absolutely necessary. This is the basis of the call to Christian families to be one body and be holy and to make holy the ecclesial community and the world.[72]

This of course brings into question the celebration of marriage outside of the Eucharist. In the East, the mandatory solemnization of marriage by a ritual was not the idea of the Church, but of the State. Justinian required the middle classes to go to church for their weddings, but this changed in 542 to include only the higher classes. It was not until the twelfth century that church ritual became the only legal form of entering marriage. The special connection between marriage and the Eucharist was gradually lost because of the general liberalization of the Canonical legislation on marriage concerning civil weddings.[73] These took place outside the Eucharist, even though they were conducted inside a church. Likewise, in the West a similar pattern can be traced. Marriage was celebrated at home, and even in medieval times marriage was celebrated in the church porch. Mass often followed, but really had no direct connection. Even at the Council of Trent, no demand was made that marriage should be celebrated with the Eucharist. In England, it was not until 1753 that marriage was required to be in church. Thus the State brought marriage into the Church.

This strange situation where the connection between marriage and the Eucharist was brought about by the State was made even more curious by the official attitude to mixed marriages. Until recently in the Catholic Church, only two Catholics could have a nuptial mass so that mixed marriages were celebrated in the sacristy, or if the priest was more liberal at a side altar. Nowadays, the marriage rite often stands alone, without the Eucharist, due to the proliferation of mixed marriages, though it is celebrated at the principal altar. The reason for omitting the Eucharist is sometimes the problem of inter-communion, but just as often it is a case of lack of practice of the faith. The latter weddings are very close to civil ceremonies conducted in church.[74] Obviously, mixed marriages without the Eucharist are theologically an impoverished sign, a fact made even clearer by the Apostolic Letter commenting on the division present in the domestic church formed by such a union. Yet the ecclesial status of mixed marriages has been recognized by the Magisterium, implying the recognition of ecclesial elements in the Protestant Church.[75] The ecclesial nature of mixed marriages cannot be denied. The domestic church exists here as well. However, as many would hope, the sign of communion could be restored so that the unity between the couple and the unity between the two families brought together by the marriage might be signified.

The Practical Implications of the Domestic Church

The threefold basis of the domestic church is that Christian marriage creates co-being, is a prophetic icon, and is salvational. Therefore, as Lehmann points out, 'the supernatural phenomenon of marriage exists because it is the covenant that allows marriage to be the means by which the eternal love of God, revealed in Jesus Christ, achieves presence in the world not just as an image but as a saving reality.' Thus, it actualizes the relationship that binds Christ to the Church in the history of salvation. The family, the domestic church, is not just a phrase implying the duties that Christian parents undertake to teach their children the faith, but is the Church in its saving dimension. The domestic church is a community that portrays community and offers salvation through this community.

It is here that the important dimension of the Eucharist in family life becomes clear. The family does not just go to church but participates as Church. It finds its highest expression in the Eucharist because: 'the Eucharist is the very source of Christian marriage, it represents Christ's covenant of love with the Church.'[76] In other words, just as Christian marriage takes part in the love of Christ for the Church, the Eucharist as a manifestation of and a participation in that love means the married have a special role in celebrating the Eucharist. The explanation that *Familiaris Consortio* gives is that baptism as the fundamental covenant becomes the source of the marriage covenant. The Eucharist as a further participation in the love of Christ becomes: 'the very source of Christian marriage ... as Christian couples encounter the source from which their marital covenant flows'.[77]

Thus to grow as Church is to grow as community; to share the life of Church is to share the life of Christ. Yet the Church is so often seen today as an institution, an organization, so that the community dimension of the local church is submerged in committees and meetings. This institutional portrayal means that the parish, diocese and the church find it difficult to signify the presence of Christ that brings forth unity. But the domestic church can portray community in all its wonder because the family is made of relationships.[78] Here unity is fashioned or weakened each day as each accepts the other in a communion of love. Thus, the domestic church brings about a civilization of love because the family is at the heart of civilization.[79] This is the hope of all who get married, even those without faith. It is evident, in church marriages, by the choice of so many brides of Paul's hymn to love (1 Cor. 13.1–13), where love is described as a better way. Co-being is the essence of Christian marriage.

Yet this co-being is a journey of life full of the shared experience of the vicissitudes of family life and faith as well as its joys in shared memories. This witness is a carrying of a daily cross of human relationships where those nearest and dearest wound the other the most. Strangers and even enemies cannot wound as deeply as one who is loved. It is here dying and rising is experienced, and the presence of Christ is witnessed to most clearly by so many Christians as they forgive and renew their love. In addition, the family bonds are seen to be real in the help that is given when one member is sick. The grandmother who goes to look after the children of a sick mother brings to life what covenantal bonds really mean. This is where the Gospel is transmitted to children, and where the family becomes the evangelizer of other families in the neighbourhood. It is the domestic church as a prophetic icon. Christian marriage has a special dimension of the priesthood of the faithful.

This special dimension finds its basis in the sacrament of baptism, because it is here the Christian enters the royal priesthood of believers. As *Lumen Gentium* teaches, the sacred nature of the priestly community is brought into operation through the sacraments and the exercise of virtues.[80] The married Christian participates in this in a special way through the marital sacrament, a participation Augustine described as being bishops in the family church. This takes place because married life is a sacramental symbol in that it signifies and shares the unity and faithful love between Christ and the Church.[81] It is the unity and faithful love of the spouses that brings this sacrament to life as can be seen in the Orthodox marriage blessing which calls upon Christ-husband, who married the holy and faithful Church, and had given to her at the Last Supper – his body and blood – to raise his right hand and bless husband and wife. Conjugal love is the basis of the domestic church.

Now the depth of meaning in the old English wedding vows can be seen. Worship literally means ascribing worth to another. This is expressed in the old English wedding vows which said 'with my body I thee worship'. Everyone knows the signs that indicate two people are a couple, the intimacy, the whole interaction between them, that proclaims their identity. Likewise, the support, the knowing what the other thinks and feels, is all part of the same reality. Love needs expression. The loving interaction between the spouses makes the marriage holy and is part of worship because the covenant of love portrays the love between Christ and His Church. It is a self-transcendency that is essential to worship because worship is the response of the creature to the eternal in spirit and in truth.[82]

In addition to this, worship is part of the essence of marriage because marriage does not just create a family, a domestic church, but brings the world in contact with the Church. As Evdokimov says, 'The laity forms an ecclesial abode which is, at the same time, of the world and of the Church.'[83] As marriage is in essence communion, being Church, worship is an expression of our being. Worship is participation. Thus, the permanent call to communion among themselves, characterized by a free and intimate relationship, is a call to worship because the partners not only share their love, but also participate through this love in the sacrifice of daily living and thus take part in the worship of the Church. This is the priestly role of the family proclaimed in *Lumen Gentium* and insisted upon in *Familiaris Consortio*. In this way, marriage is true worship and a prophetic icon.

Thus the house church of the Early Church has gone full circle. The domestic church is where Christ resides and can be most clearly seen. Some married couples may feel this is a step too far as they reflect on their own family with all its stresses, strains, quarrels and divisions. But from the beginning God brought about 'one flesh' in marriage so that we might see, as the Fathers of the Church taught, the Incarnation of Christ. The good news is that married life is sanctified and made a source of sanctity for the family.[84] As part of the Church, the domestic church is the bringer of God's gifts; gifts are entrusted to it so that down through the ages each generation may experience the love and cleansing action of God.[85] This is the better way come about through the presence of Christ within the marriage. [86]

Notes

1   He commanded His Apostles to preach to all peoples the Gospel's message that the human race was to become the Family of God, in which the fullness of the Law would be love. *Gaudium et Spes* n. 32.

2   'Thus the Christian family, which springs from marriage as a reflection of the loving covenant uniting Christ with the Church, and as a participation in that covenant will manifest to all people the Saviour's living presence in the world, and the genuine nature of the Church. This the family will do by the mutual love of the spouses, by their generous fruitfulness, their solidarity and faithfulness, and by the loving way in which all the members of the family work together.' *Lumen Gentium* n. 11.

3   *Gaudium et Spes* n. 48

4   This is clear from the verses of Psalm 20, which are used. 'You have set upon their heads crowns of precious stones; they asked you for life and you gave it to them.'

5   Mackin comments: 'It gives the spouses a participation in the mystical marriage by which the Son is incarnated in the humanity of Christ, the marriage by which the Church itself becomes reciprocally the body, the flesh of Christ.' Mackin T., *The Marital Sacrament*, Paulist Press, New Jersey, 1989, p. 595

6   Treggiari says, 'The Romans conventionally regarded marriage as an institution designed for the production of legitimate children.' Treggiari S., *Roman Marriage*, Clarendon Press, Oxford, 1993, p. 8

7   Treggiari, *Roman Marriage*, p. 11 for a list of quotes that lay behind these phrases.

8   Tertullian, *Ad Uxor* Book 2, Ch. 4, p. 6.

9   Tertullian, *Of the Inconveniences in a Marriage between an Unbelieving Husband and a Christian Wife* 4.1. *The Human Couple in the Fathers*, Pauline Books, New York, 1999, p. 155. Summary taken from Osiek C., *The Family in Early Christianity: 'Family Values' Revisited*, Catholic Biblical Quarterly, 1996, 15.

10   Tertullian wrote *De spectaculus* to prove why Christians should not go to them.

11   Phil. 3.20, Heb. 11.9–16.

12   Paul in his instruction on choosing elders for the Church
      reflects this by saying the choice of Church elder should
      depend on how they run their family (1 Tim. 3.1–13).
13   Fasola U. M., *Catacombs and Basilicas: The Early Christians in
      Rome*, Pontifical Commission of Sacred Archaeology, Scala,
      Florence, 1981, p. 58.
14   Osiek C, *The Family in Early Christianity*, 1–24.
15   Some Gnostics permitted unproductive sex and some
      banned sex all together.
16   Mackin, *The Marital Sacrament*, p. 91. It has become tradi-
      tional to blame St Augustine for a negative approach to
      marriage. Yet this negative attitude predates him by a very
      long time.
17   Brown P., *The Body and Society: Men, Women and Sexual
      Renunciation in early Christianity*, Columbia University,
      New York, 1988, pp. 77–82.
18   'Fidelity means that one avoids all sexual activity apart
      from one's marriage. Offspring means that a child is
      accepted in love, nurtured in affection, brought up in reli-
      gion. Sacrament means that the marriage is not severed nor
      the spouse abandoned, not even so that the abandoner or
      the abandoned may remarry for the sake of children. This
      is the kind of rule set for marriage by which nature's fruit-
      fulness is honoured and vicious sexual vagrancy is
      restrained.' Augustine, *Commentary on the Literal Meaning
      of Genesis* 9.7.12.
19   As Mackin shows Augustine lists the 'goods' three times in
      his writing, although not always in the same order. Twice
      fidelity comes first, once children come first. Yet it is clear
      from his treatise *On Original Sin* Bk 2, chap. 9 that in
      Augustine's mind fidelity is first. This was often lost in the
      following centuries when the Church wished to emphasize
      that the primary end of marriage was procreation. Mackin
      T., *What is Marriage?*, Paulist Press, New York, 1982, p. 129.
20   'Because of fidelity in chastity a wife has no authority over
      her body but her husband has: as likewise a husband has
      no authority over his body but his wife has it.' *On Original
      Sin*, Bk 2, chap. 9.
21   Although Augustine did write: 'the propagation of chil-
      dren is the first, the natural and the principle purpose of
      marriage' (Augustine, *On Adulterous Marriages*, Bk 2, chap.

12) when he was reacting to a Gnostic tendency to have no children. Yet in his mind fidelity came before children as he expressed a Roman view of marriage.

22 Sacramentum meant both an indissoluble bond of sacred obligations and a sacred sign because Augustine was using a Roman legal term meaning a religious commitment where one put oneself under a personal and sacred bond to carry something out. It did not indicate a sacrament in the modern sense of the word.

23 Augustine uses the term not simply to underline the indissolubility of marriage but also of the indissoluble obligations of baptism. *De nuptiis et conc.*, 1,11, n. 13 [PL 40,394].

24 This was based on his interpretation of Eph. 5.21–32. For Augustine remarriage was impossible because of a *quiddam coniugale* – the bond. (*De nuptiis et conc.* 1,11,12 [PL 44,420–1]). Cf. also the distinction between the *bonum fidei* and *bonum sacramentum*. Cf. Schillebeeckx E., *Marriage: Human Reality and Saving Mystery*, Sheed & Ward Stagbooks, London, 1965, pp. 282–283. Orsy hints that the Pauline privilege also dates from about the same time.

25 But permanence did not equal indissolubility, as divorce was tolerated. Augustine regarded a man who had dismissed his wife and married again as guilty of a light sin. Likewise, the council of Arles 314 stated that young men who had put away their wives for adultery should be advised not to marry again as long as their first wife was living. No compulsion to carry this out was foreseen. Similarly, in the Eastern Church the practice of indulgence, *oikonomia*, is claimed to date from the fourth century following St Basil and St Epiphanius. Gregory of Nazianus taught that 'A first marriage is in full conformity with the law [of the Church]; a second marriage is tolerated by indulgence; a third marriage is harmful. A fourth marriage makes one resemble a pig.' Yet all this did not mean that the permanence of marriage was disregarded. Rather, they acknowledged the permanence of marriage but accepted that marriage could die.

26 Even today Eastern theologians are most insistent that children cannot be the goal of marriage as that would degrade marriage to a bestial level.

27 Ulpianus used the Latin terms *coniunctio* and *maritalis affec-*

tio. Different theologians translated these differently. The scholastics changed the original so that *coniunctio* referred to the permanence of the union. Cf. Mackin, *What is Marriage?*, p. 172.

28   For example Ulpianus wrote: 'Marriage or matrimony is a union of a man and a woman, a union involving a single sharing of life.' Cf. Mackin, *What is Marriage?*, p. 73.

29   J.-P. Martin in 1844 said the ancient definition was deficient. Martin, J.-P., *De Matrimonio Potestate Ipsum Dirimendi Ecclesiae Soli Exclusive Propria*. Cf. Mackin, *What is Marriage?*, p. 202.

30   Kislinger M., *Bauernherrlichkeit*, Oberösterrichisher Landesverlag, Linz, 1976, p. 65.

31   St Cyril of Alexandria spoke of the married partners as not simply divinely sanctioned animality, but a reflection in creaturely form of God the Trinity – a life of perfect openness and personal communion. Chrysostom said that when husband and wife cleave to each other there is a remnant of paradise. Hom. 20, Patrologia Graece (hereafter PG), 51, col. 221.

32   Erickson J. H., *The Challenge of our Past*, St Vladimir's Seminary Press, New York, 1991, p. 41.

33   Charalambidis, S., 'Marriage in the Orthodox Church', *One in Christ*, vol. 15 (1979), 206–207.

34   St John Chrysostom, Epist. I ad Cor Homily XXXIII, PG 61:280; Epist. Ad Colossians. Cap. IV, Homily XII, PG 62:387.

35   John Chrysostom: 'When husband and wife are united in marriage, they form an image of no earthly reality but of God himself.' Thus perfect and perpetual monogamy is the norm of marriage.

36   Meyendorff J., *Byzantine Theology: Historical Trends and Doctrinal Themes*, (2nd edn), Fordham University Press, New York, 1983, pp. 197–198.

37   P. G. 40:228. Migne JP., *Patrologia Latina* 1844.

38   When harmony prevails, the children are raised well, the household is kept in order, and neighbours, friends and relatives praise the result. Great benefits, both for families and states are produced. Quoted in *St John Chrysostom on Marriage and Family Life*, St Vladimir's Seminary Press, New York, 1986, p. 57.

39   For further clarification on this see Guroian V., *Family and Christian Virtue in a Post-Christendom World: Reflections on the Ecclesial Vision of John Chrysostom*, St Vladimir's Theological Quarterly, 35(1991) 327–350.

40   St John Chrysostom, *Homily XX On Ephesians* 5:22–33.

41   Gregory Nazianzus, *Sermon 37 on Matthew*. PG.36:290–291.

42   Stravropoulos A. M., 'The understanding of marriage in the Orthodox Church', *One in Christ*, vol. 15 (1979), 59. However, it is not possible to follow Stravropoulos in his next sentence as he goes on to say: *The Church is set before them as a model as they are invited to build their 'little domestic church' together as they seek the unity, catholicity and apostolicity of the Great Church.* This is not what Chrysostom would have taught as he saw the Church not as an image for them, but something they partook of because it was that which gave the sacramental character to marriage.

43   Stylianopoulos T., 'Toward a Theology of Marriage in the Orthodox Church', *The Greek Orthodox Theological Review* 22(1977), 276.

44   Quoted in Guroian, *Family Virtue in Post-Christendom World* 333–334. The original is a doctorial dissertation: Christo G., *The Church's Identity Established Through Images According to St. John Chrysostom*, University of Durham, 1990.

45   Chrysostom J., *The Homilies of St. John Chrysostom on the Acts of the Apostles*, in *A Select Library of Nicene and Post-Nicene Fathers of the Christian Church*, First Series vol. 11, Homily 26, Eerdmans, Grand Rapids, 1956, p. 127.

46   Stephanopoulos R. G., 'Marriage and Family in Ecumenical Perspective', *St Vladimir's Theological Quarterly* 25(1981), 27.

47   Rahner K., *Theological Investigation, 10*, Darton, Longman & Todd, London, 1973, p. 220.

48   Although Blastares states that marriage is established 'through a blessing, or crowning, or contract', it is the engagement that is the object of the contract. This contract involved penalties for those who broke off a formal engagement ceremony. It must be remembered that before the eleventh century, the formal betrothal was a separate ceremony involving the exchange of rings. See Viscuso P., *The Formation of Marriage in Late Byzantium*, St Vladimir's Theological Quarterly, vol. 35(1991), 310–312.

49   *Acta Synodalia* vol. II pars II session L: 21–23. Cf. also 'Il Concilio Vaticano II Secondo Periodo', 1963–1964 vol. III, *La Civiltà Cattolica*, Rome, 1966, p. 117.

50   Tamden coniuges christiani, virtute matrimonii sacramenti, quo mysterium unitatis et fecundi amoris inter Christum et Ecclesiam significant atque participant (cf. Eph. 5.32), se invicem in vita coniugale necnon prolis susceptione et educatione ad sanctitatem adiuvant, adeoque in suo vitae statu et ordine proprium suum in Populo Dei donum habent. Ex hoc enim connubio procedit familia, in qua nascuntur novi societatis humanae cives, qui per Spiritus Sancti gratiam, ad Populum Dei saeculorum decursu perpetuandum, baptismo in filios Dei constituuntur. In hac velut Ecclesia domestica parentes verbo et exemplo sint pro filiis suis primi fidei praecones, et vocationem unicuique propriam, sacram vero peculiari cura, foveant oportet. 'Finally, Christian spouses, in virtue of the sacrament of Matrimony, signify and partake of the mystery of that unity and fruitful love which exists between Christ and His Church (Eph. 5.32), help each other to attain to holiness in their married life and in the rearing and education of their children. By reason of their state and rank in life, they have their own special gift among the people of God (1 Cor. 7.7). From the wedlock of Christians there comes the family, in which new citizens of human society are born, who by the grace of the Holy Spirit received in baptism are made children of God, thus perpetuating the People of God through the centuries. The family is, so to speak, the domestic Church.' *Lumen Gentium* n. 11.

51   Vorgimler H. (ed.), *Commentary on the Documents of Vatican II*, vol. 1. Burns & Oates, London, 1967, p. 164. This is very clear from the reference to St Augustine and the literal translation of the text. 'In this just as (velut) in the domestic church the parents are by word and example the first heralds of the faith with regard to their children, and must foster the vocation which is proper to each child and with truly special care if it be religion.'

52   Simbahayan Philippine Bishops' website. http://www.simbahayan.ph/teachings.html

53   *Familiaris Consortio* 21. The previous lines are: The Christian family is also called to experience a new and original

communion, which confirms and perfects natural and human communion. In fact the grace of Jesus Christ, 'the first-born among many brethren' (56) is by its nature and interior dynamism 'a grace of brotherhood,' as St Thomas Aquinas calls it. (57) The Holy Spirit, who is poured forth in the celebration of the sacraments, is the living source and inexhaustible sustenance of the supernatural communion that gathers believers and links them with Christ and with each other in the unity of the Church of God.

54   This is very clear from the explanations of the role of the domestic church that follows in nn. 50ff.

55   The use of the term 'Orthodox' is generic rather than specific. Technically, there is no such thing as an Orthodox Church, rather there are the orthodox churches of Eastern Europe, Russia and America. Yet they do have a common approach to the theology of marriage and hence the use of 'Orthodox' here as a generic term.

56   Timothy Buckley's book *What binds Marriage?: Roman Catholic Theology in Practice,* Geoffrey Chapman, London, 1997, is a clear example of the difficulties such an approach brings.

57   See Charalambidis S., 'Marriage in the Orthodox Church', *One in Christ,* 15(1979), 207–208, n. 8.

58   Meyendorff J., 'Mariage et Eucharistie', *Le Messenger Orthodoxe,* Paris, 49–50 (1970), 15.

59   Charalambidis, 'Marriage in the Orthodox Church', 209.

60   *Familiaris Consortio* emphasizes the same point. The Christian family is grafted into the mystery of the Church to such a degree as to become a sharer, in its own way, in the saving mission proper to the Church: by virtue of the sacrament, Christian married couples and parents 'in their state and way of life have their own special gift among the People of God'. For this reason they not only receive the love of Christ and become a saved community, but they are also called upon to communicate Christ's love to their brethren, thus becoming a saving community. In this way, while the Christian family is a fruit and sign of the supernatural fecundity of the Church, it stands also as a symbol, witness and participant of the Church's motherhood.

61   Obviously there is more than one Orthodox wedding service with sometimes different prayers. The following is

based on the Greek Orthodox rite. For other rites see Kenneth Stevenson, *Nuptial Blessing*, Alcuin Club/SPCK, London, 1982.

62   Evdokimov P., *The Sacrament of Love: The Nuptial Mystery in the light of the Orthodox Tradition*, St Vladimirs Seminary Press, Crestwood, NY, 1985, p. 118.

63   It quotes Rom. 9.25–26; Eph. 2.11–22, 3.3–6; Hos. 1 & 2. Cf Stylianopoulos, *Towards a Theology of Marriage in the Orthodox Church*, 253.

64   Evdokimov, *The Sacrament of Love*, 1985, p. 158.

65   The reception of communion was the ideal. However, in modern times the Eucharist is not always received by the couple, particularly if this is a second or third marriage.

66   Chrysostom J., PG 62, 387.

67   *Familiaris Consortio* n. 50.

68   The gift of Jesus Christ is not exhausted in the actual celebration of the sacrament of marriage, but rather accompanies the married couple throughout their lives. *Familiaris Consortio* n. 56. See also *Gaudium et Spes* n. 48.

69   Those who come for a second or third marriage are not given Holy Communion but a cup of blessing. See St John Chrysostom. Stylianopoulos, *Towards a Theology of Marriage in the Orthodox Church*, pp. 262–263 quotes Trembelas as finding its origin in the Pre-Sanctified Liturgy. He also observes that the common cup of wine given to the couple is a very ancient tradition found in Jewish marriages. For several centuries both a common cup of milk and honey and communion were given to the married couple. Tertullian and Hippolitus bear witness to this. A thorough historical study of the cup has not yet been done.

70   Charalambidis, *Marriage in the Orthodox Church*, 210.

71   *Familiaris Consortio*, n. 57.

72   *Familiaris Consortio*, nn. 55, 57.

73   Smireensky A. N., *The Evolution of the Present Rite of Matrimony and Parallel Canonical Developments*, St Vladimir's Seminary Quarterly, 8(1964), 44.

74   Although canon law requires a Catholic to marry according to the Catholic Rite of marriage unless a dispensation is given, and sees every marriage according to the Rite between Catholics as sacramental, there is an ongoing controversy over this stand. Some canon lawyers such as

Lawler require faith for this to be true. See Lawler M. G., *Marriage and Sacrament: A Theology of Christian Marriage*, Liturgical Press, Collegeville, 1993.

75 Paul VI's Apostolic Letter on *Mixed Marriages* in 1970 acknowledged the validity, sacredness and lawfulness of these marriages even if they were presided over by a Protestant minister provided the necessary dispensations have been obtained. It should be noted that the document specifically excludes the Orthodox churches, which are exempt from the canonical form. *Orientalium Ecclesiarum* n. 13. Schmaus M., *Dogma 5 The Church as Sacrament*, Sheed & Ward, London, 1975, p. 279, says this is based on the recognition of Vatican II of the major non-Catholic Christian communities as church.

76 *Familiaris Consortio* n. 57.

77 Ibid.

78 *Familiaris Consortio* n. 50.

79 *Gratissimam Sane* n. 13.

80 *Lumen Gentium* n. 11.

81 Ibid.

82 Underhill E., *Worship*, Crossroad Publishing Company, New York, 1936, p. 3.

83 Evdokimov P., *The Sacrament of Love*, p. 87. This is exactly contrary to those who view the bishop/priest as unworldly and holy in contrast to the laity who are worldly and unholy.

84 *Familiaris Consortio* n. 51.

85 Ibid., n. 56.

86 This is achieved because 'Christ ... fully discloses man to himself and unfolds his noble calling' *Gaudium et Spes* n. 22.

Chapter Six

The Marital Sacrament

As has been noted before, marriage is a complex domain where civil and canon law, moral and sacramental theology intersect. This is because marriage is both a civil and religious reality. This double reality has often bedevilled descriptions regarding the sacrament of marriage and led to many different explanations depending on where the emphasis is placed. As a civil reality, the determinant is the contract; as a religious reality, marriage is a covenant. Thus, some theologians have concluded that means the basis of the sacrament is found, either in the contract or in the covenant, a choice between understanding marriage as the sacrament of the bond – a contract, or as a sacrament of love – a covenant that unites the couple. However, this approach presents a false dichotomy, as marriage is both these realities at the same time. The tendency, because of this, is to speak of parallel realities so that the solution can be found in identifying the sacrament with the contract, as it is a parallel reality to a covenant. The result has been that in the past the explanation of the sacramentality of marriage has been dominated by its legal reality so much so that the essence of marriage as a sacrament has been difficult to discern. However, the difficulty is not only that legalism obscures sacramentality, but also the whole approach is unacceptable as the scriptural image of marriage is the love that Christ has for His Church, which implies a covenant not a contract. Failure to appreciate this scriptural image has caused a whole series of difficulties. When other theological preconceptions are added to the picture, it is not surprising that the marital sacrament had an impoverished theology.

One of the preconceptions was the Augustinian vision of human sexuality vitiated by concupiscence. In medieval times it led to the idea that marriage was a remedy for concupiscence so Albert the Great and many others speak of a multiple institution of marriage. It is important to point out that in Augustinian thought concupiscence was both a theological and biological concept. As a theological concept it was original sin, and as a biological concept it was the disorder that reigned among the senses that was particularly evident in sexual attraction and the urge to breed. Thus, marriage was instituted in the Garden of Eden, but because of the sin of Adam and Eve that gave rise to concupiscence it was re-instituted as a remedy for concupiscence. In modern times, the idea continued causing sexual acts to be seen as outside the sacramental sphere. Theologians like Martelet, who composed a large part of *Humanae Vitae*, understood married love to be limited and sexual acts to be an obstacle to the full conversion of conjugal love into charity because of its physical dimension. The cause of this is the transitory nature of physical love and its inherent pleasure, and the fact that Christ does not have a physical love for the Church. For Martelet, true love is a dispossession of self, which physical love reacts against. Yet those who are married find marital relationships call not for dispossession, but for union where the other is accepted in every way. Nor can the couple exclude physical love from the relationship. They find no rapport with Martelet's analysis.

This is not the only problem. Further difficulties arose from the choice of marital consent as the essence of marriage. A common medieval practice was to hold marriage in the Church porch where enquires were made about impediments and freedom to marry and consent exchanged. More often than not, the newly married couple then went into the church for mass and a blessing, but this was not obligatory. Though the blessing and the veiling of the bride went back to Roman times, a religious ceremony was not compulsory as marriage did not technically need a specific blessing to become a sacrament, because for early Christians, life was already blessed and grace-filled. So, in the thirteenth century when scholastic theologians used Aristotelian metaphysics to look for the sign of marriage, they did not take the blessing, but the consent between the spouses as the sign. The reason behind this was not only custom, but also the fact that if the blessing were necessary, it meant that the sacrament of marriage was transitory and would not be a continuing source of grace, or a personal union with God, or a help to fulfil the duties of married life. Yet if the blessing were unnecessary, marriage would be, as Luther later claimed, a secular affair. To avoid all this, the majority taught the marital bond formed by consent was the essence of the sacrament.

However, consent, as the basis of the sacrament, led to a further interpretation where the priest was unnecessary for a marriage to be sacramental. Thomas Aquinas wrote: 'But in marriage [the spouses'] acts are the sufficient cause for producing the proximate effect, which is the bond (*obligatio*), because whoever is of age (*sui juris*) can bind himself to another. Hence the priest's blessing is not needed in marriage for the essence of the sacrament.'[1] The conclusion was that the contract brought about the sacrament. So it is not surprising, with this interpretation, that celebrating marriage before a priest was not obligatory in the West before the Council of Trent, and only thereafter to avoid clandestine marriages. Nor is it surprising that what followed was the secularization of marriage as all that remained was the contractual view of marriage. So, the long-term effect was that marriage became a sacrament in search of a theology. What was left was the phrase 'Christ raised marriage to the dignity of a sacrament' and a long debate over whether the sacrament was merely a blessing, separate from the contract – if this was true, the contractual part of marriage was purely secular, and the blessing purely religious – or whether the sacrament was the contract, or in someway irrevocably joined to the contract. The conclusion was the latter, but this only led to further difficulties.

Thus it is not surprising that recently, a prominent canon lawyer stated that: 'Marriage as such has no religion. It is neither Jewish, nor Catholic nor even civil.'[2] In one sense this is true. Those who marry at a Register Office often believe this, and canon lawyers speak of the Church exercising jurisdiction over the marriages of the faithful. Legally, marriage has no religion. But culturally and theologically this is false. Marriage is always connected to certain ceremonies; and marriage was not invented by humankind, but is the express design of God.[3] The intuitive sense of human society that marriage has a deep religious significance cannot be ignored.

Yet the expression and understanding of this religious significance has been very weak. The clearest example of this is the explanation that Christian marriage only differs from that of the unbaptized by Christ's decree raising Christian marriage to the status of a sacrament. This declaration was merely external and did not affect the nature of the union, so the special graces of the married state are attached as a kind of appendage understood by the spouses as a blessing on their marriage. In everyday terms, a man marries a woman, which is a civil act that is raised to a sacrament by the blessing of the priest. The sacrament is an external embellishment.[4] This approach fits exactly the underlying position of those who see marriage in church as a beautiful ceremony to which they have a right because they were baptized even though they no longer practise or believe. Their right is to come and get their marriage blessed. It is also evident in the civil sphere, for example in France, where a civil ceremony at the mayor's office takes place before a religious ceremony in the church.

By the middle of the nineteenth century a theological cul-de-sac had been reached in the Latin Church whereby marriage was left as a sacrament almost without a theology. A new beginning was necessary that asked what happened if the sacrament did affect the marriage. But exploring this was not easy as theologians were weighed down by previous concepts, particularly the union of contract and sacrament in Christian marriage. The difficulty was that all the baptized who exchange wedding vows create not only a contract but also a sacrament. This meant the theologian had to answer a three-part question. First, what makes a natural marital contract become a sacramental sign and how is this a sign of the relationship of Christ to His Church? Second, how can the marriages of Christians be a sacrament when they have no religious practice and show no sign of faith? Third, how can lapsed Christians participate in the sacrament as a means of holiness especially when they are the ministers of the sacrament? Have Christians nothing to contribute to the sacrament beyond consent? [5]

Development flowed from the first question, which asked what is the link between the sacramental sign of marriage and the relationship between Christ and His Church? Various theories were put forward. Billot in 1897 proposed a Christological answer in that Christ has a physical union with human nature, and a spiritual union with the Church. Likewise, marriage has a physical union in the body and a spiritual union with Church. Thus marriage was seen to be similar to the union of Christ and His Church. But Scheeben in 1880 had already made a more fruitful suggestion by concentrating on Christian marriage as a visible sign of the relationship of Christ to His Church because marriage is the great mystery of Ephesians 5.32.[6] Therefore Christian marriage is not just a sign or an external example of the mystery of Christ and the Church, as Billot held, instead Christian marriage is 'rooted in this mystery and organically connected to it and so partakes of its nature and mysterious character ...

Marriage does not merely symbolize that mystery. It really represents it in itself and represents it by showing itself to be active and effective in it.'[7] This occurs because the union of the baptized through their baptism makes them part of the mystical body of Christ. Thus marriage partakes in the sacramental sphere because of this and must represent the union of Christ and His Church for the same reason.

The import of this insight was to be decisive. The move from an image concept of Billot to the participatory concept of Scheeben meant that a purely contractual understanding of marriage was impossible because there was no contract between Christ and His Church. Instead, the participation in the love of Christ for His Church could only take place if marriage was seen as a covenant. Love was shared because the covenant was shared. However to share in the love of Christ for His Church, it was necessary to be part of the mystical body of Christ through baptism. By sharing in the mystical body, the Church, the marriage covenant took on a different aspect. The covenant now became a sacramental reality. Thus, Christian marriage is rooted in the covenant of baptism, which blossoms through the total self-giving of the spouses into the covenant of marriage. A renewed theological foundation of marriage had been identified that was to form the basis of modern theological reflection.

However, the second question concerning marriages of Christians who do not practise and show no sign of faith was far more difficult to resolve. Its basis is still enshrined today in Canon 1055. This canon states that: 'the marriage covenant … has between the baptized been raised to the dignity of a sacrament'. Then it continues 'Consequently, a valid marriage contract cannot exist between baptized persons without its being by that very fact a sacrament.' Accordingly, is marriage between the baptized a sacrament because of their baptism alone when the non-practice, even unbelief of many baptized today is taken into account? The practice of infant baptism has led to those who do not know the Christian faith, let alone practise it and have almost no contact with the Church except to be baptized, married and buried. Have Christians nothing to contribute to the sacrament of marriage beyond consent?

Any answer to this question had to take two factors into account, the role of faith and the realization that baptism is the basis of the sacrament of marriage. As regards the role of baptism there was unanimous agreement that this is the basis of the sacrament, although what this implied is rarely clearly spelt out. As regards faith, the problem was that the idea of marriage as a contract had correctly identified the necessity of a gift of self as the basis of marriage, but failed to discern that for such a gift to be sacramental it needed more than baptism. The vital question was: 'What is a real human act on a sacramental plane?' The intention to marry showed what was taking place, but how did faith enter into such an act so that it became a sacramental act, particularly as the spouses are ministers of the sacrament. In other words, is faith necessary for an efficacious sign, or does the very fact of their baptism makes the spouse's consent an efficacious sign of the sacrament of marriage? In 1977 the International Theological Commission said: 'The intention of carrying out what Christ and the Church desire is the minimum condition required before the consent is considered to be a "real human act" on the sacramental plane. The problem of the intention and that of personal faith of the contracting parties must not be confused, but they must not be totally separated either. In the last analysis the real intention is born from and feeds on living faith.'[8] Thus the intention to do what the Church requires by using the marriage rite is not sufficient. A living faith must enliven this act.[9] So, canonists like Orsy and Lawler reject that marriage between the baptized is a sacrament because of their baptism alone.[10]

What is implied here is that a contract cannot adequately portray the marital sacrament. Although the phrase 'Christ the Lord raised the matrimonial contract

between baptized persons to the level of a sacrament'
found in the 1917 Code has its origin in the Council of
Trent's desire to defend the sacramentality of marriage,
theologians before the second Vatican Council were
uneasy about how a contract became a sacrament. In fact,
while the Latin Church chose the sign of contract, the
Orthodox Church chose the sign of the marriage blessing
to indicate the sacrament.[11] Unfortunately, the sign of
contract obscured the sacrament, and the sign of the
marital blessing alone tended to make the sacrament
external to the marriage, so a different approach was
necessary. Such a different approach is implied in the
third question because if the ministers of the sacrament of
marriage are those exchanging vows, what differentiates
their marriage from those doing exactly the same who are
unbaptized? What do Christians contribute beyond
consent?

The answer given was that baptism means that the
Christian participates in Christ, and thus the giving of
consent is sacramental. Rondet and Scheeben use the
phrase 'insertion of the spouses in the body of Christ' and
suggest the sacrament of marriage works because
marriage is a second insertion into the body of Christ.
Mersch explains that the nature of the union of Christ to
humanity shows marriage as a participation in the life of
Christ. Martelet insists it is not the man and the woman
who make marriage a sacrament, but Christ who makes
the union a sacrament. All the human person can do is to
dispose themselves for such a union.[12] Schillebeeckx takes
this further by saying in baptism the Christian not only
participates in Christ, but also participates in Christ the
Sacrament so that the baptized person becomes a manifestation of Christ. So, the spouses' self-giving is an exercise
of priesthood in the Church.[13] Later, *Lumen Gentium*,
which had placed the sacrament of marriage within the
priesthood of the laity, said: 'spouses in virtue of the sacrament of matrimony signify and partake of the mystery of
that unity and fruitful love which exists between Christ

and His Church.'[14] Thus a living faith means the ability to participate in the life of Christ. Hence, the traditional intuition that the foundation for Christian marriage is baptism is correct, not as Gaalaas points out, as a general basis for any sacrament, but as the reason why marriage is a sacrament.[15] What was necessary was an explanation of how the sacrament of marriage develops from the sacrament of baptism.

To answer this it is necessary to explore three points. First, to ask does the concept of marriage as a natural sacrament, which can be found in the early medieval theologians, form a basis for marriage to be a Christian sacrament? If this is so, then the natural conjugal love expressed in marital consent is raised to the level of a sacrament. Second, a re-examination of Ephesians 5.21–33 reinforces Scheeben's conclusion that marriage is more than a visible sign of the relationship of Christ to His Church. Christian marriage springs forth from this relationship as human love is transformed because the root of marriage is in baptism and this baptismal root blossoms in marriage through the self-giving of the spouses. Third, a sacrament that gives grace must transform the receiver. In the case of Christian marriage this takes place because of the abiding presence of Christ with the spouses throughout their life. Thus Christian marriage is salvational because as Cooke argues there is a hermeneutic of experience where a family story is a Christ-like story.[16]

These three points reflect the approach found in the documents of Vatican II. Before the Council the main concern was how the marriage contract was sacramental. Since the Council the emphasis has been on the ecclesial basis of the sacrament of marriage, and what this means. In doing this, theologians had to explore the inter-connection between the baptism and marriage, and probe the meaning of why Ephesians used the analogy of the love of Christ for His Church to explain Christian marriage. Obviously this is a huge agenda of which theologians have only recently begun to scratch the surface. But already it is revealing insights into the sacrament that have been forgotten or not explored for centuries.

Marriage is a Natural Sacrament

The first logical step is to ask: What is the connection between non-sacramental and sacramental marriage?[17] The traditional answer to this was that Christ raised marriage to the level of a sacrament by blessing an existing institution. But how was this possible? What was the basis in natural marriage so that it is possible for it to be a sacrament? The traditional solution found in the writings of St Albert and the early scholastic theologians was that marriage is a natural sacrament.[18] Albert held that the sacrament was instituted in the Garden of Eden because both the essential characteristics of marriage are present here. As an *officium*, a duty, it was instituted in the bringing together of the first man and woman. As a sacrament it is found in the indestructibility of the words: 'This one at last is bone of my bones and flesh of my flesh.' For Albert, Christ confirms this by saying: 'What God has joined together man must not separate.' Thus marriage begins from the natural complementarity of man and woman which takes on a new reality in a permanent relationship. This explanation reflects the Roman definition of *coniunctio*, the union that is a sharing of life.

With the change of the meaning of *coniunctio* to the permanence of the union and the emphasis on procreation by the later theologians, the import of this natural complementarity was hardly ever explored until Dietrich von Hildebrand resurrected the earlier meaning through his study of St Albert the Great. If marriage is a sharing of life, the natural complementarity of man and woman, it meant that marriage is not for something; rather it is a communion of persons with a meaning and a value within itself. As von Hildebrand said: 'Marriage is an I-Thou relationship, a face to face relationship, a becoming-one of two persons. It is not a side-by-side relationship ordered to reaching some goal outside of itself.'[19] This is what Genesis meant when it describes the communion of Adam and Eve as 'they are no longer two, but one flesh'. By applying Christian Personalism to marriage and asking what this special relationship meant, von Hildebrand identified the essence of marriage: getting married is to live in love. This key idea, later to be taken up at the Second Vatican Council, means that marriage is not to be simply interpreted as ordained to procreation. Children are the fruit of sexual intercourse, but the essence of marriage is conjugal love because this expresses the total self-giving of the spouses not merely in a physical sense, but also in a personal sense. This approach saw sexual acts in marriage in a different light – as *Gaudium et Spes* says: 'a man and a woman, who by the marriage covenant of conjugal love "are no longer two, but one flesh" render mutual service to each other through an intimate union of their persons and of their actions, and experience and grow in the meaning of their oneness, day by day.'[20]

Usually, the effect of this rehabilitation of sexuality is thought to apply only to the sexual ethics of marriage. In fact, it is a crucial part of the renewal of the theology of marriage. By understanding the completeness of the transformation that the sacrament achieves in Christian marriage, because no part of the relationship between the spouses could be excluded, even the physical expression of marital love was graced.[21] For example in 1927 von Hildebrand wrote: 'In as much as it is wedded love it can incorporate organically the act of marital union into the life of the person. In as much as it is love it can specifically ennoble ... Love alone represents an activity, an actualisation of the spiritual person so central and intensely conscious through and through that it keeps up with the supreme activity or actuation of the body in the act of wedlock. Hence love alone can even at this moment maintain the sovereignty of the spirit over the body.'[22] Yet this thesis could not be accepted immediately. The majority of theologians still clung to the Augustinian analysis that marriage was a remedy for concupiscence. The concept of a graced physical expression of marital love was not really accepted until the 1970s even though the thesis of *Gaudium et Spes* is that: 'the divine law reveals and protects the integral meaning of conjugal love, and impels it toward a truly human fulfilment'.[23]

What has happened is this. Instead of seeing all sexual acts as driven by lust, the Church now accepts that physical sexual acts should arise from love and are expressions of that love. As expressions of that love, such acts are graced. So a major change had taken place. By beginning, as von Hildebrand did, from marriage as a natural sacrament, relationship gives meaning to marriage. This relationship is worked out during a marriage as sexual desire is absorbed into married love. There is no longer a distinction between *amor*, sex and *caritas*, love because marriage as a sign of the love of Christ and His Church is a glimpse and a participation in divine love. Sexuality in marriage is a good in itself. However, this does not mean that any sexual act even within marriage is right. The correct basis will always be self-gift and loving reception. Thus lust, the seeking of pleasure for itself and not as a gift to the other is wrong. Self-seeking is always destructive of two-in-oneness. Total self-giving is very different as it imitates the total self-gift that Christ made of himself for the Church.

Therefore, marriage begins from the natural complementarity of man and woman, which takes on a new reality in a permanent relationship.[24] This is expressed in a self-gift that is lovingly received, that is completely transformed by the sacrament so that no part of the relationship between the spouses is excluded. Even the physical relationship between them is graced. Christian marriage is under the reign of grace. These conclusions form the basis of further reflection. Yet this is only the beginning. To take this further it is necessary to explain how Christ is the basis of the sacrament of marriage as found in the letter to the Ephesians.

Marriage is a Visible Sign of the Relationship of Christ to His Church

Already there was a long tradition of Christ being the basis of Christian marriage. For example, when Albert the Great speaks of marriage becoming a sacrament, he uses a traditional explanation found in the Early Church. The two natures of Christ changed natural marriage into Christian marriage because by becoming man, Christ was able to draw together the divine and the earthly of marriage so it became a sacrament. The joining together in one flesh was not merely the union of the couple but a participation in Christ, highlighting the humanness that is changed in the marital sacrament. By uniting the couple in Christ, the sacrament of marriage brings about a new reality, as Ephesians teaches, because the basis of Ephesians is the proclamation of the *Mysterion*, Christ the sacrament. The flesh of Christ brought about the gift of new life (Ephesians 2.14–18) and Christians share in this new life by being incorporated into the flesh of Christ by baptism. The spouses, by being two in one flesh in Christian marriage share in the same mystery, Ephesians 5.21–33. Thus Christian marriage does not merely represent this mystery but enfleshes the mystery.

These statements need unpacking, as they are the way into the great mystery of Christian marriage. Ephesians portrays Christ as the *Mysterion*, the door to a new existence. Those who open this door through baptism become incorporated into the Church because Christ married the Church and through the image of a marriage bath (baptism) the Church is saved. But Christ is not simply the door; he is the new existence whose basis is love. Christ's love of the Church both typifies what Christian life is and is the new existence. Applying this to Christian marriage, Ephesians writes: 'Husbands love your wives as Christ loved the Church and gave himself for her to make her holy, in that he purified her by cleansing in the water by the Word to prepare the Church in splendour for himself without spot or wrinkle or any such thing but rather that she might be holy and blameless' (Eph. 5.26–27).[25] In other words, the baptized who marry, because they are already incorporated into Christ, integrate their marriage into the Church so that when a Christian man marries a Christian woman through their baptism and their love they enter a new life that is not only externally visible to all as a couple, but also portrays a new Christian reality.

Fundamental to this being a new reality is the sacrament of baptism. The problem is that baptism is often portrayed as a necessity for the other sacraments without examining the meaning of the relationship it establishes with them. Traditionally baptism is a putting on of Christ. The baptized becomes a child of God and a member of the Church. It is only through this incorporation into Christ and into the Church that the Christian enters into the world of grace and can participate in the other sacraments. It must be underlined that the incorporation is not simply into Christ, but of necessity implies becoming part of the Church because Christ is present today through His Church. Moreover, participation in the world of grace is not simply through membership, as if the Christian is merely a receiver. The integration into the Church is real so that the Christian is able to participate in the life of Christ. Thus sacramental relationships come through the Church.

When this approach is applied to the relationship between the sacraments of baptism and marriage, several strands of meaning appear illuminating what two-in-one flesh means. First, the relationship between baptism and marriage as sacraments is based on the fact that Christian marriage does not simply flow from baptism, but is a flowering of the covenant of baptism through the covenant of marriage. The putting on of Christ in baptism is the most basic covenant of all. In itself, it is a two-in-oneness as the baptized is joined to Christ. For a Christian, this covenant through faith and love is relived in the marriage covenant. Just as the first covenant brings about a two-in-oneness of being joined to Christ, the marriage covenant brings about a similar two-in-oneness in being joined to each other through Christ. This occurs because in every sign there are two layers of meaning. All who marry in their desire for unity fulfil the literal sense of the marriage covenant. The sacramental sense takes this unity a step further in that personal two-in-oneness becomes a union in Christ and in His Church. This is why Ephesians teaches that married love partakes of the love of Christ for His Church.

This approach is clearly seen in the John Paul II's *Theology of the Body*. A long biblical tradition, which underlines marriage as a sacramental sign, finds its origin in the covenant between God and His people. This union goes far beyond a pact because it is a personal bond that can only be expressed by the word, covenant.[26] The spousal bond, two-in-one-flesh means the body speaks in the language of a personal gift, a covenant. As this covenant is a participation in the union of Christ and the Church, this language is the language of love.[27]

Taking this analysis a step further, it must be remembered that every sacrament is a sharing in Christ the sacrament, because every sacrament reveals a different dimension of the Paschal Mystery of Christ's dying and rising. In baptism, the symbolism is the descent into the water and the rising out of the water to new life. Marriage as a sacrament reveals the Paschal Mystery both in the sacrifices married life brings and the experience of the ups and downs of the relationship. The sacrifice that love demands of Christ is dying and rising. The sacrifice that love demands in marriage is also a dying to self and rising to togetherness. Yet this is not the only parallel that is present in Christian marriage because marriage also reveals the Paschal mystery as a participation in the Church, a way of salvation. Thus, nothing in marriage is purely secular; everything has a salvific purpose in God's plan for humanity.

To understand these parallels, it is necessary to accept that marriage as the loving union between Christ and His

Church is more than a metaphor. Marriage objectively represents this love of God for His Church partaking of this love so that marriage becomes the sign of that love. Marriage enfleshes divine love.[28] For this to be a reality, Rahner says three factors are essential. First, that the will of God working in the reality of marriage itself gives rise to genuine personal human relationships in conjugal love. The key here is the interconnection between the spouses. The divine model of this is the conjugal love that exists between Christ and the Church, a genuine love based on the sacrifice of the Cross. Marriage calls for the same sacrifice, possible because the participation in divine love raises human love to a new level, a sacramental level.

This sacramental participation cannot simply be reduced to the duties and responsibilities of married life. Love is expressed through human feelings and actions. The participation in the Paschal Mystery calls for the whole person to take part, so the spouses portray this mystery physically, mentally and spiritually in their life. This union of persons in a two-in-oneness gives sexuality a new meaning where sexual pleasure takes on its true sense of a remnant of paradise and a participation in creation. This is present in the self-sacrifice that such love demands; it is there in the total self-giving which is the basis of conjugal love, and is there in the bond such a relationship causes to be felt by the partners. This can be seen in the way a couple interact and gives special meaning to touching, embracing and kissing. They give the phrase 'personal love' a very special meaning and bind together the couple. Each interlocks with the other to show that feelings are transmitted more completely by actions than words. In every way they show that describing human relationships as mating on a purely biological or logical sphere is seriously inaccurate.[29] Rather, marriage through human feeling and actions portrays a gift of oneself. In everyday terms, real love costs, hurts, binds and gives pleasure.

Second, Rahner said, marriage has a real capacity to

represent or typify God's love in Christ for the 'one humanity', the Church, which he made holy. Marriage is in the order of salvation. It makes redemption possible for the spouses as well as the community because both take part in the mystery of Christ's love being made visible in the couple's love for each other. In this way the spouses sanctify one another and sanctify the community. Here is the origin of family in every sense. It is in this sense that baptism brings about the family of God and it is in terms of family that the human race was to become children of God.[30] As the essence of family is the web of relationships, the human image of family portrays a divine mystery of relationships to the extent that some theologians speak of the Trinitarian aspect of marriage.

This portrayal of relationships as an embodiment of the mystery of divine relationships is an insight into the inter-relationship of the sacraments of baptism and marriage that is rarely explored. Certainly, in terms of family, the Old Testament understood the relationship between Yahweh and His people Israel, and took the human concept of marriage to express this relationship. Likewise, the union between Christ and His Church is an expression of family. Thus the union between husband and wife is the basis of family in several senses where family has both a biological and spiritual dimension. It is in this co-opera-tion with the Creator that the family is creative in bringing forth new life that is not only biological, but also spiritual in that their children through baptism also share in the life of Christ. But there is another level here that can easily be overlooked. Family relationships are covenantal relation-ships not only because of blood relationships but also because of the kind of links a marriage brings about. A wedding unites two different family groups in a special relationship, a mutual gift and acceptance of persons imposing fidelity and an unbreakable oneness. Even though these relationships may substantially change, the knot of covenantal relationships remains, which is so often evident at funerals where relatives and friends appear that never meet except at these occasions. These relationships are part of a special providence in the plan of God.

These dimensions are the reason why Rahner holds that love is not an idea, or something external to God, but a lived reality. This is the third factor found in the union of humanity in Christ that brings forth the Church. As Rahner says, humanity is incarnated in the Church because through the Incarnation of the Son of God, the Church is able to exist.[31] Thus taking Scheeben's concept of marriage, being a participation in the Body of Christ, to its logical conclusion, Christian marriage partakes of the nature and the mysterious character of Christ's union with his Church because baptism as the foundation of Christian marriage incorporates a Christian marriage into the Church. This means that the mysterious character of Christ's union with the Church makes it possible for the unity of man and wife to be transformed into a new reality in the Kingdom of God, the kingdom present in the nuptial community. They do not just symbolize the mystery and love of Christ for his Church but communicate this mystery. In fact, as Mersch says: 'The marital home is not a domestic church because it is there the children first learn about God. Rather, the marital home is a domestic church because the spouses participate in the Church and their marital acts are acts of the Church.'[32]

Few married Christians realize that their marriage is a realization and a participation in the Church as sacrament. Yet this fact of being Church and showing what the Church is, is portrayed in several ways. First, the spouses realize the marital church through the gift of themselves they give to each other. This reflects Christ as sacrament because he is sacrament because of his self-communication not just through words or signs, but in that Christ gives his own self. Second, sacraments are only possible because Christ became man and joined humanity with God. It is this presence in their marriage that makes their marriage a sacrament. Third, the domestic church is a unique revelation of this sacramental action because the domestic church stresses relationships. By doing this it underlines the meaning of covenant as belonging to a family. In many ways, the marriage covenant finds its flowering in the domestic church because marriage makes real the unity and love of Christ within the Church. Likewise, baptism finds one of its most potent expressions in the domestic church because it portrays the essence of baptism, family in every sense – family as creative, family within the life giving Church. It is in this way that Christian marriage is a sacrament because it brings to life the love of Christ.

While this participation in the Church through the domestic church is a specific realization of baptism,[33] a further strand in the relationship between baptism and marriage is found in the participation marriage has in the baptismal character. A character is the signature of a sacrament showing the consecration that has taken place.[34] In simple terms, it shows that a sacrament has been participated in: in baptism this character is a sign of being assimilated into Christ. It signifies a new state of life that is so permanent baptism could never be repeated. Likewise, marriage signifies a new state of life; Augustine taught marriage was a sacred pledge between husband and wife, a bond of fidelity that is akin to a character or mark that permanently united them. This throws light on the permanence of marriage. This permanence is not caused because the marriage imitates the permanent love of Christ for his Church, or simply because marriage is a covenant; nor does this permanence come from a marriage character because such a character does not have an independent existence. Rather, participating in the marital sacrament changes the character of baptism. Through the exchange of conjugal love the marriage participates in the love of Christ for His Church in a special way and so has a different relationship in the church and acquires a different signature. It is this new signature that is permanent and is commonly called the marital bond.

This approach is not new. Scheeben describes the

marriage character as 'the signature, which makes known that the members of God-man's mystical body belong to their divine-human head by assimilating them to Him, and testifies to their organic origin union with Him.'[35] This union only takes place because the two natures of Christ that can join together the divine and the human, so that in some way the marriage character is an analogy of the union of the two natures of Christ. As the two natures of Christ change natural marriage into Christian marriage, the signature of Christian marriage is different. Yet this does not mean that Christian marriage is perfect. While Christ's character is flooded with grace, our character only absorbs a tiny fraction because of human weakness and resistance. While it is necessary to understand the great height God intended for Christian marriage, the reality is sadly often very different. Yet comfort can be drawn from the Greek Fathers of the Church, who said the union to Christ still continues even when the partners are having a row.

Thus, covenant and conjugal love take on a new reality in Christian marriage through baptism. Total self-giving signifies this new reality because the model is the love Christ has for His Church. The two-in-oneness of the spouses is a new existence, a new Christian reality. Their incorporation into Christ and His Church through baptism flowers in the new sacramental relationship of the sacrament of marriage. They are joined to each other through Christ and because of that share in the Paschal Mystery of dying and rising. From this sharing in the Paschal Mystery they share in the Church. That is why a Christian family is a domestic church. Thus in Ephesians, marriage is more than a metaphor, it is a sacramental reality of the love of Christ for His Church. The spouses participate in divine love and typify through their love, God's love for us. But more than that, they enflesh this divine relationship so that their family and all its connections are brought into this relationship. Marriage is a participation story.

Marriage is a Salvation Story

Marriage is a sacrament for life, not just a blessing on the wedding day. It is not just a ceremony in church, but a total self-giving where baptism gives a new meaning to this gift incorporating the gift into the Church and into a new life. Conjugal love is changed so that *Gaudium et Spes* describes this new experience as merging the human with the divine.[36] Such a gift cannot be a single event, but is a continuous offering so that 'due to the unity of body and soul found in mutual help and service the partners sense an increase and fulfilment of their unity'.[37] Thus, the sacrament is participated in at each act of service and love and through these acts the marriage grows. The concept of marriage growth is nothing new. Psychologists have long identified certain key events in the life of the couple that alter the relationship between them. Principally these events are becoming parents, finding themselves alone again and becoming grandparents as well as the major traumas of life such as the death of parents, children's accidents and the death of a spouse. However, it is forgotten that in all these events the sacrament is present moulding and giving the spouses strength to change. There is a different experience of the sacrament of marriage at different stages of life. Yet traditionally little attention has been paid to the effect of the sacrament during married life, beyond exhortations to faithfulness and the bringing up of children in the faith, because the emphasis has been on what causes marriage. To explore the marital sacrament as a lived experience of grace requires rediscovering somewhat forgotten theological truths.

Before the twelfth century the number of sacraments was disputed. The vague definition of St Augustine that a sacrament was a sacred sign, or the definition of St Isidore that emphasized the hidden or mysterious power a sacrament had, resulted in different lists that included monastic profession and funerals.[38] The combination of these two approaches at the beginning of the Middle Ages meant that a sacrament depended on the sacred sign being an efficacious sign of grace that is important for salvation. The school of Abelard considered marriage a sacrament not because it conferred saving grace directly, but because it remedied an obstacle to salvation, concupiscence.[39] Later, Peter Lombard argued that concupiscence could never be suppressed without grace. Thus, matrimony must impart grace. Although the arguments had started from what we now know was a doubtful premise, concupiscence, the intuition of those theologians who followed was correct. The sacrament of marriage continues throughout life and transforms those who receive it; otherwise it is powerless.

If this is true, the presence of this sacrament should be discernable, particularly when it is remembered that 'sacraments are meant to be a special avenue of insight into the reality of God'.[40] Yet finding the sacramental sign for marriage has always proved difficult whether this was the sign of a marriage beginning or a marriage in existence. The Roman civil sign of marriage at its inception was consent, while, as St Ambrose shows, the religious sign was the veiling and blessing of the bride. However, these ancient religious signs were lost in the Middle Ages and consent became the religious sign, which under the influence of Duns Scotus developed into the handing over of exclusive sexual rights. Today, this has been converted into the total self-giving of the spouses to each other. But the sign of marriage is still the consent expressed in the marriage vows. The blessing of the spouses still takes place but it is a blessing of a marriage that has already taken place as consent has already been given by the spouses.

The mixture of civil and therefore legal signs with sacramental signs raises several problems. As the contract is a civil sign that can give rise to a non-sacramental marriage as well as a sacramental marriage, and as the sacrament of marriage does not only require baptism as a precondition for the sacrament, but also requires those marrying to live

their baptism, consent alone is an inadequate sign of
Christian marriage. Neither can the civil sign of a marriage
contract be the sacramental sign because it only brings the
marriage into existence and does not show how mutual
help and love sustains the whole of married life. If we look
at the natural signs of marriage, the human experience of
finding a partner begins with physical attraction based on
signs that a man and a woman find the other attractive.
Pairing then begins, as the couple begin to mutually
explore their relationship. Growth in this relationship, and
the stress such growth generates is obvious both in rows
and in making up. What is taking place at this stage is
finding out whether they are compatible. Only if this
succeeds will the question of marriage be approached. The
signs here are obvious: commitment to each other based
on compatibility, which leads to an absolute commitment
to each other. It is this commitment called love that is the
sign of marriage.

The transformation of this natural sign into a sacramental sign takes place because of baptism. Sacramentally,
marriage is a communion of both partners because the
covenant naturally forms a bond because of its basis in
baptism. This is why both Rahner and Cooke suggest that
the sign of the sacrament of marriage is the special friendship between husband and wife.[41] Doms calls this 'two-in-
oneness'. This should not be surprising if it is remembered
that we can only come into contact with spiritual realities
through our human experience.

A similar answer is evident if the problem of the sign of
marriage is approached from a different direction. Both
the practice of *economia* by the Eastern churches and the
approach of the three German bishops in 1993 to those in
second unions come to the same conclusion. Working
from the premise that a sacramental marriage is discernable in everyday life, they both asked: What are the signs
of a graced union? While most commonly *economia* is used
to discern the presence of baptism (a baptismal certificate
from a non-orthodox church is not sufficient), it is also

used to discern the presence or not of the sacrament of marriage where a marriage has broken down. Evidence of belief, prayer, and practice, particularly the celebration of the great feasts of Christmas and Easter is required because the pastoral discernment seeks evidence of the special relationship between husband and wife and the Church. This may be surprising to Western minds because the pastoral discernment does not only seek to find whether the couple are irreconcilable; it also finds whether the attachment to the Church is discernable because the marriage partakes in the Church. Likewise, the three German bishops put forward a similar approach. They required evidence of an enduring relationship and belonging to the Church through prayer, practice and repentance.[42] This double discernment of relationships shows that the sign of the enduring sacrament of marriage cannot simply be conjugal love; instead the participation in the Church and the bonds that the sacrament brings are part of the sign of marriage.

What is being sought here is evidence of the action of God. For a sacramental sign to be adequate it must reveal a dimension of the Paschal Mystery of Christ's dying, rising and ascension so that we can participate in His life. As the reality of God found in marriage is conjugal love, which is the special friendship that exists between husband and wife, this love is the way the spouses gain a special insight into the love of God. Yet marriage objectively represents this love of God for His Church and the spouses partake of this love so that their marriage becomes the sign of the Church. For Ephesians makes clear that Christ's relationship is not just a model for marriage but a participation in marriage. As Karl Rahner wrote:

> If conjugal unity and love only served in some vague sense as a simile for the loving union between Christ and the Church, if the two realities were only related metaphorically, the whole matter would be a very

incidental one. That cannot be the intention. Marriage and the covenant between God and humanity in Christ can not only be compared by us, they stand objectively in such a relation that matrimony objectively represents this love of God in Christ for the Church; the relation and the attitude of Christ to the Church is the model for the relation and attitude that belongs to marriage, and is mirrored by imitation in marriage so that the latter is something contained or involved in the former.[43]

This is why the special relationship between the spouses goes further in the sense that marriage is not just a new dynamic between two people, but is a new state of life.

Civilly and legally this is indicated in a variety of ways summed up in the term 'institution'. Yet, while the word institution accurately sums up the civil and legal reality, it conceals marriage's sacramental dimension because sacramentally this new state of life is summed up in the term, family, not in the sense of having children, but in the sense of the saving ties and links marriage brings about. It is these ties and links that are the couple's salvation story. Thus, marriage as a sacrament finds its origin in the spouses participating in Christ through baptism by means of the covenant they make. This participation in Christ means their marriage is integrated into the Church because marriage has an ecclesial reality as well as a personal reality. Their two-in-oneness is a sharing in the two-in-oneness of Christ so they both reveal the love of Christ and the reality of the Church. In Cooke's phrase they are: 'a word that expresses Christ's love for each of them' so that they are sacrament to each other and all that knows them.[44] Because of this married Christians bring the sacramental presence of Christ to the world.

But if Christian marriage is a sacrament it also means the sacrament transforms those who receive it. The life-long sacrament of marriage brings about change because sacraments are never static. The strengthening, maturing of the spouses' relationship, even though it may never reach its true perfection, is the work of the sacrament because Christ, the sacrament, brings unity to the marriage. He is the sacrament of oneness breaking down walls and rebuilding broken relationships. Only our human weakness prevents this from happening. Likewise, Christ the sacrament makes the idea of family a reality. While husband and wife are the basis of family, and family extends beyond the blood relations of this family in its links with other relatives, these links are covenantal relationships and therefore salvational relationships. In God's plan each link joins together and makes a strong unit portraying God's love and care for humankind. First, this is portrayed in the relationship between husband and wife where each partner strengthens the other, and makes Christ present to the other. Second, their children learn what love means by being loved. It is the school for the next generation. Third, relatives can draw comfort and strength in their life from the links family brings. God's plan was that family carried the sacrament of His love. Marriage was to be an evolving salvation story.

Yet sometimes this is not the case. Modern living separates families, and some members become detached. Not only that, human relationships can go badly wrong where some relatives are left out in the cold and children can be put out of the home. To this must be added the stresses and false expectations of modern life that leave the spouses badly bruised. It is the healing of these problems that the sacrament promotes in its saving dimension of reconciliation. Forgiving one another is an essential part of conjugal love and is a natural attribute of that love. However, this is only possible because human love participates in divine love. Forgiveness is a gift of God. It is in this sense that marriage as a natural sacrament reconciles. Christian marriage goes further not only because of the example of Christ who won for us the gift of reconciliation, but also because His presence in Christian marriage heals and repairs relationships. More exactly, the Christian marriage is incorporated into Christ and because of this takes part in the saving action of Christ.

Therefore, marriage is a salvation story where it is possible to discern the action of Christ within married life. The experience of love that heals and binds, and the experience of family life with all its joys and sadness make a tapestry where the changes brought about through the sacrament can be seen. Marriage is a real experience of the Paschal Mystery in its sorrows and joys. Likewise, marriage shows the work of God in bringing forth new life in every sense, not only in the birth of children, but also in the constant rebirth of the relationships marriage demands. The breakdown of any of the relationships, whether it is a quarrel with a brother or sister, or a serious dispute between the spouses that is difficult to heal, is experienced as the negation of all that marriage means. Going through death is not too strong an expression for that experience. Yet these are the salvational moments in married life because 'sacraments are meant to be a special avenue of insight into the reality of God'.[45] Healing is one of the principle works of the marital sacrament. All this cannot take place without realizing that it is the presence of Christ in marriage which is crucial to marriage being a salvation story. The acceptance of Christ's presence is central to marriage being a salvation story.

God's Vision of Marriage

Thus, God's design from the beginning was to sustain life and love; echoed by *Gaudium et Spes* in its definition of marriage as a community of life and love. From the beginning, marriage was a natural sacrament because it was an image of God's family. The first couple are made in the image and likeness of God and become one flesh. This union is only revealed in all its mystery with the coming of Christ, God's son, who became flesh for us because Christ was able to draw together the divine and the earthly of marriage so it became a sacrament. The result is a new reality, as the union of the couple becomes a unity in Christ, the sacrament. Our humanness is changed in the marital sacrament so that to speak of a new state of life is underlining not only a legal change, but also a spiritual change in the couple. Their life together is more than an image of Christ's relationship to the Church. They are a domestic church. The covenant that a Christian couple makes of a total self-gift of life and love becomes part of the love Christ has for His Church and so they enflesh the presence of Christ in Christian marriage and bring about the salvation of their family in its widest sense.

All this is possible because the basis of the marital sacrament is baptism. Baptism began their incorporation into Christ and this participation was raised to a new level of God's family, part of the Church through Christian marriage. Through marriage Christians have a new signature, a new level of being children of God because the spouses are in a more intimate way members of God's family. It can be seen in conjugal love where they show what divine love means. It is clearly expressed in the marriage covenant that demands a total self-gift so that trust is an integral part of marriage, and it is clearly present in that marriage is creative not only of life, but also of family. The new integration into God's family means that Father, Son and Spirit are present in Christian marriage. The Father is creative; the Son is reconciling; the Spirit gives love. A Christian family is in a special way God's family and therefore Christian marriage is a salvation story. God reveals himself as a family in many senses. There is the Trinity of persons, the desire to have children, the selfless gift of love, all of which point to family realities. This is why the word 'marriage' in the Old Testament indicated a divine relationship; it is also why home was to live with God. Similarly, Jesus taught us to call God our father, and that father has prepared a home for each one of us in heaven. Family is the chosen image of God and God created marriage to be that image of God on earth.

Yet marriage is more than an image of God's family, it

is God's family, and just as in any human family God as parent cares for his children. He is the true ancestor, giving life and bringing each child back to Himself. This fundamental desire that everyone would be saved brought about through Christ is realized in a special way in Christian marriage. In Christian marriage salvation takes place because the couple are incorporated into Christ and take part in the saving action of Christ. The two-in-oneness of the spouses is a new existence, a new Christian reality. Moreover, this incorporation makes them part of the Church in that they are joined to each other through Christ and because of that share in the Paschal Mystery of dying and rising. From this sharing in the Paschal Mystery they share in the Church. That is why a Christian family is a domestic church. As married Christians are the Church and reveal the Church by the gift of themselves to each other, they reflect the total gift of Christ to His Church. In their portrayal of the love of Christ, they communicate that love to others and stress the relationship that gives meaning to the covenant they made, a covenant that makes family and shows the essence of baptism – being part of God's family. These are the divine realities expressed in Christian marriage and the reason why marriage is a sacrament.

Notes

1   St Thomas Aquinas, In IV Sententiarum, Distinctio 28, Quaestio unica. n. 15. English Translation Dominicans.
2   Page R., 'Marriage: Sacrament of Love or Sacrament of Bond?' Studia Canonica, vol. 34 (2000) 5–22.
3   Leo XIII, *Arcanum*, Pius XI *Casti Connubii*, etc.
4   This attitude predates the 1917 code. See Scheeben M., *The Mysteries of Christianity*, B. Herder Book Co., London, 1954, p. 593.
5   I have followed the formulation of these questions as found in Mackin T., *The Marital Sacrament*, Paulist Press, New York, 1989, pp. 579–580.

6   The interpretation of Ephesians 5.32 is fraught with diffi-
     culty because the Greek text is ambiguous. Billot saw the
     great mystery as the relationship between Christ and His
     Church – a perfectly respectable interpretation; Scheeben
     saw Christian marriage as the great mystery, also a
     respectable interpretation. Certainly the text of Ephesians
     5.21–33 lays side by side the love of Christ for His Church
     and human love in marriage, and in many ways
     Scheeben's theology flows from this.

7   Scheeben, *The Mysteries of Christianity*, p. 601.

8   Quoted by Orsy L., 'Faith, Sacrament, Contract and Chris-
     tian Marriage: Disputed Questions', *Theological Studies*
     43(1982), 385

9   Rahner K., *Theological Investigations IV*, Darton, Longman
     & Todd, London, 1966, p. 267.

10   Lawler M. G., *Secular Marriage Christian Sacrament*,
     Twenty-Third Publications, Mystic, 1992, p. 61; Orsy,
     Faith, Sacrament, Contract and Christian Marriage, 387.

11   Code of Canon Law 1917, canon 1012. This canon was
     widely criticized and today would be interpreted as Orsy
     does in *Faith, Sacrament, Contract and Christian Marriage*,
     394, n. 15

12   Mackin, *The Marital Sacrament*, pp. 592–593 gives a
     summary of these opinions.

13   Schillebeeckx E., *Le Marriage est un Sacrament*, La Pensée
     Catholique, Brussels, 1961 pp. 41–42.

14   *Lumen Gentium* n. 11.

15   Gaalaas P., 'In What Sense can Marriage be called a Sacra-
     ment?', *Louvain Studies*, vol. 8 (1980–81) 403–409.

16   Cooke B., *Sacrament & Sacramentality*, Twenty-Third Publi-
     cations, Mystic, 1994, pp. 29–43.

17   Historically, this was not the first step. Instead, the first
     step was that of Scheeben who began to re-explore the
     meaning of Ephesians 5.21–33 in 1880. The question of
     natural marriage being the basis of the sacrament did not
     occur until 1929 with von Hildebrand.

18   In *IV Sententiarum*, arts 1 & 6. He was not the first to
     propose this as Mackin shows. Peter of Poitiers, Alexander
     of Hales, Pope Alexander III and Peter Lombard held the
     same opinion in a rather literal reading of Genesis 1 & 2.
     See Mackin, *The Marital Sacrament*, pp. 331–332.

224 *The Mystery of Christian Marriage*

19   Mackin T., *What is Marriage?*, p. 227.

20   *Gaudium et Spes* n. 48.

21   Given the premise that the sacrament is simply the natural relationship made a grace-giving image of the relationship of Christ and the Church, a relationship of perfect, self-giving love, one must conclude that the imaging, the self-giving, the gracing are done most effectively in sexual lovemaking climaxing in intercourse. Mackin, *The Marital Sacrament*, p. 598.

22   von Hildebrand D., *In Defence of Purity*, Sheed & Ward, London, 1931, p. 100. It is a translation of *Reinheit und Jungfraulichkeit*, Munich, 1927.

23   *Gaudium et Spes* n. 48. Taylor, M J. (ed) The sacraments N. Y. Alba House 1981 pp 193–204

24   Boff L., 'The Sacrament of Marriage', in Taylor, M. J., *The Sacraments*, Alba House, New York, 1981, pp. 193–204.

25   Gaalaas, *In What Sense can Marriage be called a Sacrament?* 404.

26   John Paul II, *The Theology of the Body*, Pauline Books, Boston 1997, p. 357.

27   Ibid., p. 361.

28   Rahner K., *The Church and the Sacraments*, Herder and Herder, New York, London, 1963, p. 107.

29   Rahner K., *The Church and the Sacraments*, Burns & Oates, London, 1974, p. 108.

30   He commanded His Apostles to preach to all peoples the Gospel's message that the human race was to become the Family of God, in which the fullness of the Law would be love. *Gaudium et Spes* n. 32.

31   'One would have to say ... that the will to humanity (incarnation) itself necessarily, formally and implicitly involved the willing of the Church.' Rahner, *The Church and the Sacraments*, 1963, p. 109.

32   Mersch E., *The Theology of the Mystical Body*, Herder Book Company St Louis, 1951, p. 574

33   Schillebeeckx, *Le Marriage est un Sacrament*, p. 36. Quoted in Mackin, *The Marital Sacrament*, p. 605.

34   Scheeben M., *The Mysteries of Christianity*, B. Herder Book Co., London, 1954, p. 574.

35   Ibid., p. 582.

36   'Conjugal love is eminently human, bringing special gifts

of healing and perfecting, exalting the gifts of grace and charity. Such love, merging the human with the divine, leads the spouses to a free and mutual gift of themselves, a gift proving itself by gentle affection and by deed, pervading the services and sacrifices of daily conjugal life.' *Gaudium et Spes* n. 49.

37   ... Intima animorum, corporum atque operum coniunctionem mutuum sibi adiutorium et serbitium paraestant, sensumque suae unitatis experiuntur et semper plenius adispiscentur. *Acta Synodalia* vol. IV pars I:478.

38   Pourrat P., *Theology of the Sacraments*, Herder, St Louis and Freiburg, 1910, pp. 256– 268, gives details of the various lists of sacraments that were held before the twelfth century.

39   Pourrat, *Theology of the Sacraments*, p. 270.

40   Cooke, *Sacraments & Sacramentality*, p. 80.

41   Rahner, *The Church and the Sacraments*, 1974, p. 108; Cooke, *Sacraments & Sacramentality*, pp. 78ff.

42   The letter of the three German bishops of 1993 proposes the following criteria: 'Only an honest accounting can lead to a responsible decision of conscience. An examination of the following criteria is therefore indispensable:
   – Where there is serious failure involved in the collapse of the first marriage, responsibility for it must be acknowledged and repented.
   – It must be convincingly established that a return to the first partner is really impossible and that with the best will the first marriage cannot be restored.
   – Restitution must be made for wrongs committed and injuries done in so far as this is possible.
   – In the first place this restitution includes fulfilment of obligations to the wife and children of the first marriage (cf. CCL, can. 1071,1.3).
   – Whether or not a partner broke his or her first marriage under great public attention and possibly even scandal should be taken into consideration.
   – The second marital partnership must have proved itself over a long period of time to represent a decisive and also publicly recognizable will to live permanently together and also acceding to the demands of marriage as a moral reality.

- Whether or not fidelity to the second relationship has become a moral obligation with regard to the spouse and children should be examined.
- It ought to be sufficiently clear – though certainly not to any greater extent than with other Christians – that the partners seek truly to live according to the Christian faith and with true motives, i.e., moved by genuinely religious desires, to participate in the sacramental life of the Church. The same holds true in the children's upbringing.

The English text can be found in Kelly K., *Divorce and Second Marriage, Facing the Challenge*, Geoffrey Chapman, London, 1996, pp. 98–117.

43   Rahner, *The Church and the Sacraments*, 1974, p. 107.
44   Cooke, *Sacraments & Sacramentality*, p. 91.
45   Ibid., p. 80.